"I can think of no one more qualified to speak to the pressing issue of Christian nationalism than Paul Miller. Despite the bleak subject, this book is full of confidence, conviction, and hope. Liberal democracy matters. The kingdom of God matters more. Those who care about either or both should read this work."
Russell Moore, Christianity Today

"In a political moment too often characterized by vitriol, distortion, and scorn, Paul D. Miller offers a refreshingly different approach. *The Religion of American Greatness* presents a careful, insightful, and charitable critique of contemporary American nationalism and points readers toward a more faithful political framework that elevates personal liberty and human dignity. A must-read for those concerned about politicized religion and its negative consequences for gospel witness."
Amy E. Black, professor of political science at Wheaton College

"There are few I trust more than Paul D. Miller on matters of national politics. He brings knowledge, vision, nuance, and understanding to a compelling vision of what it means (and doesn't mean) to live as faithful Christians in this nation, today and into the future, for the good of all."
Karen Swallow Prior, research professor of English and Christianity & Culture at Southeastern Baptist Theological Seminary and author of *On Reading Well: Finding the Good Life Through Great Books*

"*The Religion of American Greatness* is a superb and essential book—engaging and fair minded, thoughtful and accessible, and oh so timely. It both explains and challenges an increasingly widespread, malicious movement—toxic Christian nationalism—that is doing great harm to America and to the Christian witness. *The Religion of American Greatness* is powerfully argued, honest, and never ungracious. It's just the book we need, and Paul D. Miller is just the person to write it."
Peter Wehner, senior fellow at the Ethics and Public Policy Center and author of *The Death of Politics*

"There are works that challenge the mind and others that speak to the heart. Paul Miller does both in this important book about the role of America's dominant religion in our national politics."
Tom Nichols, author of *Our Own Worst Enemy*

"Paul Miller draws from an impressive range of sources to show the theological, historical, and cultural errors of Christian nationalism while still suggesting how American Christians can pursue with each other and their neighbors a common American identity and shared aspirations for the future of the country."
John Inazu, Sally D. Danforth Distinguished Professor of Law and Religion at Washington University in St. Louis

"A much-needed and astute analysis of a major reality in the United States, a reality that challenges the very heart of this nation and of Christianity. Dr. Paul Miller brings to bear years of political experience, a deep commitment to Christian understanding, and a wellspring of scholarly comprehension to help us see what ultimately is wrong with Christian nationalism. A must-read."

Michael O. Emerson, professor and sociology department head at the University of Illinois Chicago and author of *Divided by Faith: Evangelical Religion and the Problem of Race in America*

"I'll be recommending this book to every thinking Christian I know who's looking to understand why nationalism, and Christian nationalism in particular, is such a danger for the church and American democracy. Beautifully written from a conservative, Christian perspective, Paul Miller carefully engages the arguments for both nationalism and Christian nationalism, and shows them to be sorely lacking. Christian nationalism is illiberal, antidemocratic, and ultimately for Christians, unbiblical and inconsistent with authentic gospel witness. Miller shows us all the better way."

Samuel L. Perry, coauthor of *Taking America Back for God: Christian Nationalism in the United States*

"I'm grateful to Paul Miller for writing this book. It stretched and challenged me. He has done a great service for all of us concerned about liberal democracy and the Christian church. At points, the writing crackles with intensity. I will be recommending this work to anyone intent on responding both theologically and politically to the threat of Christian nationalism."

Andrew Whitehead, associate professor of sociology at Indiana University-Purdue University Indianapolis and coauthor of *Taking America Back for God: Christian Nationalism in the United States*

"Paul D. Miller crafts his message with confident humility, taking an honest look at the virus of Christian nationalism plaguing our politics and our pulpits. He presents difficult truths in palatable forms that reveal his genuine love for Christ and the church. Read this treatise with an open heart and mind, with the goal of seeing God's kingdom come and will be done."

Samuel Rodriguez, lead pastor of New Season Church and president and CEO of the National Hispanic Christian Leadership Conference

THE RELIGION
OF AMERICAN
GREATNESS

WHAT'S WRONG
WITH CHRISTIAN
NATIONALISM

PAUL D. MILLER

FOREWORD BY
DAVID FRENCH

Academic
An imprint of InterVarsity Press
Downers Grove, Illinois

InterVarsity Press
P.O. Box 1400 | Downers Grove, IL 60515-1426
ivpress.com | email@ivpress.com

InterVarsity Press® is the publishing division of InterVarsity Christian Fellowship/USA®.
For information, visit intervarsity.org.

Scripture quotations, unless otherwise noted, are from The Holy Bible, English Standard Version, copyright © 2001 by Crossway Bibles, a division of Good News Publishers. Used by permission. All rights reserved.

Cover design and image composite: David Fassett
Interior design: Jeanna Wiggins

ISBN 978-1-5140-0026-7 (print) | ISBN 978-1-5140-0027-4 (digital)

Printed in the United States of America ♾

Library of Congress Cataloging-in-Publication Data
Names: Miller, Paul David, 1978- author.
Title: The religion of American greatness : what's wrong with Christian
   nationalism / Paul D. Miller.
Description: Downers Grove, IL : InterVarsity Press, [2022] | Includes
   bibliographical references and index.
Identifiers: LCCN 2022007907 (print) | LCCN 2022007908 (ebook) | ISBN
   9781514000267 (print) | ISBN 9781514000274 (digital)
Subjects: LCSH: Christianity and politics–United States. |
   Nationalism–United States–Religious aspects–Christianity. |
   Patriotism–United States–Religious aspects–Christianity.
Classification: LCC BR516 .M5426 2022 (print) | LCC BR516 (ebook) | DDC
   261.70973–dc23/eng/20220314
LC record available at https://lccn.loc.gov/2022007907
LC ebook record available at https://lccn.loc.gov/2022007908

26   25   24   23   22 | 6   5   4   3   2   1

This book is dedicated to my wife, Jennilee.

Thank you for going on this adventure with me.

CONTENTS

FOREWORD

David French

If you live in the South—or almost anywhere in rural America—you've seen the images of Christian nationalism. Perhaps it's a billboard that says "God strong" with an image of a faded and battle-damaged American flag between the words. Or perhaps you spot a pickup truck or two that has an American-flag-draped cross painted on the back, with the words *stand for the flag, kneel for the cross* stenciled on the tailgate.

Starting in late June, you'll see different sights. In preparation for the Fourth of July, some churches will hold "faith and freedom" Sundays and cover their grounds with American flags. You'll see flags inside the sanctuary as well. They're always in some churches. Others bring them in to celebrate the nation's birth. Pastors will ask veterans to stand, and the congregation will cheer.

All these sights and sounds are the tangible, telltale evidence of a deep and profound bond that exists in the hearts of countless millions of Americans, a bond between church and nation that is experienced far more viscerally than it is intellectually or theologically.

There is a deep conviction that America has a specific, divinely ordained purpose that is distinct from and superior to the divine purpose for other nations. There is a connection to a version of the past that renders the nation uniquely virtuous, and there is a profound feeling that the fate of the church itself is bound up in the fate of the nation—that as America becomes less "American" it will invariably become less Christian.

This version of Christian nationalism has existed for a very long time in American history, but prior to the Trump administration it was often suppressed or channeled through establishment Republican politics. For decades it was harnessed to the great national cause to contain and ultimately defeat an atheist and oppressive Soviet empire.

Figures like Ronald Reagan, George H. W. Bush, and George W. Bush could appeal to Christian nationalists while still advancing a version of classical liberal conservatism that rejected nationalist extremes. Nationalists were part of the GOP coalition, but they did not dominate it. They did not define it.

But while Christian nationalism could be more or less malignant in American life, it could never truly be benign. It warps both religion and patriotism, and when turned against fellow Americans, it's a force potent enough to rupture the fabric of American political life—and possibly even the American republic itself.

The effort to overturn the 2020 presidential election—culminating in the president of the United States pressuring the vice president to disrupt the counting of the electoral votes and hundreds of vocal Christian "patriots" storming the Capitol—represented the most tangible evidence of Christian nationalism's dark influence.

Most Americans were shocked by what they witnessed on January 6, but in hindsight we shouldn't have been. Months of apocalyptic rhetoric and prophecy—including rhetoric and prophecies explicitly tying the Trump presidency to the very life and health of both nation and church—had deceived millions and radicalized tens of thousands. All the signs of violence were there, including explicit admonitions to fight for God and country. But this time the fight wasn't against the North Koreans, or the Viet Cong, or al-Qaeda, or ISIS; it was against "the media," Joe Biden, and the left. It was American versus American.

The conflict is still American versus American. The nationalist fever is not breaking. Christian nationalism has long had a hold over millions of Christian hearts, and it is increasing its hold over Christian minds. Right-wing Christians are increasingly rethinking the American classical liberal founding itself, and they're girding Christians to fight a "cold civil war" to defend and restore a particular (and largely mythical) version of America's Christian past.

Thus, there is no better time for Professor Miller's book. It's arriving exactly when an increasing number of America's religious and political leaders need to understand exactly what Christian nationalism is and why it's manifestly dangerous to both the church and nation it seeks to save.

This book takes Christian nationalism seriously. By that I mean that it takes both the ideas and the threat seriously. It engages the ideas critically and respectfully. There are no straw men in these pages. Professor Miller understands that there are reasons why so many millions of Americans are captured by Christian nationalism's themes, and reasons why so many millions of Americans feel as if both the church and their idealized version of the state are under threat.

And if there is no better time for Professor Miller's book, there is no better person to make the argument. All too many books about American Christianity are written from the outside looking in, as if the writer is encountering and struggling to understand a strange new people group. Outsider perspectives can be helpful, but they're often not heard. In a nation so torn between left and right, red and blue, all too many Americans simply refuse to hear from anyone who is not in their tribe.

Miller, however, is a theologically orthodox Christian with a deep history in America's conservative churches. He's a veteran. He's a longtime Republican. He's not writing about a people he doesn't know or ideas he's just encountered. He's writing, instead, about members of his own community, and he doesn't just observe their concerns about the direction of the nation and the ideology of the American left; he shares their concerns.

Critically, Miller is also a patriot. He doesn't scorn this nation. His eyes are open to its flaws, but he has also served it in uniform. He has served it as a member of a Republican administration. In the pages of the book, he articulates a patriotic alternative to nationalism, one that is grounded in a love of home but does not tie the fate of the church to the fate of the nation or indulge the notion that America is God's special land.

Christian nationalism is deeply embedded in too many Christian hearts. Professor Miller doesn't pretend that his book can reach every man with a flagged-draped cross painted on his truck or every woman who plants flags on the church grounds the night before faith and freedom Sunday, but he does know that leaders matter, and America's Christian shepherds are now facing temptations to follow their flocks rather than lead them away from a dangerous path.

Equipped by the arguments in this book, leaders rightly alarmed by Christian nationalism can offer an informed critique of nationalist excess and support a superior Christian vision for faithful and patriotic engagement in the public square. Come for the understanding of Christian nationalism. Stay for the inspiration necessary to propose an alternative idea. This book will leave you with a clear conviction that Christians don't have to surrender to the authoritarian spirit of a nationalist age. There is a better way.

PREFACE

THIS IS A WORK OF CHRISTIAN POLITICAL THEORY. It is the first part of a larger argument—the other two-thirds of which exists, so far, solely in my head. This volume is a sustained argument against nationalism, especially American nationalism, especially American Christian nationalism. But I felt, writing this book, as if I were participating in an incomplete conversation. So much of contemporary nationalism is framed as opposition to progressivism, the other major voice in this argument, that it was difficult for me to critique nationalism without taking some notice of its critique of progressivism—much of which I agree with. But because I could not do justice to the discussion about progressivism while still maintaining focus and brevity, I have largely ignored the progressive left and focused on the nationalist right in this book. I hope someday to write a sustained argument against progressivism. If I focus first on the nationalist right, it is because, having spent most of my life on the right, I feel a special burden to examine the plank in my eye before critiquing the speck—or plank—in the eye of the progressive. A third volume—a far distant shore at the time of this writing—would be a vindication, defense, and apology for what I view as the best framework for ordering our political life together, a framework of ordered liberty that we might call Christian democracy, Christian republicanism, or Augustinian liberalism.

The argument of the trilogy as a whole is that the progressive left and the nationalist right are both illiberal political movements. By *illiberal*, I mean, "not classically liberal, inconsistent with republicanism, and incompatible with ordered liberty." By *liberal*, I do not mean "the American political left," or "the Democratic Party," for which I reserve the term *progressive*. Rather, I am using *liberal* as shorthand for a framework of ordered liberty: the institutions of political and economic liberty and republicanism that arose in Europe and gradually took shape in the early modern era—especially in the United Kingdom in the eighteenth century—and that played the predominant role in shaping the American founding. I use *liberalism* and *republicanism* in this book as loose terms to include democracy, majority rule plus minority protections, free enterprise and private property, the rule of law, the separation of powers, and limited government. I recognize that the word *liberalism* has been stretched and abused so much as to make its use often the cause of more confusion than clarity—specifically, many people assume that liberalism means "the philosophy of John Locke and John Rawls," which is not what I mean, so I have tried to use it sparingly. By whatever label, a framework of ordered liberty rests on an ideology of constitutional government and human dignity. When I say that the progressive left and the nationalist right are both illiberal, I mean that both ideologies are inconsistent with the ideals of the American founding, with political liberty, and with human dignity.

Progressivism and nationalism are both examples of what Thomas Sowell has called "unconstrained visions" of human life and political purpose.[1] To be blunt, both ideologies disregard important American ideals, and both are in tension, at least, with a biblical understanding of justice. The two share much in common: they both embrace a sort of bureaucratic authoritarianism in which the state is given responsibility for reengineering American life and culture. Progressives envision a utopian future; nationalists, a romantic past. Progressives want to usher in their promised land of autonomous individuals empowered to express any identity they prefer, with the state responsible for providing primary goods, punishing dissent, and policing identity choices. At the extreme, it has deteriorated into a hectoring, authoritarian movement that seeks to enforce its ideals through legal bullying, speech codes, and "cancel culture." Nationalists want to re-create the imagined culture of American greatness, usually envisioned as the era of 1950s White, middle class, Protestant America—the greatness of America as a "Christian nation."

---

[1]Thomas Sowell, *A Conflict of Visions: Ideological Origins of Political Struggles* (New York: Basic Books, 2002).

They equate the nation with the majority culture in a way that leaves little room for the diversity of subcultures in America. Both movements believe Washington, DC, is responsible for bringing about their preferred social and cultural vision, and they are prepared to grant it as much power as necessary to accomplish their goals. They only differ on the direction of the state's social engineering programs.

Against the progressive left and nationalist right, I want to defend ordered liberty, liberal institutions, and civic republicanism, particularly a specific kind that I think is consistent with Christianity. This is an unfashionable stance to take. From the right, nationalists, including many Christians, think every kind of liberalism is a Trojan horse for progressivism.[2] They feel that Christian cooperation with liberalism has only led to decades, even centuries, of continuous cultural and legal defeat, and that if Christians are to save civilization from itself, they must return to an older, more structured framework for ordering society. Whether pursued under the banner of nationalism, Catholic integralism, or nostalgic calls to renew Western civilization or Christendom, all stem from the same impetus. From the left, progressives critique liberalism for being inadequately progressive. Liberalism, they say, is hopelessly compromised with the racism and imperialism that indisputably overlapped with the early liberal past, compounded and replicated by the inequalities of global capitalism. In order to achieve true justice—understood now as diversity, equity, and inclusion for the historically marginalized and oppressed—we must be willing to rethink and even reject the liberal institutions that (they mistakenly believe) allowed such injustices to happen in the first place.

I reject these critiques. Political liberty begins with the belief that human beings possess inherent dignity and moral worth. Crucially, our moral worth resides in our essential humanity—which we share equally with everyone else. God has commissioned all of us equally as his image bearers, stewards of creation, and participants in the Noahic covenant. No one of us is inherently superior by virtue of birth, lineage, rank, wealth, ethnicity, religion, intelligence, sex, or any other attribute to merit special treatment by the government or special access to power. If none of us merits political power by virtue of some innate trait, we all deserve an equal say in how we are governed. Unless we live in a city-state small enough for participatory, direct democracy, this

---

[2]Patrick J. Deneen, *Why Liberalism Failed* (New Haven, CT: Yale University Press, 2019).

situation leads us to collectively entrust power to a subset of people who govern on our behalf. And so we arrive at some form of representative rule, accountable governance, and majoritarian decision-making. At the same time, since even those in the minority are equal under law, there are limits to what the majority can do to them. And so we also arrive at a concept of inviolable and individual rights that fundamentally limit the state's jurisdiction.[3]

This basic starting point is what distinguishes ordered liberty and republicanism from monarchy, aristocracy, oligarchy, dictatorship, theocracy, and other forms of hierarchical, illiberal government. Every ideological justification for rejecting liberal institutions, if brought to its logical conclusion, ultimately must assert that some people are intrinsically worthier of ruling than other people. No matter how you dress that up in arguments about national identity, culture, heritage, or history (as the right does) or intersectionality and diversity, equity, and inclusion (as the left does), it is complete and utter nonsense. If you believe in human equality and its political consequences, you end up supporting some notion of ordered liberty. I hope to make the full argument someday.

---

[3]Paul D. Miller, "Augustinian Liberalism," *Providence Magazine*, September 2, 2019.

ACKNOWLEDGMENTS

I'D LIKE TO THANK ANDREW WALKER for hosting an invaluable colloquium on a draft of this book in December 2020. Thank you to the participants: John Wilsey, George Marsden, Daniel K. Williams, Randall Balmer, Mark David Hall, Nathan Finn, Kristen Kobes du Mez, Matthew Hall, Jonathan Leeman, David van Drunen, Thabiti Anyabwile, Philip Gorski, Matthew Franck, Rogers Smith, Andrew Whitehead, John Owen, and Amy Black. Listening to you interrogate my book for four or five hours was an extraordinary privilege—and deeply humbling. Thank you for your intellectual companionship and accountability and for your investment in me. I'd also like to thank Kendrick Kuo, O. Alan Noble, Jon Askonas, Coyle Neal, Megan Reiss, Luke Perez, and above all my wife, Jennilee Miller, for reviewing various drafts. Your insights were invaluable as I occasionally lost the ability to think straight in the early phase of this project. Thinking about evangelicals, Trump, and American identity was a profoundly personal and difficult task, and I am grateful to those who sat down to think together with me.

Parts of this book rely on research first conducted for a project with the Ethics and Religious Liberty Commission (ERLC). The material is used here with permission. This book is independent of the ERLC, which does not endorse or support this book or any of its analyses or conclusions. No member of the ERLC vetted this work before publication for institutional equities. This book also reprints parts of the following articles, which are used with permission: Paul D. Miller, "The Vice of Nationalism," *Orbis* 63, no. 2 (2019):

291-97; Paul D. Miller, "Non-'Western' Liberalism and the Resilience of the Liberal International Order," *The Washington Quarterly* 41, no. 2 (2018): 137-53; Paul D. Miller, "Against 'Conservative Democracy,'" *Providence Magazine*, June 19, 2019; Paul D. Miller, "America: Creedal or Tribal?," *Providence Magazine*, January 21, 2020; Paul D. Miller, "The Jedi Are Selfless: Nationalism, Identity, the Humanities, and Liberalism," *Mere Orthodoxy*, May 8, 2019.

CHRISTIANITY AND AMERICAN IDENTITY

1

"AMERICA IS WINNING AGAIN. America is respected again. Because we are putting America first. . . . We're taking care of ourselves for a change, folks. . . . You know they have a word, it sort of became old fashioned, it's called a 'nationalist.' And I say, really? We're not supposed to use that word. You know what I am? I'm a nationalist. Okay? I'm a nationalist." President Donald J. Trump proudly spoke these words to a crowd in Houston in October 2018. The crowd roared its approval and broke into a chant: "USA! USA! USA!"[1]

The media treated this as news, but to close observers it had been evident for a long time.[2] Trump plainly was not a conservative as defined by the political right since the 1950s. It was at first hard to identify Trump's place on the political map because nationalism had been underground, so to speak, for a few generations. In its place, conservatism, as articulated by thinkers like William Buckley and Russell Kirk and practiced by statesmen like Ronald Reagan and George H. W. Bush, served as the quasi-official ideology of the political right. Conservatism stressed the paramount value of human liberty within a framework of limited government. But Trump had at various points endorsed abortion, trade restrictions, gun control, and other positions at odds with the modern Republican Party and the conservative movement. Trump did not use the rhetoric of liberty, limited government, or constitutionalism. He

---

[1] CBS News, "Trump: 'I'm a Nationalist,'" YouTube video, posted October 22, 2018, www.youtube .com/watch?v=sazitj4x6YI.

[2] Thomas Wright, "Trump's 19th Century Foreign Policy," *Politico Magazine*, January 20, 2016.

talked about national greatness, cutting advantageous trade deals, and looking out for "America First." Trump's success illustrated a broader phenomenon. By 2016 it had become evident that "conservatism"—its intellectual coherence, philosophical depth and rigor, and the consonance some saw between it and biblical political theology—was the working ideology of a tiny circle of intellectuals, not the voice of a broad movement. The political right was—and, in fact, had long been—far more indebted to nationalism than to conservatism. Donald Trump recognized this reality and rode it to the White House.[3]

American nationalism is infused with the rhetoric and symbols of Christianity. When Trump pitched himself as a champion of regular Americans, he repeatedly and explicitly cast it as an appeal to Christians. In June 2016 he told the Faith and Freedom Coalition, "We will respect and defend Christian Americans."[4] In August 2016, he told a group of pastors in Orlando, "Your power has been totally taken away," but under a Trump administration, "you'll have great power to do good things."[5] In September 2016, Trump told the Values Voters Summit, "[In] a Trump administration, our Christian heritage will be cherished, protected, defended, like you've never seen before. Believe me."[6] At the same venue the following year, after his election, Trump reminded them of his promise. "I pledged that, in a Trump administration, our nation's religious heritage would be cherished, protected, and defended like you have never seen before," he claimed. "That's what's happening. . . . We are stopping cold the attacks on Judeo-Christian values. . . . We will defend our faith and protect our traditions."[7] In June 2020, amid nationwide protests against police brutality and racial injustice, Trump posed for a photo holding a Bible in front of St. John's Church, a historic church one block north of the White House (after police forcibly evicted protesters in the area) to "show a message of

---

[3] Anatol Lievin noted as early as 2004, more than a decade before Trump, that the Republican Party was more accurately understood as the American Nationalist Party; see his *America Right or Wrong: An Anatomy of American Nationalism* (New York: Oxford University Press, 2004).

[4] Donald Trump, "Remarks at Faith and Freedom Coalition Conference," June 10, 2016, www .c-span.org/video/?410912-4/donald-trump-addresses-faith-freedom-coalition-conference.

[5] Donald Trump, "Remarks in Orlando, Florida," August 11, 2016, www.c-span.org/video/?413877-1 /donald-trump-addresses-evangelical-leaders-orlando-florida.

[6] Donald Trump, "Values Voter Summit Remarks," September 9, 2016, www.politico.com /story/2016/09/full-text-trump-values-voter-summit-remarks-227977.

[7] Donald Trump, "Remarks by President Trump at the 2017 Values Voter Summit," October 13, 2017, www1.cbn.com/cbnnews/politics/2017/october/president-trumps-entire-faith-filled-speech -at-the-values-voters-summit.

resilience and determination" according to the White House Press Secretary. Days later Trump said he believed "Christians think it was a beautiful picture."

Nor is this recent: American Christians have long merged their religious faith with American identity. In the seventeenth, eighteenth, and nineteenth centuries, Americans regularly described the United States as a "new Israel"; in the twentieth century, as a "Christian nation." When they do so, they are expressing a collection of beliefs: that to be a faithful Christian in America, one must be loyal to the American nation; that the American nation is defined in part by Christian values and Christian culture; that it is, in some sense, the outworking of Christianity in political form; that it may enjoy a special relationship with God; and that American Christians should ensure their government keeps Christianity as the predominant ordering framework for our public life. American national identity has long been defined by many Americans to include Christianity as a necessary part of it. Since at least the Civil War, Americans have regularly read 2 Chronicles 7:14 ("If my people who are called by my name humble themselves, and pray and seek my face and turn from their wicked ways, then I will hear from heaven and will forgive their sin and heal their land") and Psalm 33:12 ("Blessed is the nation whose God is the LORD") and applied it to themselves and the United States: Americans are the people called by God's name, and the United States is the nation whose God is the Lord. Seen in this light, the Christian Right, a broad social and political movement that arose in the late 1970s, is not new in its effort to define the United States as a Christian nation. Rather, the movement stands solidly within the tradition of American Christians—mostly White—who define their sacred and secular identities in terms of each other. The Christian Right is the latest in a long line of White Protestant American nationalists.

In response to Trump's campaign pitch aimed at them, 81 percent of White, self-identified evangelical voters cast their votes for him, and they remained a core base of his support throughout his presidency. Their acceptance of Trump suggests that many American evangelicals have accepted nationalism as their political philosophy: at a minimum, as something that is consistent with their faith; at most, as the necessary political implication of Christian belief and practice. In a recent survey, a staggering 65 percent of Americans believed it was "fairly" or "very" important that a citizen be a Christian to be "truly American," including 75 percent of those scoring highest on measures of nationalism.[8] In other recent polls, 29 percent of Americans believed that "the federal government should declare the United States a Christian nation," and almost two-thirds that "God has granted America a special role in human history."[9]

Christian nationalism asserts that there is something identifiable as an American "nation," distinct from other nations; that American nationhood is and should remain defined by Christianity or Christian cultural norms; and that the American people and their government should actively work to defend, sustain, and cultivate America's Christian culture, heritage, and values. Historians have often argued that a generic Protestant Christianity served as the *de facto* established religion of the United States until the 1960s. A Christian nationalist is someone who believes that historical fact is normative for today, that the United States should return to the days of a quasi-official, nondenominational (Judeo-)Christian establishment that privileges Christian norms, values, symbols, culture, and rhetoric in American public life and public policy. They do not advocate repeal of the First Amendment, but they do favor a strongly "accommodationist" interpretation of it in which the government is permitted to favor religion over irreligion, and even favor America's historically predominant religious tradition (i.e., Christianity) over new or different ones. Christian nationalists believe that the American nation was, is, *and should remain* a "Christian nation"—that America's identity as a Christian nation is not merely a historical fact but a moral imperative, an ideological goal, and a policy program for the future, which also means that defining the nation's religious and cultural identity is rightfully part of the government's responsibility.

What are the origins, historical development, key beliefs, and political and cultural implications of American Christian nationalism? Is it a good thing or a bad thing? What is its relationship to the ideals of the American experiment? What does nationalist governance look like in practice, and what effects has it had on American society and the world when they have had opportunities to pursue their agenda in the past? What is the difference, if any, between nationalism and patriotism? What is the right way to love one's country? To these

---

[8]Bart Bonikowski and Paul DiMaggio, "Varieties of American Popular Nationalism," *American Sociological Review* 81, no. 5 (2016): 949-80.

[9]Andrew L. Whitehead and Samuel L. Perry, *Taking America Back for God: Christian Nationalism in the United States* (New York: Oxford University Press, 2020), 10.

historical and political questions, we can add a host of theological ones. What is the relationship between Christian nationalism and Christianity? Between Christian nationalism and other forms of Christian political engagement? Does the Christian faith permit, or possibly even require, its adherents to believe in the tenets of nationalism? In short, do American Christians have to be nationalists? Do Americans have to be Christians? These questions raise broader and deeper questions about the relationship between religion and politics, questions that have been asked ever since the Pharisees used a question about taxes to suss out Jesus' take on collaboration versus resistance toward civil government, and about humankind's ultimate loyalties.

THE ARGUMENTS OF THIS BOOK

This is a book about the historical development, key beliefs, and political, cultural, and theological implications of Christian nationalism. I argue that Christian nationalism is a bad political theory, illiberal in theory and practice, and at odds with key features of the American experiment. In chapter two I clarify what exactly nationalism is, broadly understood. I review the conventional distinction between nationalism and patriotism, and I affirm the positive value of patriotism for both practical and theological reasons. I start with an affirmation of patriotism because I want to stress that my critique of nationalism is not a rejection of all forms of loyalty and affection for our worldly communities and, in fact, some kind of local affection is an important safeguard against the unhealthy kind. I then review the academic literature on nationalism to define the concept, draw its boundaries, and help distinguish it from patriotism. Nationalism is the belief that humanity is divisible into internally coherent, mutually distinct cultural units which merit political independence and human loyalty because of their purported ability to provide meaning, purpose, and value in human life; and that governments are supposed to protect and promote the cultural identities of their respective nations.

I then take up the difficult question of American nationalism and its relationship to Christianity. In chapter three I review the arguments from advocates of Christian nationalism to define the ideology. American Christian nationalism defines America as the cultural nation of "Anglo-Protestantism," as some of its scholarly advocates have recently avowed. Christian nationalists believe that the American government should sustain and defend the nation's Anglo-Protestant cultural identity to remain faithful to America's past, ensure the survival of American liberty, and secure God's blessing.

I then move on to critique Christian nationalism. In chapters four and five I argue that there are some clear problems with any form of nationalism: cultures have blurry boundaries, which means they are a poor foundation for political boundaries. When governments try to force political and cultural boundaries to overlap, the effort inevitably leads them down an illiberal path. Governments end up treating minorities—ethnic, racial, religious, linguistic, or otherwise—as second-class citizens, or worse. I argue that governments should not try to promote or enforce a national cultural template. State-sponsored cultural engineering involves the government tilting the playing field, or putting its thumb on the scales, to favor one cultural template and disfavor others. Far from promoting national unity, the effort promotes national division and fragmentation because nationalism is simply another form of identity politics.

Christian nationalism is, in effect, identity politics for tribal evangelicals who confuse their particular culture for the nation as a whole. Evangelicalism, when it indulges in this kind of political engagement, is acting less like a religious community seeking to embody the universal faith than one among many particularistic or tribal ethnoreligious sects lobbying for power and prestige. In short, nationalism, considered as a political theory, is arbitrary, incoherent, and illiberal. If taken to its logical conclusion, nationalism undermines the foundations of a free and open society, including religious freedom and racial or ethnic pluralism. I also show that Anglo-Protestant culture is *not* necessary to sustain the political institutions of liberalism and democracy. In chapter six I review "nations" and "peoples" in the Bible, critique nationalists' misuse of the Bible, and discuss how Christians today should think about "the nations" and about ancient Israel. I suggest that nationalism, in its ideal form, is a kind of idolatry.

In chapters seven and eight I argue that, in light of the previous chapters, it is easier to see the Christian Right as the latest instance of White Christians' efforts to push for a strong Christian American identity—or, to put it another way, the Christian Right has always included a strong element of nationalism among its goals, mixing uneasily with Christian republicanism. To the extent that it is nationalist, the movement's political agenda is rooted more in cultural particularity than theological universality. Much of American evangelicalism is acting more like a cultural tribe, an ethnoreligious sect advocating for its own power and protection, rather than a people from every tribe and nation advocating for universal principles of justice, flourishing, and the common good.

That is troubling by itself, but there is another problem. Many evangelicals do not recognize the difference between their particular culture and the common good; they believe that advocating for one must include the other. The effort to pass off their particular culture as a universal template for the nation is fraught with dangers, both for itself and for the nation. The movement is illiberal, as other nationalist movements around the world and its predecessors in American history have been. Even though the Christian Right today does not overtly appeal to racist or sectarian arguments in the same way as past nationalist movements in American history, it is nonetheless complicit with *illiberalism*—an illiberality that continues to show up in how nationalists think about race, racial inequality, and our responsibility (or lack thereof) to remedy the sins of the past. In chapter nine I use this way of understanding the Christian Right to explain its relationship to Donald Trump.

In chapter ten I suggest the outlines of what I hope is a sounder theology of the nation. Despite my critique of nationalism, I do not believe the answer is to reject nationality altogether. We can find some suggestion in the Bible that God blessed humanity with corporate political memberships as one layer among many in our multifaceted identities. The challenge is to find a way to embrace and celebrate our particular differences while avoiding the idolatry that so often attaches to them. Nations are not evil, but the record of nationalism in history is overwhelmingly one of idolatry and oppression. I conclude with a broader reflection on American politics and culture and with a note on the role that pastors and churches might play in the work of repair.

Is the marriage of Christianity with American nationalism a forgivable quirk over an unimportant doctrinal matter, a lovable excess in patriotism and piety? The burden of this book is to show that nationalism is incoherent in theory, illiberal in practice, and, I fear, often idolatrous in our hearts. Christian nationalism in American history has been devastating to both church and state, in the nation's race relations, its foreign policy, and in the church's witness. The marriage represents an American and evangelical version of Caesaropapism, the appropriation of the church's moral authority and evangelical zeal to the cause of secular greatness. It can be hard for Christians to recognize this because, truthfully, America is unique and, compared to other great powers today and in ages past, relatively just and humane—and of course it is true that Christianity has been extraordinarily influential in the nation's history, politics, and culture. But that is part of the problem: When America is most just, it is most tempting for Americans to treat it as a precursor to the kingdom of God, reducing the church to the chaplaincy of American nationalism. The opposite case is an even greater problem: When America is at its worst, when it does not live up to its creed—as happens sadly all too often—American Christians nonetheless continue to act as cheerleaders and defenders of the nation, Christians have blessed sin and called evil good. We have taken the name of Christ as a moral fig leaf while shilling for the whore of Babylon.

DEFINING TERMS

This book deals with abstract concepts like culture, religion, heritage, ideology, and more. One of the key points of discussion is whether and to what extent "ideology" is separable from "culture"—whether the ideas of ordered liberty, democracy, and human rights can be separated from the Anglo-Protestant culture from which they first arose. This discussion will hardly be intelligible unless I spend a few moments defining terms. These definitions are not exclusive of one another.

Ideology is a linked set of normative ideas about the social and political order, specifically ideas about how society and politics *ought* to be ordered. It is a set of beliefs about justice, the right ordering of human societies. Communism is an ideology that claims justice is the abolition of class distinctions and private property and the organization of society under the dictatorship of the proletariat. Fascism is an ideology that claims justice is the empowerment and unity of a race, nation, or people under an authoritarian government that has total control to regulate all aspects of society for the good of its nation, usually involving militarism and forcible repression of dissent. Classical liberalism is an ideology that claims justice is majority rule plus minority rights, as ordered by a limited government under the rule of law (virtually all Americans are "liberal" in the classical sense; as noted in the preface, I use the term *progressivism* to refer to the American political left). Other ideologies include republicanism, progressivism, Islamism, conservatism, socialism, and

—depending on one's definition—multiculturalism, authoritarianism, and more. (Another terminological clarification: I use *republicanism* and *civic republicanism* with a small *r* to denote a belief in republican forms of government, including features such as popular sovereignty, the rule of law, checks and balances among divided branches of government, and so on. I use *Republican* with a capital *R* to denote the Republican Party, which is decreasingly republican in outlook.) This book is primarily an examination of the ideology of nationalism, especially American nationalism, especially the kind that uses Christian symbols and rhetoric.

What about religion? The famous anthropologist Clifford Geertz defined religion as "a system of symbols which acts to establish powerful, pervasive, and long-lasting moods and motivations in men by formulating conceptions of a general order of existence and clothing these conceptions with such an aura of factuality that the moods and motivations seem uniquely realistic."[10] Religion is a set of beliefs and practices about what is most basic, fundamental and important in human life. Christianity is obviously a religion—the one true religion, I believe—alongside many other religions. What is the relationship between religion and ideology? Many, perhaps most, ideologies emerge from prior religious commitments, though that does not mean there is a deterministic relationship between them. More importantly, some ideologies are themselves simply substitute religions. Read the definition of religion again and note how well it might describe communism, fascism, or even progressivism. In chapter six I suggest that the ideal type of nationalism also falls into this category.

One argument nationalists regularly make is that they want to preserve their nation's heritage. Our "heritage" is our inheritance, a thing passed down from generations and valued for its representation of the past and its ability to give us a vicarious linkage to our ancestors. In that sense, nationalists claim they simply want to preserve what came before, to honor the past. In chapter ten I will strongly endorse the idea of *history* as a component of national identity, but not quite in the way nationalists mean when they invoke *heritage*. History is the contemporary, scholarly effort to reconstruct the past as faithfully as possible based on surviving artifacts and documents. By contrast, nationalists often use the word *heritage* as a catchall for the parts of the past they

[10]Clifford Geertz, *Interpretation of Cultures* (New York: Basic Books, 1973), 90.

prefer, or for a fabricated version of the past that never really existed. As one scholar put it, partisans invent heritage by "mining the historical record for identity traits that the interpreter believes should be key ingredients in the recipe for present-day identity."[11] And they invoke heritage to justify their policy preferences in the present, as a way of claiming that their political agenda—their ideology—is actually rooted in the past and carries its authority: they make "heritage" part of "ideology." Nationalists end up *dis*honoring the past because they weaponize it, select only the parts most flattering to themselves, or, somewhat contradictorily, assert that we must honor our heritage regardless of its content.

Another argument nationalists make is that liberal ideas and liberal ideology is rooted in Western or Anglo-Protestant "culture" and cannot survive apart from it. What is culture? This is probably the hardest word to define, but also the most important for my argument. Nationalists are sometimes guilty of tautology, of simply defining their terms to include one another. If culture includes all of ideology—if ideology is nothing but a subset of culture—then by definition ideology cannot be separated from culture, and nationalists can claim victory. Geertz's famous definition is that culture is "an historically transmitted pattern of meanings embodied in symbols, a system of inherited conceptions expressed in symbolic forms by means of which men communicate, perpetuate, and develop their knowledge about and attitudes toward life." More concisely, "Man is an animal suspended in webs of significance he himself has spun. I take culture to be those webs."[12] If culture encompasses all possible "patterns of meanings," then religion and ideology and heritage are all parts of a culture.

I am not satisfied with this way of thinking about culture, at least not for the purposes of this book. Nationalists rarely recognize or discuss the important but rather abstract relationship between ideas and culture. Can ideas have agency outside of their home culture? The irony is that the advocates for nationalism claim they are the ones who take ideas seriously and who are working hardest to protect the ideals of the American creed. They believe that protecting the creed means protecting the culture and heritage from which it first sprang. But that approach treats ideas as wholly dependent on cultural

---

[11]Nathan Finn, email to author, December 18, 2020.
[12]Geertz, *Interpretation of Cultures*, 89, 5.

circumstances. In fact, their stance does not take ideas seriously at all; they do not believe ideas exert an independent effect on the world. To them, ideas are a byproduct, an epiphenomenon, a function of something deeper and more fundamental: "culture." Culture does all the work; once we get the culture right, ideas inexorably follow—and by extension, they believe ideas cannot survive without their supporting culture.

I am not satisfied with this because, as I discuss in chapter four, it is simply not true. History, evidence, and social science easily show that some of the major defining ideas of classical liberalism, at least, have been transmitted across cultural lines. Advocates of classical liberalism treat ideas with more seriousness. We believe ideas can, in principle, be independent of culture and heritage; that ideas can break free of the cultural and historical circumstances in which they were first articulated; that ideas can be reappropriated and rein-terpreted in other cultural and historical circumstances in ways that still pre-serve the unity and consistency of those ideas. Since that is true, we have to recognize that ideology can be at least partly independent of culture, and thus culture does not wholly subsume ideology. There is a part of ideology that is acultural, not wholly determined by and dependent on culture. Nor is that true only of liberalism: socialism, Christianity, and nationalism itself have all jumped cultural borders and found new homes and new meanings in different lands. Try a common-sense test: have you ever learned from a book written in a dif-ferent culture or historical context? Did you benefit from Aristotle's discussion of the virtues or Plato's dialogue on justice, from Dante's poetry, Shakespeare's plays, or Dostoevsky's novels? If so, recognize that though you do not live in ancient Greece, medieval Italy, renaissance England, or czarist Russia, you were able to take ideas and stories from those eras and make them meaningful in your context. Ideas can take on meaning outside of their originating culture.

By the same token, there must be a nonideological component of culture. If culture is "patterns of meaning," they are not all meanings about politics and society. There are meanings about life and death, the gods, our ancestors, what it means to be a good husband or wife, how to live well, the meaning of good friendship, what makes a good joke, how to face tragedy and suffer well, how to greet a guest and offer hospitality, what counts as good food or appropriate clothing, how to show respect and disrespect to others, and so forth. Our in-herited patterns of meaning make up the whole of life, and the whole of life is vastly larger than the domain of politics and our meager political ideologies.

If you are having a hard time grasping that there are nonpolitical, nonideological aspects of life, you spend too much time on Twitter. The nonideological component of culture is, in principle, very large: it includes all the habits, mores, customs, quirks, foibles, preferences, peccadilloes, and idiosyncrasies that makes one place or people distinct from another.

The nationalist argument boils to down an assertion that ideology cannot survive if disconnected from these nonideological components of culture. We will lose who we are, they say, and imperil our experiment in free government if our culture changes too much. Taken to its logical extreme, their argument reduces to the belief that liberal democracy depends for its survival on the cultured habits of eighteenth-century English gentlemen. If that were true, democracy would have died a quick death a long time ago. Instead, it has enjoyed an almost miraculous global spread over the past two centuries, suggesting that the nationalist theory of the relationship between ideas and culture is wrong.

One last term, or set of terms, needs clarification. What is an *evangelical*, and why does it matter that so often we speak specifically of *White* evangelicals distinct from the non-White kind? Throughout this book I use the terms *White evangelical, White Christian, and Anglo-Protestant*, and critics may be uncomfortable with the imprecision implied by my usage. Who exactly are these people? The imprecision is built into my argument: in chapter four I argue that cultures have blurry boundaries and that they overlap and intermingle in ways that make strong demarcations impractical. The same is true of the historic ethnoreligious group marked by Anglo-American culture and by the norms and values (if not always the dogma) of early modern protesting Christianity—which is the group I generally have in mind when I use the terms *White evangelical* or *Anglo-Protestant*.

I am precise in one respect: by *evangelical*, I generally do not mean people who conform to the Bebbington quadrilateral—biblicism, crucicentrism, conversionism, and activism—which is the standard scholarly definition of evangelicalism as defined religiously or theologically.[13] *Evangelical* has a long history and originally was a purely religious term that meant something like "Protestant who wishes to share the good news of Jesus Christ." But in the

---

[13]David W. Bebbington, *Evangelicalism in Modern Britain: A History from the 1730s to the 1980s* (New York: Routledge, 2003).

twentieth- and twenty-first-century American context, the word *evangelical* now has a cultural, tribal, and political meaning. Samuel Huntington calls this culture "Anglo-Protestantism" to emphasize the Anglo-American roots of this tradition. It is important to note that this is a cultural or tribal unit, not a religious or racial one, and so it is possible for this culture to include non-Anglos, non-Whites, non-Protestants, and even non-Christians who otherwise conform to Anglo-Protestant culture, values, and norms. Much of this book is a sort of anthropology of cultural or tribal evangelicalism.

I generally use Huntington's term "Anglo-Protestant" and *White Protestant* to refer to the dominant American national culture prior to the 1960s. (I am not using it in reference only to the northeastern political and economic upper class of White Anglo-Saxon Protestants, or WASPs, as is sometimes done.) I generally use *White evangelical* or *conservative White Christian* synonymously to refer to the post-1965 cultural and tribal (not theological) community of self-identified, politically engaged conservative White Christians regardless of their actual theological beliefs or religious practices (which is why it comes to include Catholics and people who do not attend church regularly). Where necessary, I distinguish between *religious evangelicals* or *churchgoing evangelicals*, on the one hand, referring to those who adhere to the historic and religious definition of evangelicalism as understood since the Reformation, and *tribal evangelicals*, referring to twentieth- and twenty-first-century American nationalists who believe America is a Christian nation and who participate in White evangelical culture, regardless of their religious beliefs. But by distinguishing between the two I do not mean to imply that they are entirely separate. They overlap more than they diverge and, I suspect, more than many White American Christians realize. Many American Christians fall into both categories; the question is not which category they belong to, but which takes precedence in their public lives. Different kinds of evangelicalism might mix in the same heart, but only one political agenda can predominate: the pursuit of tribal privilege and power, or the principled pursuit of justice for all.

A NOTE TO DIFFERENT AUDIENCES

I argue that Christian nationalism is a bad thing, inconsistent with both the ideals of the American experiment and important tenets of biblical

Christianity. But I face a dilemma in writing this book. The people who I believe most need its message are least likely to read it. Christian nationalists tend to be older, less educated, and more rural (and Whiter), not the typical target audience for an academic book of social science, history, political theory, and theology. This sort of book is likely to attract college students, seminarians, young pastors, urbanites, the educated general-interest reader, journalists, other scholars—all of whom are likely to already believe that Christian nationalism is a bad thing. Over 60 percent of millennials already reject Christian nationalism, according to one scholar.[14] I recognize that this book might be a long exercise in preaching to the choir.

But even the choir needs good teaching. I hope this book is useful for readers who already agree with its basic message by clarifying exactly what Christian nationalism is, *why* Christian nationalism is bad, and what its damaging implications are, thus equipping you to be better Christian witnesses in the public square and better teachers in your own churches, families, and schools—places where there almost certainly are a number of true believers in Christian nationalism. The most influential political discussions in America take place around the dinner table, at the local school, and during potluck after Sunday church services (or whatever the equivalent is to potluck for non-Baptists). I hope this book gives you more confidence and more knowledge to have those discussions. I also hope it is a model for how to engage the other side with good grace. You have a responsibility to be wise, gracious ambassadors of both true Christianity and a humble, affectionate, open patriotism.

I hope this book is useful for pastors, seminarians, church leaders, and other professional Christians for the same reason—leaders who often have more political influence than they are comfortable with. Some Christian leaders—especially White Christian pastors—who recognize the dangers of Christian nationalism have absorbed a functional quietism about politics, believing it to be inappropriate to engage too directly or too explicitly about political issues except abortion and religious liberty. "Just preach the gospel" is their common refrain. But quietism is itself a public, political stance: your congregants absorb the lesson that Christianity has no particular political implications except to endorse the pro-life movement, and thus there is no particular problem with

---

[14]Whitehead and Perry, *Taking America Back for God*, 50.

the de facto Christian nationalism that dominates much of White evangelical political life. That implicit message is false. African American pastors are rarely drawn to quietism because their churches were vital in the fight for civil rights and have always been much more central to the social and political lives of their members. In other words, some White members of this choir sing too softly: I hope this book helps you see the inevitable and important responsibility we have to explicitly and vocally oppose the misuse of our faith in the public square, to proclaim the distinction between cultural evangelicalism and biblical Christianity.

Another set of readers might not stop at agreeing with this book's basic message. Many millennials, for example, have already come to their own conclusions about the dangers of Christian involvement in American politics—and some are overreacting by rejecting patriotism in addition to nationalism, by giving up on America altogether, leaving the Christian faith, or gravitating to other political ideologies that are as dangerous and foolish as the nationalism they reject. They are singing the wrong tune, and I would hope to gently bring them back to the score written in these pages. I have no desire to write another book of evangelical self-flagellation, or to give another ex-evangelical budding socialist a talking point to explain why he left the faith. While this book amounts to a pointed critique of Christian nationalism, readers should understand that I am writing about my own people, as I share in my story below. This book is (I hope) not an exercise in self-righteous judgment intoned from on high, but a pastoral and reflective engagement on a serious political theory that has deep roots in American history. I feel obligated as a Christian, a patriot, and a public intellectual to treat my interlocutors, no matter how gravely mistaken I believe them to be, with respect and charity. Readers expecting the frisson of Twitter snark will come away (mostly) disappointed. (You can follow me on Twitter—@pauldmiller2—for that.)

It is precisely because I assume most of my readers already agree with my basic argument, and some are at risk of going too far—of throwing the baby out with the bathwater—that I have included a positive vision of a healthy kind of patriotism and the outline of a theology of nationhood. This is the part of the book that may strike a discordant note with readers who are already skeptical of Christian nationalism. Truthfully, I am not fully comfortable doing so because of the curious dynamics that surround public debate. Readers usually filter what they read through the experience of contemporary events. If I say anything positive about America or suggest there is any validity to national identity, some will jump to the conclusion that I am shilling for Trump or the Republican Party. In the face of contemporary realities—the ascendency of nationalism on the right—I feel a specific burden to focus my energy on critiquing, not justifying, the nationalist program. Even still, I argue that patriotism and American ideals are generally good. I do so because I believe these things to be true, because I believe this to be a message that millennials and younger readers specifically need to hear—and also because, as George Orwell argued, a healthy patriotism is the best inoculation against the dangers of nationalism. Some readers are probably so skeptical of group identity, so cynical about American history, and so alienated by the Trump presidency that they see no merit at all in American identity or national solidarity. I think this is a serious mistake both because it is theologically erroneous and also because it is politically counterproductive. If you want to oppose nationalism most effectively, you need to be a patriot. I have written this book to show that we can and should reject nationalism without rejecting America, and to illustrate that patriotism is not the slippery slope to nationalism but the best guardrail against it.

A note to two other potential audiences. If you are a Christian nationalist, I hope you find a faithful, accurate, and fair reconstruction of your ideology in chapter three—because I know you will also find an unstinting, blunt critique of it throughout the rest of the book. Please understand that I approach debate with a certain ethos: charity and magnanimity toward people I believe to be mistaken; but to mistaken *ideas*, no mercy. When I encounter ideas I believe to be mistaken, it is my job, my vocation, and my calling as a teacher and public intellectual to dissect those ideas, show them for their error, warn against them, and illustrate how damaging and destructive they can be, with every bit of evidence, reasoning, and rhetoric I can muster. Please do not take my intellectual zeal as personal contempt. I love you and pray for you, and I think your ideology is unjust, unwise, and dangerous.

Finally, it is possible that some readers come from outside this conversation. Progressives, Democrats, socialists, and Americans of other faiths or no faith at all might pick up this book. If so, you are welcome to listen in on this debate that is largely among evangelical Christians and Americans on the political right. Indeed, I hope you do, because the stakes of this debate are high for everyone, not just for conservative American Christians. Our intramural debate has profound consequences for the nation as a whole. In passing, you will find occasional references to you and your movements and beliefs, but not in great detail. I obviously am not a progressive and I disagree with virtually everything the left stands for. You may be dissatisfied with my dismissive asides to your movement. That is not for lack of interest or belief in the importance of your ideas. Rather, engaging with your ideas is so important I intend to leave it for a separate book altogether.

MY STORY

I am a White American Christian. I am politically and theologically conservative (more on what that word actually means later). I was raised in what most observers would call a fundamentalist household. I've attended Baptist and nondenominational churches throughout my life. I "prayed the prayer" at the age of five. As a teenager I went to a Billy Graham Crusade in Portland, Oregon, in 1992. I was baptized in the Willamette River two years later in a scene of old-time religion straight out of *O Brother, Where Art Thou?* Politically, I was born and bred into social conservatism and the Republican Party, learning to vote on the basis of abortion and family values. My wife and I met and married at a Southern Baptist church at which we were happily members for ten years. To this day I am a theological traditionalist: I hold old-fashioned views about sin, hell, and the exclusivity of Christianity's truth claims. I am proudly pro-life and I am a zealot for religious liberty. I served for several years as an elder at a small Baptist church in Texas. I love eating at Chick-fil-A.

I am also a patriot. I served in the United States Army and I am a veteran of the war in Afghanistan. I spent nearly a decade working for the US government, including working in the White House for President George W. Bush. I read the Declaration of Independence to my kids on the Fourth of July (the famous bits, at least), and a selection of presidential Thanksgiving Day proclamations over turkey each November. I've lived in nine states and three countries and I am immensely proud to be an American (though I don't care for Lee Greenwood's schmaltzy country hymn) and grateful for the privilege of raising my three children here. If I sometimes doubt that the United States is the absolute single greatest country in the history of the universe, it is because I have an almost childlike admiration for the United Kingdom.

I firmly believe in the exceptional nature of the American experiment. This is an unpopular thing to say among my fellow scholars, for many of whom

American exceptionalism is a dirty word, an indication that I am probably a rube, possibly a bigot. Their suspicion isn't wholly unfounded: as I'll discuss later, there are many versions of American exceptionalism, some of which actually mean the opposite of what I mean. What I mean is this: as a matter of historical fact, the circumstances of America's founding are unique; the United States, unlike any other nation in the world at the time, claimed to be defined by a set of ideas; and those ideas have proven to be the most successful for ordered liberty, for the peaceful transfer of power, and for human flourishing in the history of human civilization.

But it is vital to recognize, despite how exceptional it was at the time, those ideals are no longer uniquely associated with America. American ideals of liberty are, in an important sense, not American. As world history since 1776 has proven, the ideals and institutions of a free society can be adapted across the world. American exceptionalism is *not* the view that we, uniquely, invented and live by the ideals of freedom and equality, or that we, uniquely, deserve freedom. Rather, it is the belief that we, uniquely, rediscovered and adapted a set of *universal* ideas to practical experience in a way that can be emulated and improved upon by the rest of humanity. As George W. Bush said in 2002, "America will lead by defending liberty and justice because they are right and true and unchanging for all people everywhere. No nation owns these aspirations, and no nation is exempt from them."[15]

I start with my religious and patriotic bona fides and my belief in American exceptionalism to help you understand that when I spend the rest of this book calling fire on Christian nationalism, I do it as an American patriot and an orthodox Christian—and I do it *because* of my patriotism and my Christian faith, not despite them. When I warn against nationalism, I am not doing so from the left. My critique of one side is not an endorsement of the other. My alienation from the Republican Party has not driven me into the arms of the opposition. I firmly call down a plague on both their houses. Not only am I pro-life, I find the Democratic Party's emerging view on religious liberty deeply alarming. I have written elsewhere at greater length about the problems I see with the left and the Democratic Party.[16] I remain more or less politically

---

[15]George W. Bush, "State of the Union," January 29, 2002.
[16]See Paul D. Miller, "The Twenty-First Century Federalist," *Perspectives on Politics* 46, no. 1 (2017): 51-57; "The Perils of Croly's Promise," *National Affairs* 39 (Spring 2019); and "Politics Is More Than Abortion vs. Character," *Mere Orthodoxy*, November 2, 2020.

conservative, in the pre-2016 sense of the word; I only lament that the Republican Party no longer is.

In other respects I am not a typical White evangelical, beginning with an upbringing and a family that—to lean on cliché—looks like America in its ethnic diversity. Later, I served in the most ethnically and racially integrated institution in America: the US Army. I've lived and worked most of my adult life in large, diverse cities that don't look like red America. I have extensive international experience. I have a passport (less than half of Americans do) and have visited a dozen foreign countries for work, education, and tourism. I served in Afghanistan alongside troops from around the world in our multinational coalition, including Afghan troops. I waited tables at a restaurant in Washington, DC, alongside a Palestinian who faithfully took breaks every few hours to lay out his rug in the basement, face east toward Mecca, and say his prayers. I taught military officers from across Africa and Asia at the National Defense University in Washington, DC. I once had to shout down two students, a Libyan and an American, who were near blows over disagreements about US foreign policy; lectured on political Islam to Egyptians and Saudis; and taught geo-strategy to Pakistanis and Indians in the same class who dutifully took notes on how to use my lessons against each other. I have graduate degrees, hold a top-secret security clearance, served in the CIA, and have attended meetings in the Oval Office.

These experiences helped me gain something of an outsiders' perspective on my community. I know my bluntness may offend some friends and family, but I also owe it to them to be honest: in my observation, middle-class White American evangelicals living in red states can be surprisingly ignorant of the rest of our country, let alone the world; deaf to self-criticism; and curiously incurious to learn about people who are different from them. The same is true, of course, of the college-educated White American progressives living in blue states with whom I have spent most of my career. The difference is that while conservatives are proud of their bubble, progressives deny they are in one.

My background, experience, and beliefs have made me politically and culturally homeless. In early 2016, I signed the "Open Letter on Donald Trump from GOP National Security Leaders."[17] My stance against Trump put me in a

---

[17]"Open Letter on Donald Trump from GOP National Security Leaders," War on the Rocks, March 2, 2016, https://warontherocks.com/2016/03/open-letter-on-donald-trump-from-gop-national-security-leaders/.

tiny minority among Republicans—and, even more so, among my fellow White evangelical Christians. Famously, 81 percent of self-identified White evangelicals reported voting for him, and Trump consistently enjoyed his highest approval rating among White evangelicals compared to any other religious or cultural group throughout his presidency. Several evangelical leaders contrived explanations for why Trump's policies were not merely morally permissible but the best and possibly only way of keeping America safe. After Trump's loss in the 2020 election, some White evangelicals were at the forefront of spreading falsehoods about the integrity of the election. The 81 percent of White evangelicals who voted for Donald Trump are my people. They are my friends, neighbors, and family, including some of the people with whom I share a pew on Sundays. I grew up with them and agree with them on the most important issues of faith and the meaning of human life.

Since I am in such a small minority, the burden of proof is on me to explain why I believe my erstwhile political comrades and coreligionists are wrong to have taken up the banner of nationalism. That requires a deeper discussion of American nationalism: its theory, its history, and its theology. It does not require rehashing our debates about Trump's personality and temperament, which are immaterial to the broader political movement he represents. To be candid, I believed in 2016 that Trump was personally unqualified for public office because of his character and temperament; I think his presidency vindicated my concerns; I publicly argued for his impeachment and conviction in 2019 because of his criminal conduct;[18] and I will repeat all of these concerns if Trump runs again in 2024. But I have mostly chosen to ignore those issues in this book and focus instead on nationalist ideology, beliefs, and the broader social and cultural movement Trump represents, which predate Trump and will outlast him. I am more concerned about what Trump stands for and what he represents, about the deeper and broader cultural wave he is riding: the wave of nationalism, especially the sort that puts a Christian gloss on American identity. Nationalism—as distinct from patriotism—is a dangerous ideology. Trump's rise and his embrace by my erstwhile political friends and allies helped me to look afresh at the American political right and at American history. This book is my effort to share what I've seen.

---

[18]Paul D. Miller, "Five Reasons Every American Should Oppose Donald Trump," *The Federalist,* February 29, 2016; Paul D. Miller, "Convict Trump: The Constitution Is More Important Than Abortion," *The Christian Post,* December 22, 2019.

NATIONALISM AND THE LOVE OF COUNTRY

WHY NATIONALISM? WHY NOW?

The resurgence of nationalism in the twenty-first century is a response to decades of weakening national identities driven by globalization and tribalization. After the end of the Cold War, capitalism and democracy appeared to be the "final form of human government," and their triumph was hailed as the "end of history," as Francis Fukuyama argued.[1] Dozens of countries in Eastern Europe, the former Soviet Union, Africa, and Latin America transitioned to some form of democratic and capitalist systems and joined the emerging global economic and trading regime. But that regime came with a price: every country that participated, including the United States, had to open itself up to foreign investment, multinational corporations, and the creative destruction—which sometimes felt more destructive than creative—of hypercompetitive global capitalism. These forces, seemingly unresponsive and unaccountable to any national governing authority, were unimpressed with local difference and cultural particularity. Globalization led to deindustrialization, the loss of manufacturing jobs, and the homogenizing and depressing sameness of "McWorld," as Benjamin Barber termed the global monoculture that was everywhere and nowhere.[2] Many consumers enjoyed lower prices and cheap goods, and hated everything else about McWorld, but also felt powerless to stop or reverse its

---

[1]Francis Fukuyama, "The End of History?," *The National Interest* 16 (1989): 3-18.
[2]Benjamin Barber, *Jihad vs. McWorld: Terrorism's Challenge to Democracy* (New York: Ballantine, 2010).

impact on their communities because it was unresponsive even to their national governments. McWorld felt condescending, arrogant, bland, imperial, and soulless.

At the same time, national identity has been weakened from below by fragmentation, balkanization, and tribalization. The Cold War had forced virtually every nation in the world to pick a side, capitalist or communist, and participate in a decades-long ideological struggle that overrode differences in culture, identity, religion, and region. When the Cold War ended, subnational identities reemerged with a vengeance. Civil war erupted in Yugoslavia and Afghanistan along ethnic and religious lines; ethnic violence and civil unrest wracked Armenia, Azerbaijan, Uzbekistan, and Tajikistan; genocide tore Rwanda apart and sent chaos tumbling into the Democratic Republic of the Congo next door, which spent most of the 1990s as the center of a major international war that left some ten million dead. In the developed world, subnational identities led to calls for autonomy, decentralization, and even secession, from the Québécois of Canada, Catalonians of Spain, and Scots of Britain, to the Flemish and Walloons of Belgium and the "velvet divorce" of Czechs from Slovaks. Though it dates at least to the end of the Cold War, the rise of reactionary, atavistic subnational identities has accelerated in recent years in response to the apparent soullessness of global capitalism, the sclerosis of liberal democracy, and the 2008 financial crisis and recession. The Covid-19 pandemic and ensuing economic downturn seem to have accelerated these trends.

In the United States, American national identity has always been conceived somewhat differently than in the rest of the world, and thus its experience of globalization and fragmentation has also been different. In globalization, it could see its own image reflected dimly in the triumph of its ideals abroad, and the American foreign policy establishment largely supported the strengthening of international ties, the creation of new international organizations (such as the World Trade Organization in 1995), and the expansion of cooperative security (through the North Atlantic Treaty Organization). But America was not immune from the same forces of cultural homogenization and deindustrialization that afflicted the rest of the world, and so Americans too eventually grew disillusioned with globalization. Tribalization found traction because of America's vastly greater pluralism, compared to Europe, and because academia gave it an official ideology in the form of multiculturalism and identity politics. Scholars and activists, mostly on the left, have increasingly argued that American identity is deeply, even irredeemably flawed because of its historical complicity with racism, slavery, and other historical crimes. Historically oppressed peoples, they argue, should cultivate an attachment to their own particular identities, advocate for the advancement of their group, and withhold loyalty to any shared sense of American identity, while scholars engage in ceaseless, unstinting critique of the American experiment.

This is the problem that nationalists want to solve. A substantial number of people—at least a plurality of Americans and a broadly similar number of Europeans—believe that their national identity is good, endangered, and worth fighting for. They feel that globalization has gone too far and tribalization is too dangerous. Nationalism is one of the main political and cultural responses to these trends, an effort to salvage and revive a meaningful sense of national identity between the global and the tribal. It is both an ideology for political action and a cultural movement seeking to revive lost (or imagined) senses of national identity and national solidarity. I sympathize with much of their critique of globalization and tribalization, and I agree that national identity can be good and healthy (see chap. 10). However, nationalists' solutions are deeply flawed: nationalism turns out to be just another form of tribalization and just as corrosive of a healthy national identity as many of the trends they rightly decry.

LOVE OF COUNTRY

What is nationalism, and how does it differ from patriotism? Why would President Trump say that "we're not supposed to use that word"? Is nationalism a good way of thinking about politics? Is there an alternative? In this book I argue that nationalism is generally a bad idea. Before I can make the argument, I need to define my terms—and here already we run into a problem. As I've developed this argument over the past several years, I've heard a common complaint: this is just a game of words that depends entirely on how we define *nationalism*. I've stacked the deck by defining nationalism in wholly negative terms, critics say, so that by the time I'm done simply defining the word, my argument that nationalism is bad is a foregone conclusion. In particular, many nationalists claim that nationalism simply means the love of country. I disagree: as I show later, the word carries a lot more meaning than that—and even nationalists who *claim* to mean nothing more than "love of country" often actually mean more because of *how they define the country*. But first I want to address the love of country, simply considered on its own terms, which I call *patriotism*. I agree that the love of country is usually good, but we still need to be on guard against some common temptations to ensure our love is rightly ordered.

Loyalty and affection for our home and our tribe is instinctive, universal, and essential for human life. C. S. Lewis praised the "love of home, of the place we grew up in . . . of all places fairly near these and fairly like them; love of old acquaintances, of familiar sights, sounds, and smells," as well as "a love for the way of life," for "the local dialect," and more.[3] Edmund Burke rightly taught that we ought to cultivate affection for our inner circles of associations as practice for the next-most outward circle: "To be attached to the subdivision, to love the little platoon we belong to in society, is the first principle (the germ as it were) of public affections."[4] More recently, Nigel Biggar, an Anglican theologian, ethicist, priest, and scholar at Oxford University, argued that "it is justifiable to feel affection, loyalty, and gratitude toward a nation whose customs and institutions have inducted us into created forms of human flourishing."[5] We have all experienced that combination of pride, fellow feeling, and grandeur that comes from being a part of something larger than ourselves, something important, some part of history. We have a natural bent for this kind of team spirit, group loyalty, or *tribalism:* a prerational, atavistic loyalty—emotional and instinctual rather than cerebral and philosophical—to the people and places that feel familiar and in which we see ourselves reflected.

This kind of love for our country goes hand-in-hand with what is sometimes called a "civil religion," a collection of traditions for collectively celebrating our patriotic attachment.[6] Virtually all of us participate in some aspects of America's civil religion—the collection of symbols, beliefs, and civic liturgies that tie Americans together and create a sense of shared experience, including the flag, the Pledge of Allegiance, the anthem, and the feast days

---

[3]C. S. Lewis, *The Four Loves* (New York: Harcourt and Brace, 1960), 41.
[4]Edmund Burke, *Reflections on the Revolution in France* (London: Penguin Classics, 1986), 135.
[5]Nigel Biggar, *Between Kin and Cosmopolis: An Ethic of the Nation* (Eugene, OR: Wipf and Stock, 2014), 13.
[6]Robert N. Bellah, "Civil Religion in America," *Daedalus* (1967): 1-21.

(Memorial Day, Independence Day, and Thanksgiving), Juneteenth, the musical *Hamilton,* days of prayer, parades, national museums, historical sites and battlefields, national cemeteries, statues of national heroes, the commemoration of achievements or shared experiences, honoring the military and its achievements, speeches about national purpose, and celebrating folkways like clothing, music, food, and dance. These are the modern form of tribalism, adapted to the large, mass politics of contemporary states.[7]

Is tribalism good or bad? This is a complicated issue because, whether it is good or bad, it is inevitable. We cannot simply get rid of it; humans will always find a tribe to be part of and to root for. Human beings are not best understood as individuals found in a state of nature. Rather, we are found first in families; then in extended families with grandparents, uncles, second cousins, and more; and then in larger units still of loosely affiliated kinship groups and communities. We even participate in tribes of our own choosing, such as schools and colleges, the fandom of sports teams, hobbyist associations, and religious groups (I am a proud member of the tribe of *Star Wars* fandom). We are tribesmen and tribeswomen before we are individuals.

Sometimes this kind of tribalism can veer into chauvinism and national idolatry—I'll spend the rest of the book warning against how nationalism tries to make us all one large tribe, which is a dangerous and utopian fantasy—but civil religion, at its best, is a sort of theatrical enactment of our solidarity and patriotism. Crucially, this pageantry has an educational and formative function. It is meant to evoke emotional loyalty to our country but also awareness of the American creed and gratitude for the best parts of our heritage. Civil religion should teach us what our country stands for and commemorate the moments in our national history when we got it right. It can shape and reinforce our collective identity as *this people,* with *this* particular history, the ones dedicated to *these sorts of ideas,* and who aspire to live up to *those good examples.* Done right, civil religion elevates mere tribalism into something more. It can also be an important occasion for catharsis, as when we collectively mourned the terrorist attacks of 2001, or when I grieved with

---

[7]These kinds of civil liturgies are akin to what Billig calls "banal nationalism," or the routine mundane ways in which nationhood is "flagged" and reproduced and how it structures citizens' unconscious assumptions about individual and "national" identity. Billig is critical of this kind of national attachment, whereas I acknowledge is it usually harmless and even necessary; see his *Banal Nationalism* (London: Sage, 1995).

my fellow soldiers at the funeral of a fallen comrade. As such, it is inescapable, necessary, and can be beneficial.

A small portion of the American population is sometimes embarrassed by Americans' simple devotion to their country. In a recent study of American sentiment toward American identity, a pair of sociologists identified a group of Americans they call the "disengaged," who made up about 17 percent of the population, but were disproportionately represented among Democrats, the highly educated, and the least religious. The disengaged said they did not feel close to America and reported the lowest levels of pride in American history, achievements, and ideals. The disengaged were the least likely to say they would rather be a US citizen than not, and the most likely to express shame in America.[8] This way of viewing American identity starts with an obviously true insight: that blind or knee-jerk loyalty to a group is not an intrinsic virtue. Lots of groups do bad things, including national groups, and the United States has committed its share of historical sins. Some groups and nations are simply bad by virtue of how they define themselves in opposition to others. Tribalism is easily distorted and turned into chauvinism, xenophobia, and racism.

But the disengaged view tends to overemphasize America's sins and failings and misunderstand the solution. This is probably the same subgroup of Americans who, after protesters tore down Confederate statues in the summer of 2020, cheered when protesters moved on to tear down statues of George Washington and Ulysses S. Grant. This mindset is what the nationalist right is reacting against—and it is partly justified. The "disengaged" should remember that American ideals are actually worth celebrating. Civil religion is what helps create the *unum* from the *pluribus.* If you are so fixated on what America got wrong that you cannot celebrate the American creed and enjoy some schmaltzy patriotism on the Fourth of July, you've entirely lost the plot. More to the point, rejecting group loyalty is the wrong answer because if it succeeds, people will simply gravitate to another group: we cannot live without some kind of group identity. More often, the effort fails and sparks a backlash and tempts people to dig in their heels, cling to ever-smaller tribal identities all the harder, and define their boundaries more exclusively. This is the origin of identity politics, including White nationalism.

---

[8]Bart Bonikowski and Paul DiMaggio, "Varieties of American Popular Nationalism," *American Sociological Review* 81, no. 5 (2016): 949-980.

But the left does have a point: we do need some way to guard against the obvious dangers of unreflective tribalism. To judge the moral quality of our group loyalties, we have to ask what our group is doing, how the group is defined, and what the group is for. And, in truth, the nationalist right needs to learn to incorporate more sobriety, humility, lament, and contrition in their celebrations of America. How do we do so? Note what Edmund Burke thought local public affections were ultimately for: "It is the first link in the series by which we proceed towards a love to our country, and to mankind."[9] Burke did not want us to stop with the little platoons. Team spirit starts with the normal, healthy, and universal affection for home, family, and tribe—but it should not end there. If our team spirit stops with the little platoons or exhausts itself with mere loyalty to local identities, we would never have a basis to stand apart from our tribe when it does something wrong, nor would we be able to grow beyond our little platoon if it grows too insular. We need something more to ensure our group affinity does not deteriorate into provincialism, groupthink, or the passions of the mob. Burke thought the little platoons were important because they helped train our hearts to be other-directed, and because we should not ultimately be concerned only with the other members of our tribe. We should, in principle, love every human being in the world. Loving the strangers whom we call countrymen helps us practice that kind of universal, disinterested love of humanity. A love of country is healthy because it trains us for spiritual cosmopolitanism, which should complement, rather than replace, local affections.

Most people, following George Orwell, call this healthy affection for one's country "patriotism." "By 'patriotism' I mean devotion to a particular place and a particular way of life," Orwell wrote, "which one believes to be the best in the world but has no wish to force on other people."[10] Anthony Smith similarly defined the patriot as "the man who is loyal and devoted to his community" and who shows "love of country."[11] Christians should recognize that patriotism is good because all of God's creation is good, and *patriotism* is another word for gratitude for and commitment to our particular place in it: our affection and loyalty to a specific part of God's

---

[9]Burke, *Reflections on the Revolution in France*, 135.

[10]George Orwell, "Notes on Nationalism," available at www.orwellfoundation.com/the-orwell -foundation/orwell/essays-and-other-works/notes-on-nationalism/.

[11]Anthony Smith, *Nationalism: Theory, Ideology, History*, 2nd ed. (Cambridge: Polity, 2010), 25.

creation helps us do the good work of cultivating and improving the part we happen to live in.

Another important way of guarding against the bad kind of tribalism is to be careful how we define the boundaries of our group. What makes us *us*? What is distinct and different about us that separates us from everyone who isn't us? Most political tribes throughout history picked a shared characteristic like race, ethnicity, heritage, or religion, which is the defining trait of nationalism. As I'll explore throughout this book, defining one's group that way leads to all sorts of problems, especially, but not only, in the American context. For our purposes, American identity is best defined by our history and by a set of ideals, not by an ethnicity, culture, or religion. Retelling our story (all of it, including the bad parts), teaching the creed of liberty and equality, and symbolizing them with the pageantry of civil religion is the best kind of patriotism. We celebrate that America, at its best, "strives to serve as a communal paragon of justice, freedom, and equality among nations," as John Wilsey argued.[12] This kind of "open exceptionalism" harnesses our natural tribal loyalties to a constitution, the rule of law, minority rights, freedom of conscience, the disestablishment of religion, and so forth. Patriotism in democratic societies achieves a unique harmony: all people feel natural affection for their own nation, but democratic patriots around the world can feel special pride because our affection and loyalty are, in part, to a set of ideals and to a moral aspiration.

Defining our national identity by a set of ideals helps guard against bad tribalism because it sets up an external standard outside and above the nation by which we can judge our nation's conduct. This enables the best kind of love for our country: when we challenge ourselves to do better. As Biggar argues, "What one owes one's family or nation is not anything or everything, but specifically respect for and promotion of their good. Such loyalty, therefore, does not involve simply doing or giving whatever is demanded."[13] In times when our nation perpetuates a great evil, our love for our country ought to lead us to oppose that evil and work to change our nation for the better—one of the clearest ways that a healthy love for country should depart from a crude tribalism or uncritical team spirit. Sadly, in 2004, 37 percent of Americans believed that "people should support their country even if their country is in the

---

[12]John D. Wilsey, *American Exceptionalism and Civil Religion: Reassessing the History of an Idea* (Downers Grove, IL: InterVarsity Press, 2015), 18.
[13]Biggar, *Between Kin and Cosmopolis*, 14.

wrong,"[14] a clear sign that many Americans' love of country is not rightly ordered. The best patriot is the one who recognizes what our nation *should* be at its best, not the one who celebrates "my country, right or wrong."

Scholars call this a variety of names, including liberal nationalism, civic nationalism, creedal nationalism, prophetic civil religion, or open exceptionalism.[15] By whatever label, its defining trait is a civic understanding of American identity, in which America is defined by the American creed—ideals that stand apart from and over the nation itself; ideals which are, in principle, universal. I'll return to this in more detail in chapter ten. When we are loyal to those ideals, we can envision the best version of our country and, simultaneously, we can see the best version of other countries that aspire to similar ideals (as about half the world now does). It is precisely these ideals that allow us to see the universal in the particular, and thus to move seamlessly from a love of our particular country to the universal love of humanity. When we love our country not merely because of its familiarity but also because of what it stands for, we are engaging in a higher kind of love, a truer love of our *patria*, our homeland. This is what G. K. Chesterton meant when he said America was a nation with "the soul of a church."

The tribalist's love of his or her tribe is instinctive and thus a lesser kind of love. Love of country *starts* with a prerational, natural, and inescapable affection for what is familiar and close, but it should not end there. Many things that are "natural" are easily distorted and need discipline and order imposed by reason, reflection, and grace. If our love of country stops with natural affection, it is no better than a child's preference for a favorite toy. Our love for country should grow and mature into something more considered and discriminating, disciplined and ordered by an understanding of our country's history and *what our country is for*, by the ideals of justice, liberty, and equality. You may be wondering if it is really necessary to write a book vindicating the ideals of freedom and equality; to many, it may sound obvious and even trite. But many Americans apparently do not understand the full implications of American ideals for issues like immigration, church-state relations, or what

---

[14]Bonikowski and DiMaggio, "Varieties of American popular nationalism," 956.
[15]Liah Greenfeld, *Nationalism and the Mind: Essays on Modern Culture* (London: Oneworld, 2006); Bonikowski and DiMaggio, "Varieties of American Popular Nationalism," 949-80; Wilsey, *American Exceptionalism*. Peter Alter's "Risorgimento" and "Reform" nationalism are also of this type. "Cultural" or "objective" nationalism are also, in principle, consistent with this kind of liberal or civic patriotism.

sort of history we should honor in the public square. In a recent study of American nationalism, scholars found that just 22 percent of Americans were truly committed to defining American identity in creedal terms.[16] Most Americans mix their admiration for American ideals with a more restrictive definition of American identity, including the importance of being a Christian or having been born in the United States.

Christians should be grateful for the nations in which we live and (under most circumstances) should be obedient to our governments. The apostle Paul reminds us that "there is no authority except from God, and those that exist have been instituted by God," and that we should therefore be "subject to the governing authorities" (Romans 13:1). He described the ruler as "God's servant" commissioned to uphold order and do justice. Peter told us to "fear God, honor the emperor" (1 Peter 2:17); Paul reminded us to pray for those in authority (1 Timothy 2:1); Jesus told us to pay our taxes (Matthew 22:21); and Jeremiah told Israel to "seek the welfare of the city" to which it had been exiled (Jeremiah 29:7). Centuries later, Augustine argued that even though the "City of Man" was thoroughly marked by sin, we should still be grateful because it creates a temporal, earthly peace within which we can raise our families, live our lives, and seek the salvation of our neighbors.

WHAT IS NATIONALISM?

Some readers may wonder, if national team spirit is generally good, or at least a version of it is defensible, what the argument over nationalism is all about. Some nationalists claim that "love of country" is all they mean by the word. If so, this book is not really responding to them, but I do ask that they use words the way most everyone else uses them. People who call themselves nationalists should be aware of what nationalism means to scholars, what it has meant in history, and what contemporary politicians mean when they use it. The word *nationalism* has a history, a scholarly definition, and a specific political resonance.

In those contexts, nationalism is not merely love of country: it is an argument about *how we define* our country, about how we draw the boundary lines and

---

[16]Bonikowski and DiMaggio, "Varieties of American Popular Nationalism." For an alternate view, including a different way of measuring nationalist sentiment, see Matthew Wright, Jack Citrin, and Jonathan Wand, "Alternative Measures of American National Identity: Implications for the Civic-Ethnic Distinction," *Political Psychology* 33, no. 4 (2012): 469-82, who concluded that between 44 and 55 percent of Americans fall into the "clearly civic" category of nationalism.

say who is part of the nation and who is not, and it is also an argument about the nature, purposes, and duties of government. Nationalism is a theory about how human communities are best organized and what are the proper bases of political organization. In this section I review the scholarly literature on nationalism—which mostly focuses on nationalism around the world over the past two centuries—and develop a definition that captures its main themes. This is not a universal definition of all types of nationalism in all ages; rather, I am following most contemporary scholarship in tracing the evolution of nationalism as it has been practiced in the past two centuries and as it appears most frequently around the world today. Nationalism is the belief that humanity is divisible into mutually distinct, internally coherent cultural groups defined by shared traits like ethnicity, language, religion, or culture; that these groups should each have their own governments; that one of the purposes of government is to promote and protect a nation's cultural identity; and that sovereign nations with strong cultures provide meaning and purpose for human beings.

Humanity is divisible into cultural units. Nationalism, what one scholar has called "the most compelling identity myth in the modern world,"[17] starts with the belief that "nations" are not simply territories under a common rule but that they are groups of people defined by a common ethnicity, language, religion, or culture. These groups constitute an "imagined political community" of people who have never met face-to-face, yet who treat each other as part of a common whole with "deep, horizontal comradeship" because of their shared traits, in the words of Benedict Anderson in his seminal study of the subject.[18] Nationalism depends on the reality of such group feeling. In this sense, a nation is a cultural identity first, a political unit second.

The group in question is variously defined. Scholars of nationalism have shown how many different traits have been proposed as the basis for national identity. Hans Kohn listed "common descent, language, territory, political entity, customs and traditions, and religion."[19] Eugen Lemberg emphasized that nations are defined by "shared language, origins, character and culture, or common subordination to a given state power."[20] Anthony Smith defined

---

[17] Anthony Smith, *National Identity* (Reno: University of Nevada Press, 1991), viii.
[18] Benedict Anderson, *Imagined Communities: Reflections on the Origin and Spread of Nationalism* (New York: Verso, 2006), 6, 7.
[19] Hans Kohn, *The Idea of Nationalism: A Study of the Origins and Background* (New York: Macmillan, 1944), 14.
[20] Quoted in Peter Alter, *Nationalism*, 2nd ed. (New York: Hodder Education, 1994), 4.

nations as peoples with "common myths and historical memories."[21] Peter Alter called nations a "social group" that "has become conscious of its coherence, political unity and particular interests," through its shared "linguistic, cultural, religious, or political" heritage.[22]

Advocates of nationalism show the same tendency to offer several candidates as the possible basis of unity without settling on any one of them. Yoram Hazony, who made one of the most recent and sophisticated attempts to vindicate nationalism and make it intellectually respectable, defines a nation as a group of people with a shared "language or religion."[23] John Mearsheimer, an international relations scholar and another advocate of nationalism, argued that nations are characterized by six features: "a powerful sense of oneness, a distinct culture, a marked sense of specialness, a historical narrative that emphasizes timelessness, a deep attachment to territory, and a strong commitment to sovereignty or self-determination."[24] Michael Lind, an advocate of (liberal) nationalism, defines the nation as "a concrete historical community, defined primarily by a common language, common folkways, and a common vernacular culture."[25] Daniel Philpott, in one of the most famous defenses of national self-determination, gives up on finding objective criteria and settles instead on a subjective one: "it simply does not matter which traits define a seceding group; we know one when it announces, campaigns, or takes up arms for its dream of self-determination."[26]

The common theme among these definitions is that the nation is defined by shared traits, and that we should define ourselves by traits we share with others. We should be loyal to others because of what we have in common with them. In

---

[21]Smith, *National Identity*, 14, 73.

[22]Alter, *Nationalism*, 11. Scholars have noted that different nationalisms define their nation by different criteria. Anthony Smith argues that Western nations tended to focus on legal status while non-Western nations emphasized ethnicity. In fact, both kinds of nationalism are now often present in an ambiguous blend in the twenty-first century resurgence of nationalism (*National Identity*, 8).

[23]Yoram Hazony, *The Virtue of Nationalism* (London: Hachette, 2018).

[24]John Mearsheimer, *The Great Delusion: Liberal Dreams and International Realities* (New Haven, CT: Yale University Press, 2018). A similar, but negative, definition comes from Peter Alter: "consciousness of the uniqueness or peculiarity of a group of people, particularly with respect to their ethnic, linguistic or religious homogeneity; emphasizing of shared socio-cultural attitudes and historical memories; a sense of common mission; disrespect for and animosity towards other peoples" (*Nationalism*, 3).

[25]Michael Lind, *The Next American Nation: The New Nationalism and the Fourth American Revolution* (New York: Simon and Schuster, 2010).

[26]Daniel Philpott, "In Defense of Self-Determination," *Ethics* 105, no. 2 (1995): 365.

this sense, *culture* and *nation* are used synonymously. In that sense, nationalism is a retreat to raw tribalism. I argued above that tribalism is natural and unavoidable, but I also argued that it is not enough, that it can go awry, and that we should seek to grow beyond mere tribalism to avoid its dangers. Nationalism rejects the effort to move beyond tribalism and asserts that tribes are not merely natural but normative and that nations should aspire to be tribes writ large.

Sovereignty is a moral imperative. Nationalism is the belief that these cultural groups should form the basis of political organization. Nationalists believe that cultural groups, and the people in them, flourish best when they govern themselves without interference from other nations, and national units should be the fundamental units of political organization and international relations. Nationalism could be defined as the pursuit of *sovereign culture*; it is the belief that the mere existence of a discrete and coherent culture is enough for it to merit political sovereignty. Hans Kohn, one of the earliest scholars of nationalism, argued that "The growth of nationalism is the process of integration of the masses of the people into a common political form,"[27] which is to say, the expansion of a given government to encompass people presumed to belong to it. Nationalism, he continued, entails "a group seeking to find its expression in what it regards as the highest form of organized activity, a sovereign state."[28] Ernst Gellner wrote that "Nationalism is a political principle, which holds that the political and the national unit should be congruent."[29] Anthony Smith argues, "The nation is the source of all political power, and loyalty to it overrides all other loyalties," and nationalism "is an ideological movement for attaining and maintaining autonomy, unity, and identity," for the nation.[30] Max Weber defined a nation as "a community of sentiment which would adequately manifest itself in a state of its own." Nigel Biggar suggested that "if being a nation is distinctively about a culturally definite people possessing a significant degree of autonomy, then nationalism is about the aspiration to acquire autonomy, increase it, or defend it."[31]

Nationalists believe that distinct cultural nations should have their own government; they should not be governed by another nation. Applied globally,

---

[27]Kohn, *Idea of Nationalism*, 4.
[28]Kohn, *Idea of Nationalism*, 19.
[29]Ernst Gellner, *Nations and Nationalism* (Ithaca, NY: Cornell University Press, 2008), 1.
[30]Smith, *Nationalism*, 10.
[31]Biggar, *Between Kin and Cosmopolis*, 91.

nationalists believe there should be a perfect correspondence between nation and state: that is why we talk today about modern "nation-states," and why *nation* and *state* are sometimes used interchangeably in nonscholarly discourse. The misuse of terms has led to some confusion: because some people think nations and states are the same thing, an argument against nationalism sounds to them like an argument against sovereignty, or even against the existence of states, which sounds absurd and impractical. After all, what would replace the sovereign state, other than a world government or a kind of neo-Medieval order? Such critics have a hard time conceiving of any kind of political order or basis for sovereignty other than national identity. For them, *nationalism* essentially becomes a synonym for *sovereignty*, an overriding emphasis on the value of sovereignty and the belief that modern nation-states are the only possible foundations of political order in the modern world. (In reality, there are many alternatives that do not involve jettisoning sovereignty or advocating for world government, as becomes clear when you understand that cultural nations are different from states, and most states govern multiple cultures.) Nationalists today argue that we have a moral imperative to sustain our national autonomy and sovereignty against supposed threats from the United Nations, the World Bank, alliances, multilateral treaties, the International Criminal Court, and other instruments of "globalism," or what most scholars call the liberal international order.

This leads to another common feature of nationalism. Nationalists cannot conceive of a cooperative international system, committed as they are to a zero-sum vision of global politics. For nationalists, international politics can only be a contest for power, prestige, and influence between nation-states, a zero-sum sport in which we root for our team because it is ours. Nationalists give "indiscriminate precedence to the interests of one nation."[32] Nationalists' emphasis on sovereignty and cultural independence often gives rise to a certain attitude of national chauvinism, a cultural pride that veers into a prickly, belligerent insistence on recognition and, eventually, superiority and a distrust of alliances and international organizations. Weber observed that nationalism is usually accompanied by intense concern for "prestige interests," motivated by a "legend of a providential 'mission'" to cultivate "the peculiarity of the group set off as a nation," under the conviction of the "superiority, or at

---

[32] Alter, *Nationalism*, 2.

least the irreplaceability," of the nation's values.[33] That is why George Orwell defined nationalism as the pursuit of "competitive prestige," and Peter Alter called it "undisguised political egoism."[34] Nationalism essentially requires nations to compare themselves to and compete with other nations. In practice, cultural chauvinism is such a widespread and common byproduct of nationalist ideology as to be essentially synonymous with it, even though they could be disentangled in theory.

States should have jurisdiction over culture. Nationalists have distinctive beliefs about the role of government—and this is perhaps where nationalism departs most dramatically from American conservatism. They believe that the government should promote and protect the nation's cultural identity, which means it should encourage whatever traits define the nation and discourage, or possibly even outlaw, other traits, whereas conservatism usually stressed that government had limited jurisdiction and should not overstep its bounds. To some extent, all governments engage in the cultural life of their nations. In pluralistic liberal democracies, this includes relatively innocuous things mentioned above in our discussion of civil religion and patriotism, such as public commemoration of holidays, traditions, and historical events; public funding for memorials, festivals, or "traditional" arts; designating a flag, motto, and national bird; and other symbolic activities that governments perform. It also involves telling a story about the nation's history. These are, for the most part, innocuous and universal parts of statehood, not distinctive to nationalist regimes. Yet even these seemingly innocuous public symbols and official gestures involve choices about who "we" are, which events and heroes to commemorate, and whose traditions count as "ours," decisions that are not neutral. Using public funds or public land for Confederate statues and memorials, for example, is deeply troubling because of what is says about "us," about the "we" who are doing the celebrating, and about the values we are honoring. Whose cultural traditions are we preserving and celebrating? Who counts as a full member of the "nation" when we use public resources that way?

But nationalism tends to go beyond these minimalist cultural policies. Nationalism typically becomes a synonym for the preservation of "traditional" cultural practices, for the cultivation and celebration of a particular heritage.

---

[33]Max Weber, "The Nation," in *Readings and Commentary on Modernity*, ed. Stephen Kalberg (Oxford: Blackwell, 2005), 228.
[34]Orwell, "Notes on Nationalism"; Alter, *Nationalism*, 118.

In this sense, nationalism is a form of state-sponsored cultural traditionalism in which nationalists get to designate what counts as "traditional." The point of traditionalism is, of course, resistance to cultural change and the elevation of one particular culture as the official culture for the nation. Many governments go further in the creation and protection of an official culture. Most designate an official language and mandate its use; some select, subsidize, and protect a body of literature, film, and art in public education and international commerce as reflective of their national character—choices which inevitably include some and exclude others. In addition to selecting a national language, some governments without a tradition of religious freedom select an official religion, establish religious institutions, and give legal privileges to its adherents. And of course many authoritarian governments have gone much further still. Some take steps to sideline, disenfranchise, outlaw, or simply eliminate cultural outsiders, including linguistic, religious, or ethnic minorities, through cultural ostracism, legal persecution, enforced hierarchies (like India's caste system or Nazi Germany's Nuremberg laws), extrajudicial detention, enforced population expulsion, or outright genocide.

It may seem too much of a stretch to lump together public funding for the arts with genocide into one category of "nationalism." The common theme is that in both cases the government understands its jurisdiction to extend to the creation and defense of an official cultural template for the nation. Those things that fit the template—whether certain works of art or members of a certain ethnicity—are favored, while those that do not—dissident art or the "wrong" sort of person—are disfavored, defunded, disenfranchised, or destroyed. Nationalists believe nations should have strong membership criteria and a thick common culture; you have to belong to the nation's defining culture to be a full member of the nation. In more tolerant nationalist regimes, minorities might be accepted but expected to leave behind their old identities and agree to assimilate to the prevailing cultural identity or accept status as a second-class citizen. Nationalists' strong membership criteria stands in stark contrast to the more open understanding of *nations* under patriotism.

Human flourishing requires membership in a nation. Nationalists believe that individuals should be willing to assimilate to the prevailing national identity because cultivating a national identity is essential to living a fulfilling, meaningful human life, and national solidarity is essential for security and well-being. The nation protects us, defines us, and enables us to fulfill our potential. Nationalism "holds the nation and the sovereign nation-state to be crucial indwelling values . . . capable of engendering hopes, emotions, and actions," as Alter says.[35] For Anthony Smith, nationalists believe that "human beings must identify with a nation if they want to be free and realize themselves," and that "a sense of national identity provides a powerful means of defining and locating individual selves in the world. . . . It is through a shared, unique culture that we are enabled to know 'who we are' in the contemporary world."[36] The organizers of the National Conservatism conference in Washington, DC, in 2019 called for "the revival of the unique national traditions that *alone* have the power to bind a people together and bring about their flourishing."[37] Nationalism rests on a view of human personhood that understands people not most fundamentally as individuals or even as members of families or local communities, but as members of a national cultural group. People flourish best when they identify with a national cultural group, they believe, and the nation draws strength from its members' loyalty.

From these definitions, it is clear that nationalism is distinct from mere love of country. Nationalism comes with a host of assumptions about how the world works, what the right form of government is, what government's responsibilities are, how governments relate to each other in international affairs, and how human life is experienced and defined—none of which are necessary to a healthy patriotism. We can patriotically love our country without believing it must be defined by language, ethnicity, religion, or culture; without believing that the jurisdiction of our government should perfectly overlap with the boundary lines of an imagined cultural group; without believing that our government should take upon itself the responsibility of protecting and promoting a universal cultural template of national identity for all citizens; without insisting on strong membership criteria for the nation; without insisting that our government engage in a competition for prestige with other nations; and without believing that the nation is essential to our identities or our fulfillment.

DONALD TRUMP AND NATIONALISM

President Donald Trump articulated many of the main themes of nationalism throughout his presidency. He emphasized the importance of national

---

[35] Alter, *Nationalism*, 4.
[36] Smith, *Nationalism*, 10; *National Identity*, 17, 74.
[37] See the conference website at https://nationalconservatism.org/about/ (emphasis added).

sovereignty in his annual speeches to the United Nations. "In foreign affairs, we are renewing this founding principle of sovereignty," against the alleged threat of globalism, he claimed in 2017. "The future does not belong to globalists," he said in 2019. "The future belongs to sovereign and independent nations who protect their citizens, respect their neighbors, and honor the differences that make each country special and unique." In 2017 he pictured a world of culturally distinct units, separated by "different values, different cultures, and different dreams." In 2018 he was more specific: "Each of us here today is the emissary of a distinct culture, a rich history, and a people bound together by ties of memory, tradition, and the values that make our homelands like nowhere else on Earth." Each sovereign nation had a distinct culture, and that culture is what made them rightful sovereigns on the world stage. And in 2017 he claimed sovereignty was essential for human flourishing: "Strong, sovereign nations let their people take ownership of the future and control their own destiny. And strong, sovereign nations allow individuals to flourish in the fullness of the life intended by God . . . the nation-state remains the best vehicle for elevating the human condition." In 2018 he described sovereignty as the "foundation" on which democracy, peace, and flourishing depend and called for a renewal of sovereignty to usher in an age of "new purpose, new resolve, and new spirit flourishing all around us, and making this a more beautiful world in which to live."[38]

Trump also articulated a specific vision of American, or Western, cultural identity. In a speech in Warsaw, Poland, in July 2017, Trump stressed the importance of history, memory, culture, and identity, and argued they are essential underpinnings of liberal values and of American and Western identity. "Our two countries share a special bond forged by unique histories and national characters," he told the Polish audience. "It's a fellowship that exists only among people who have fought and bled and died for freedom." Trump invoked freedom, but not as a universal value. Freedom is rooted in a "special bond" and

---

[38]Donald Trump, "Remarks by President Trump to the 72nd Session of the United Nations," September 19, 2017, https://trumpwhitehouse.archives.gov/briefings-statements/remarks -president-trump-72nd-session-united-nations-general-assembly/; Donald Trump, "Remarks by President Trump to the 73rd Session of the United Nations," September 25, 2018, https:// trumpwhitehouse.archives.gov/briefings-statements/remarks-president-trump-73rd-session -united-nations-general-assembly-new-york-ny/; Donald Trump, "Remarks by President Trump to the 74th Session of the United Nations," September 25, 2019, https://trumpwhitehouse.archives .gov/briefings-statements/remarks-president-trump-74th-session-united-nations-general -assembly/.

"unique histories" and "national characters." He spoke of the threats that might "undermine these values and erase the bonds of culture, faith and tradition *that make us who we are.*" Note that we are defined by culture, faith, and tradition, which are in turn the source of liberal values. In the key line of the speech, Trump articulated the heart of nationalism: "Our freedom, our civilization, and our survival depend on these bonds of history, culture, and memory." Freedom depends on Western culture. Trump was saying that Western values depend on Western heritage and that liberalism is better understood as a cultural outgrowth of European history, not universalizable ideals that can be adopted by non-Western nations. Faced with the choice of defining the West as a heritage or a set of ideals, he answered that the ideals depend on the heritage. Understanding liberalism as a particular cultural practice, not a universal ideal, is also why Trump repeatedly and explicitly told audiences that America did not care how other nations governed themselves and would not "force" its way of life on others, that other nations' cultures might lead them to be governed differently, and that America would not and should not try to encourage democracy abroad.[39]

Trump's understanding of American identity—and the role of American ideals in shaping our identity—was also evident in a pair of Independence Day speeches on July 3 and 4, 2020. While both speeches contained a lot of unobjectionable, if bombastic, patriotic content, they also reflected Trump's nationalist ideology. In the first speech, he affirmed that "our country was founded on Judeo-Christian principles," which is more or less true, if in need of some nuance. But the next day, in a separate speech, he affirmed that "we will safeguard our values, traditions, customs, and beliefs," which together articulate the core of nationalist ideology, the idea that governments should protect and sustain their nation's unique cultural identity; that America is *and must remain* defined by its Christian heritage. In the July 3 speech in front of Mount Rushmore in South Dakota, Trump went further. After rehearsing the deeds of famous Americans and praising American history (a "miraculous story") and heritage (as a "land of legends"), Trump promised that our children will know "that nothing can stop them, and that no one can hold them down. They will know that in America, you can do anything, you can be anything, and together, we can achieve anything," and that "this country will be everything that our

---

[39]Donald Trump, "Speech in Warsaw," July 6, 2017, www.cnn.com/2017/07/06/politics/trump-speech-poland-transcript/index.html.

citizens have hoped for," suggesting a quasi-mystical understanding of American greatness that fulfills human purpose and meaning. But the most revealing comment came next. "American freedom," Trump announced, "exists for American greatness." National power, national renown, and national greatness was the point; freedom was just the means to get there. In this, Trump got things exactly backward.[40]

AMERICAN NATIONALISM

Nationalists believe there are things called nations defined by a shared culture, language, history, religion, or ethnicity. How does this apply to the United States? What does American nationalism look like? The American case is difficult because of the circumstances of its founding, the role that liberal ideals have played in American self-consciousness, and the contested relationship between those ideals and the culture in which they originated. Is there an American nation? Is the United States best defined by a common culture, as nationalists contend? If so, what is the specific cultural content of the American nation? And what is the relationship between an American identity rooted in shared culture and an American identity rooted in liberal ideals?

In response to this Gordian knot, scholars have offered a plethora of definitions, typologies, and schematics of American nationalism. Classically, scholars used to distinguish between "ethnic" and "civic" nationalism, the first rooted in shared culture, heritage, or ethnicity, and the second in notions of civic identity or liberal ideals,[41] and they argue that both kinds have been found among Americans. This way of thinking about American nationalism is oversimplified. The problem with the "ethnic" versus "civic" distinction is that it rhetorically stacks the deck by pitting good civic nationalists against bad ethnic nationalists, as if Americans fall into two camps—Jeffersonian philosophers or White supremacists. In this simplistic view, there are good Americans who believe in the creedal version of American identity and bad Americans who are racists. This dichotomy is part of the reason that the left reflexively

---

[40]Donald Trump, "Remarks by President Trump at South Dakota's 2020 Fireworks Celebration," July 3, 2020, https://trumpwhitehouse.archives.gov/briefings-statements/remarks-president -trump-south-dakotas-2020-mount-rushmore-fireworks-celebration-keystone-south-dakota/. Donald Trump, "Remarks by President Trump at the 2020 Salute to America," July 4, 2020, https://ge.usembassy.gov/remarks-by-president-trump-at-the-2020-salute-to-america-july-4/.
[41]Kohn, *Idea of Nationalism*. Kohn believed that civic nationalism was prevalent in the West while ethnic nationalism was typical in the East.

accuses its opponents of racism. They cannot comprehend any other basis on which someone might disagree with them.

To improve on the simplistic ethnic-civic dichotomy, scholars have suggested a number of ways to think of American identity and to categorize Americans' experience of it. Jack Citrin distinguishes between cosmopolitan liberalism, nativism, and multiculturalism.[42] Bonikowski and DiMaggio distinguish between ardent nationalism, restrictive nationalism, creedal nationalism, and disengagement.[43] Michael Lind describes multiculturalism, democratic universalism, nativism, and (his preference) liberal nationalism. Lind also periodizes the history of American national identity, telling a story of how an Anglo-American nation evolved into a Euro-American nation, and then into a multicultural nation.[44] Philip Gorski advocates for a "prophetic republican" civil religious tradition as an alternative to both religious nationalism and radical secularism (and further distinguishes among civic republicanism, Hebraic republicanism, liberalism, and more). Andrew Whitehead and Samuel Perry, focusing specifically on American Christian nationalism, distinguish between ambassadors, accommodators, resisters, and rejectors.[45] John Wiley draws a distinction between "open exceptionalism" and "closed exceptionalism."[46]

These typologies helpfully highlight that most Americans experience their national loyalty and national identity differently than the stark division between "ethnic" and "civic" would indicate. I suggest that instead of two types of national identity, there are at least three different *sources* of American national identity, and they mix and mingle to create a broad spectrum of how Americans feel about their nationality. In addition to ethnic and civic sources of national identity, *religion* is a third important headwater that feeds into the broad river of American national identity. At various points different people have defined America as a nation of White European immigrants, a nation of Protestants, or a nation of all people within the territory of the United States who pledge loyalty to the US Constitution. But that does not mean there are

[42]Jack Citrin et al., "Is American Nationalism Changing? Implications for Foreign Policy," *International Studies Quarterly* 38, no. 1 (1994): 1-31.

[43]Bonikowski and DiMaggio, "Varieties of American Popular Nationalism."

[44]Lind, *Next American Nation.*

[45]Andrew L. Whitehead and Samuel L. Perry, *Taking America Back for God: Christian Nationalism in the United States* (New York: Oxford University Press, 2020).

[46]Wilsey, *American Exceptionalism.*

simply three kinds of American nationalism (ethnic, religious, and civic) instead of two. Rather, most Americans hold a shifting, inconsistent combination of all three views in different degrees that change over time, across generations, and in response to different circumstances, as the various scholarly typologies rightly suggest. It also suggests there is a sliding scale of nationalism that can be more or less intense.

Which one is "right"? Most readers probably gravitate to the idea that being American means being loyal to our Constitution because that is what we are taught in our high school civics classes. But at various points in American history, that idea was probably the minority view, and it was strongly opposed by many American Christians (specifically by White Protestants). That is why the question of American identity can be especially confusing and difficult for American Christians. For many of us, we simply absorbed from our family upbringing that America is, was, and should remain a Christian nation. That implicit familial transmission has its source in the historical fact that American Christians, for generations, saw the project of American nation building as a Christian project and religious duty. White American Protestants have felt a sense of ownership over and responsibility for the American experiment and have tried to build that ownership into their understanding of American identity, as if we are the rightful owners of the American brand and are entitled to a preeminence of place in American culture. The creedal understanding of American identity continues to be contested among many evangelicals today because of its implicit criticism of a sectarian understanding of American identity and because of how the disestablishment of religion has played out in American history. In response, some insist on defining America in "traditional" terms, which means religious terms. American nationalism has always been profoundly religious, merging with Americans' traditional religious beliefs—which is to say, with Protestant Christianity. Although there are many varieties and flavors of American nationalism, most of them, to one extent or another, involve Christianity. It is to this blend of Christianity and American nationalism we now turn.

3

THE CASE FOR
CHRISTIAN NATIONALISM

WHAT IS CHRISTIAN NATIONALISM? To answer that question, I want to give the stage first to its advocates and defenders. I do so to guard against the temptation to caricature or misrepresent the movement. There is an avalanche of literature on Christians' engagement in American politics and Christian nationalism from long before the Trump era, much of which succumbs to this temptation. In some critics' eyes, conservative Christian political activism is not a movement to be studied or taken seriously. Rather, it is an aggressive faction bent on cultural and political dominance, a movement of racists and theocrats; misogynistic, homophobic fascists who hate freedom, science, and reason; in response to whom there is no understanding, only victory or defeat.

Lest the reader think I am exaggerating, let me cite a few examples of such criticism. Michelle Goldberg, a journalist, wrote in 2006 of the Christian Right that "the movement aims at the destruction of secular society and the political enforcement of its theology," warned against its "totalitarian resonances," and predicted that it would lead to "the curtailment of the civil rights that gay people, women, and religious minorities have won in the last few decades."[1] Similarly, in 2006 Chris Hedges warned against "American fascism." He argued the Christian Right was defined by "theocratic" dominionist theology, which he claimed was the predominant force in the Southern Baptist Convention. Dominionists were "taking over the machinery of US state and

---

[1]Michelle Goldberg, *Kingdom Coming: The Rise of Christian Nationalism* (New York: Norton, 2006), 182, 184, 191.

religious institutions," motivated by their "fierce utopian vision, fanaticism [and] ruthlessness," as seen in "calls for widespread repression of non-believers." This amounts to "an American theocracy, a Christian fascism," or "America's new state religion, a Christo-fascism" devoted to "holy war," against its enemies. He unashamedly drew a straightforward analogy to the Nazis: "Similar apocalyptic visions of a world cleansed through violence and extermination nourished the Nazis." The solution was clear: "There arise moments when those who would destroy the tolerance that makes an open society possible should no longer be tolerated," because "the radical Christian Right is a sworn and potent enemy of the open society." There is no room for conservative Christians in American democracy because, Hedges believes, "Debate with the radical Christian Right is useless. . . . This movement is bent on our destruction."[2]

Finally, in 2020, Katherine Stewart wrote in *Power Worshippers* that Christian nationalism "does not seek to add another voice to America's pluralistic democracy but to replace our foundational democratic principles and institutions with a state grounded on a particular version of Christianity," and that the movement "does not appear to have much respect for representative democracy." Stewart dismisses Christians' concern for religious freedom: to her, it is obvious that such calls are rooted in "a sincerely held belief that conservative Christians should be permitted to discriminate against LGBT people and members of religious minority groups," which is bad enough, but more fundamentally such calls reflect "the fear among movement leaders that their discriminatory inclinations might cost them their lucrative tax deductions and subsidies."[3] These critiques are rather extreme and almost comical examples of beating up on straw men—or would be, if they weren't also fear-mongering, scurrilous libel masquerading as scholarship.

Part of the problem stems from critics' tendency to engage with Christian nationalism solely as a partisan movement and a sociological phenomenon, not as a political theory. It is both, of course, a bottom-up embodied cultural phenomenon and a top-down articulated ideology. But focusing only on the movement—broad social and cultural trends exemplified by colorful and

---

[2]Chris Hedges, *American Fascists: The Christian Right and the War on America* (New York: Simon and Schuster, 2008), 19, 21, 29, 149, 31, 33, 202, 207.
[3]Katherine Stewart, *The Power Worshippers: Inside the Dangerous Rise of Religious Nationalism* (Bloomsbury, 2020), 8, 11, 12.

controversial politicians and personalities, and dramatized by highly contentious events, issues, or elections—glosses over the ideas, beliefs, and convictions that animate Christian nationalism. I will look at the embodied cultural movement later (chaps. 7–9), but I first want to engage with the ideas of its formal, articulated ideology, the top-down version of Christian nationalism. The movement has serious ideas which have serious problems and require serious debate. That means we need to engage with the strongest possible version of Christian nationalist ideology to understand it and its weaknesses. In this section I want to listen to the arguments from the best contemporary advocates of Christian nationalism. I have chosen a Harvard political scientist, a British Anglican theologian and Oxford professor, two American magazine editors, and an Israeli Jewish political theorist. This diverse selection shows that Christian nationalism is not limited to White American evangelicals and it has a serious intellectual pedigree. It also shows that Christian nationalism has a lot of internal variety.

The common thread is that when faced with the question of how to define American identity, they converge on two points: Christianity and English, British, or European heritage (and sometimes they equate the two, treating "Christian" and "European" as interchangeable). Some scholars and advocates call the combination, for short, "Anglo-Protestantism," the unique mix of early modern Britishness and protesting Christianity that marked the era of America's founding. (Anglo-Protestantism in this sense is broader than the "White, Anglo-Saxon Protestants" that made up the old WASP establishment of the East Coast. I use the broader meaning throughout this book.) They do not argue that citizens must be biological descendants of British immigrants or that the government must establish Protestant doctrine; rather, they argue that America should remain shaped by the cultural norms, the "patterns of meanings," "inherited conceptions," and "webs of significance," (to draw on Geertz again) of eighteenth-century Protestant Britain and White Protestant America. American nationalists argue that because America was founded by Anglo-Protestants, and because its prevailing culture was dominated by Anglo-Protestantism for much of its history, the United States government should privilege, protect, and promote Anglo-Protestant norms and culture. Advocates of this view offer a range of explanations for why we should preserve our culture, including that every government should protect and promote its own culture, that a cohesive national culture is essential for national survival;

that a cohesive national culture is vital for human flourishing; that Anglo-Protestant culture in particular is the essential precondition for our form of government; or that God blesses nations that recognize and honor him.

SAMUEL HUNTINGTON

The first scholarly advocate of Anglo-Protestant nationalism I want to review is Samuel Huntington. Huntington was a political scientist at Harvard University, most famous for his 1996 book *The Clash of Civilizations and the Remaking of World Order*. Some of Huntington's earlier works were widely praised, critiqued, and commented on within his field, including *Political Order in Changing Societies* (1968) and *The Third Wave* (1991). But his final book, *Who Are We?* (2004), published four years before his death, met a different reception because of its unpopular thesis. Building on the idea in *Clash* that culture and religion had become the fundamental lines of division and conflict in world politics, Huntington argued in *Who Are We?* that changes in American culture and religion threatened to change American identity beyond recognition and possibly end the American experiment in free government.

Most of Huntington's work in this book is descriptive and historical. He argues that the United States is, and has always been, an Anglo-Protestant nation. The American founding

> was rooted in and a product of the Anglo-American Protestant society and culture that had developed over the intervening one and a half centuries. . . . The central elements of that culture can be defined in a variety of ways but include the Christian religion, Protestant values and moralism, a work ethic, the English language, British traditions of law, justice, and the limits of government power, and a legacy of European art, literature, philosophy, and music.[4]

Anglo-Protestant culture also includes Protestant dissent, liberty and equality, individualism, and the reform ethic. In other words, Anglo-Protestantism is the habits, tastes, and beliefs of a well-educated, eighteenth- or nineteenth-century English gentleman. If America has the "soul of a church," to use G. K. Chesterton's phrase, Huntington argues it is a church "that is profoundly Christian in its origins, symbolism, spirit, accoutrements, and most importantly, its basic assumptions about the nature of man, history, right and wrong.

---

[4]Samuel P. Huntington, *Who Are We?: The Challenges to America's National Identity* (New York: Simon and Schuster, 2004), 40.

The Christian Bible, Christian references, biblical allusions and metaphors, permeate expressions of the civil religion."[5]

Huntington's description of American history and predominant culture is relatively anodyne and should be uncontroversial. His picture probably could be improved with some qualifications and more recognition of the non-Anglo and non-Protestant contributions to American life, but Huntington is responding to how it has become unfashionable to draw attention to the overwhelming importance of Britishness and Christianity in American history and culture. However, the historical details are less important to my argument. The real problem starts when Huntington argues that America's Anglo-Protestant heritage is eroding because of multiculturalism, globalization, and Hispanic immigration (the part of the book that provoked a backlash from critics), and that the United States should work to counter those trends—including by restricting immigration—to sustain its Anglo-Protestant cultural heritage.

Though Huntington does not lay out the reasons we should sustain Anglo-Protestantism in a systematic fashion, he seems to appeal to two different justifications. First, he argues that Anglo-Protestantism is the foundation for American democracy and the American creed. He notes that classical liberalism originated in seventeenth- and eighteenth-century British Protestantism. Anglo-American ideas about liberty and limited government were "the product of the distinct Anglo-Protestant culture of the founding settlers of America in the seventeenth and eighteenth centuries." He argues, "Almost all the central ideas of the Creed have their origins in dissenting Protestantism [because of] the emphasis on the individual conscience." "The American Creed, in short, is Protestantism without God." Because the ideas came from a specific cultural context, Huntington believes, the ideas are unlikely to survive if the culture changes. "The Creed was the product of people with a distinct Anglo-Protestant culture. . . . The Creed is unlikely to retain its salience if Americans abandon the Anglo-Protestant culture in which it has been rooted. A multicultural America will, in time, become a multicreedal America, with groups with different cultures espousing distinctive political values and principles rooted in their particular cultures."[6] This is a key point—that ideas depend on culture and thus American democracy

---

[5]Huntington, *Who Are We?*, 106
[6]Huntington, *Who Are We?*, xvi, 68-69, 340.

depends on Anglo-Protestant heritage—that is undertheorized in Huntington and other advocates of Christian nationalism, and I will examine it carefully in chapter four.

Second, Huntington seems to argue that the creed is not enough to keep America together and ensure national survival. Implicitly, he seems to argue that nations require strong common cultures to exist. He argues against the idea that "a nation can be based on only a political contract among individuals lacking any other commonality," as he thinks the creed assumes. "History and psychology, however, suggest that it is unlikely to be enough to sustain a nation for long," he says and invokes the Austro-Hungarian Empire as an example of a multiethnic polity that dissolved because it had no common culture to keep it together. Huntington asks whether "America will continue to be a country with a single national language and a common Anglo-Protestant mainstream culture" and warns that "a bifurcated America with two languages and two cultures will be fundamentally different from the America with one language and one core Anglo-Protestant culture that has existed for over three centuries." It will not only be fundamentally different; it might cease to exist. Huntington notes that communist states were also creedal, but they proved fragile: "People can with relative ease change their political ideologies. . . . A nation defined only by political ideology is a fragile nation." (Huntington is surprisingly pessimistic about his fellow Americans. In my view, it is not a stretch to believe that Americans have made liberty far more central to our identity, and will cling to it far more tightly, than Russians have to communism.) Given enough cultural change, America might cease to be recognizably American—and might simply cease to be. A nation exists because of its cultural inheritance and continues so long as the nation votes, so to speak, in a "daily plebiscite" (Ernst Renan's phrase) to sustain that inheritance. "Without that inheritance, no nation exists, and if the plebiscite rejects that inheritance, the nation ends."[7]

To avert this fate, "Americans of all races and ethnicities could attempt to reinvigorate their core culture. This would mean a recommitment to America as a religious and primarily Christian country, encompassing several religious minorities, adhering to Anglo-Protestant values, speaking English, maintaining its European cultural heritage, and committed to the principles

---

[7]Huntington, *Who Are We?*, 19, 318, 324, 338-39.

of the Creed."[8] He calls for us to recognize that "America is different, and that difference is defined in large part by its Anglo-Protestant culture and its religiosity" and to cultivate a "nationalism devoted to the preservation and enhancement of those qualities that have defined America since its founding."[9] Huntington's book appeared a dozen years before the 2016 presidential election and the foregrounding of nationalism in American politics, which helps distance the argument from current partisan squabbles and from the Trump administration.

NIGEL BIGGAR

Another work, probably less well known to American audiences, appeared just before the 2016 election and has the added benefit of coming from a non-American. The best contemporary argument in favor of a soft form of cultural nationalism rooted in Christianity is from Anglican theologian, ethicist, and scholar Nigel Biggar. Biggar is the Regius Professor of Moral and Pastoral Theology at Christ Church, Oxford University, and director of the MacDonald Centre for Theology, Ethics, and Public Life. He has written extensively on issues at the intersection of politics, theology, ethics, and statecraft. Biggar argued in his 2014 work *Between Kin and Cosmopolis* for a middle ground between the hard tribalism of chauvinistic nationalism and the utopian cosmopolitanism of progressive dreams, in favor of national loyalty and national patriotism. I leaned on parts of Biggar's argument in the previous chapter when I argued in favor of love of country and a simple kind of patriotism; there is much to agree with in Biggar's thoughtful argument. But Biggar does not stop with the love of country. He gives some of the theoretical foundations lacking in Huntington's argument for why he thinks a given set of ideas and institutions needs a corresponding cultural foundation. Unfortunately, he also argues that the state needs to adopt and endorse—we Americans would say "establish"—one particular cultural and religious framework in order to sustain healthy liberal institutions.

Biggar begins by affirming our need to embrace a common history. "Since a particular constitution and its institutional components derive their particular meaning from the history of their development, fully to affirm that

---

[8]Huntington, *Who Are We?*, 20.
[9]Huntington, *Who Are We?*, 365.

constitution involves understanding its history and owning its heroes."[10] If limited to history and heroes, Biggar is on solid ground; he goes on, however, to apply the point broadly and argues that because political institutions are steeped in history and memory, embedded in the cultural habits, mores, and institutions that evolve in a society over generations, sustaining our political culture requires sustaining the cultural foundation. As I noted in chapter one, it is important to recognize that there are nonideological components of culture and acultural components of ideology. Biggar seems to disagree, or to argue that the connection between liberal ideology and Anglo-Protestant culture is indissoluble.

Biggar is arguing against multiculturalists for whom any talk about the superiority of one culture over another is anathema. "In over-reaction against crude notions of racial superiority, multiculturalism tends to assert the moral equality of all cultures. Consequently, it refuses to recognize the legitimacy of defending the integrity of a national culture and its continued dominance over sub-cultures." Biggar is right that pure neutrality among cultures is impossible (see chap. 5) and moral equivalence is foolish. If we value democracy and freedom, we should endorse and encourage classically liberal ideals (again, "liberal" here means the political values of the Enlightenment, not the political left). "Public institutions cannot afford to be neutral about which larger views of the world dominate public culture," he argues. "Public institutions that would stay liberal need actively to promote a liberal ethos." Not only can they not afford to be neutral, but in a sense the effort is impossible. "*No* society can avoid asserting the authority of an orthodoxy against its heterodoxies."[11]

Biggar is right that liberal societies need to privilege liberal ideas and institutions against their opponents to survive. But he argues that to endorse liberal ideals at all, states must choose and endorse a specific, sectarian vision of the good that happens to overlap with liberal ideals. He rejects the idea that the state should limit itself to the "overlapping consensus" among various visions of justice. He claims that "liberal public institutions and rituals cannot limit their affirmation simply to a common ethic," and so "they must choose one supportive humanist worldview to represent."[12] Biggar's objection to the

---

[10]Nigel Biggar, *Between Kin and Cosmopolis: An Ethic of the Nation* (Eugene, OR: Wipf and Stock, 2014), 17.

[11]Biggar, *Between Kin and Cosmopolis*, 25, 35, 37, 42.

[12]Biggar, *Between Kin and Cosmopolis*, 35.

"overlapping consensus" seems to be that it does not have enough resources to protect us from ourselves. An overlapping consensus is a lowest-common-denominator version of human freedom in which we do whatever we want so long as it does not interfere with what others want to do. But "a libertarian version of liberal society is actually self-subverting," because it allows people "to degrade themselves" with "poor choices" and causes "wider social damage," through the atrophy of civic virtue and self-control. He does not address the obviously problematic historical record of a stronger, sectarian foundation for liberal values.

Thus, "we need a certain humanism to be established by the national authorities or by the state as a public orthodoxy," to supplement a minimalist liberalism.[13] Biggar believes this kind of humanism—a high view of human dignity, the groundwork for human rights—requires sectarian support, such as Britain's Anglican establishment, or what he calls America's "ecumenical monotheism."[14] Only a religious buttress—specifically, either Christianity or its close derivative—can keep civil liberties from eroding their own foundations. Though he does not put it in these terms, Biggar is making an argument about civic virtue and social capital, those unquantifiable qualities that capture a people's sense of responsibility, public spiritedness, and relational networks. Such virtues are required to sustain democracy and, Biggar believes, they can only come from and be safeguarded by the traditional religious culture of the English-speaking Protestant world. Biggar's argument is attractive because of how much he gets right and how he strives for a middle ground between chauvinistic nationalism and multiculturalism. But Biggar's distinctive argument—that a religious establishment, even an informal one, is required to sustain a liberal society—is also where he goes wrong.

R. R. RENO

Huntington and Biggar wrote before Trump's arrival on the political stage. Since Trump, more writers and thinkers have stepped forward to offer their apology for tenets of nationalism, such as R. R. Reno, editor of *First Things*, the preeminent periodical of religion and public life in the United States. Founded by Fr. Richard John Neuhaus in 1990, the magazine is predominantly Catholic

---

[13]Biggar, *Between Kin and Cosmopolis*, 30.
[14]Biggar, *Between Kin and Cosmopolis*, 36.

in outlook but self-consciously cultivated an ecumenical and broadminded perspective, attracting Protestant, Orthodox, and Jewish readers and contributors. Reno, a conservative Catholic, took the helm in 2011 following Neuhaus's death in 2009. Under Neuhaus, *First Things* was a voice for religiously infused conservatism, including paleo- and neo-conservatives. Under Reno's editorship, *First Things* has gravitated toward a kind of nationalism in recent years, though one refracted through its distinctively Roman Catholic voice. Reno articulated his viewpoint most fully in his 2019 book, *Return of the Strong Gods*.

Most of Reno's book is a critique of progressivism and its attendant *-isms*, including postmodernism, multiculturalism, identity politics and identity studies, and related movements. Reno frames this as a critique of the post–World War II movement toward "weakening" and "openness." As Reno tells it, postwar intellectuals concluded that the war had its roots in fascism's strong beliefs, the solution to which was for the world to learn to believe things less strongly. Following the guidance of writers like Karl Popper, the West cultivated a habit of critiquing itself, avoiding strong beliefs, opening its borders and its students' minds, and relentlessly praising the virtues of diversity and pluralism, all in the service of antifascism. Reno agrees that much of this was, of course, needful and appropriate but believes things have gone too far. In reaction to the excesses of self-critique, Reno believes some version of nationalism—the "strong god" whose return he welcomes—is necessary: "The open society leave[s] no room for the concept of the nation and the cultural solidarity it nurtures."[15]

Reno's approach to defending a version of Christian nationalism is different from those of Huntington, Biggar, and others. His main argument is that some kind of mixture of politics and religion is inevitable and that it can be either healthy or dangerous. We should consciously cultivate the healthiest kind of religious nationalism to forestall the dangerous kind. And he argues that a religiously infused polity is essential for full human flourishing. "The sacralizing impulse in public life is fundamental. Our social consensus always reaches for transcendent legitimacy," he argues. "Public life requires the aroma of the sacred." This tendency is baked into our very nature as human beings. "To be human is to seek transcendent warrants and sacred sources for our

---

[15]R. R. Reno, *Return of the Strong Gods: Nationalism, Populism, and the Future of the West* (New York: Simon and Schuster, 2019), 147.

social existence." Since the tendency is inescapable, the effort to banish religion from the public square is dangerously naive and utopian. While some kinds of religious politics lead to a religious utopianism, "a too rigorously anti-utopian outlook is itself dangerously utopian." Specifically, it becomes "the utopianism of imagining that societies can survive on facts without myths, on authority without rituals, and on reality without dreams." In short, "We yearn to join ourselves to others, not only in the bond of matrimony but in civic and religious bonds as well. The 'we' arises out of love, a ferocious power that seeks to rest in something greater than oneself."[16]

If religious politics are inevitable, Reno counsels that we simply accept that fact as given. Fighting against our natural inclination to infuse politics with religious legitimacy goes against human nature and leaves us spiritually impoverished and susceptible to ever more extreme religious and political appeals. "Are we able to restore a shared moral community that protects the undisciplined among us from self-destructive vices?" he asks, warning that "a deconsolidated, fragmented nation can be as great a threat to human dignity as an over-consolidated, conformist one."[17] If, instead, we consciously cultivate the right kind of religious politics, if we accept the nation and its religious claims, it elevates us and helps give our lives a sense of meaning, belonging, and purpose:

> The strong god of the nation draws us out of our "little worlds." Our shared loves—love of our land, our history, our founding myths, our warriors and heroes—raise us to a higher vantage point. We see our private interest as part of a larger whole, the "we" that calls upon our freedom to serve the body politic with intelligence and loyalty. As Aristotle recognized, this loyalty is intrinsically fulfilling, for it satisfies the human desire for transcendence.[18]

Reno's view that loyalty to the nation is "intrinsically fulfilling" and "satisfies the human desire for transcendence" is remarkable for its explicit statement, and embrace, of the religious nature of nationalism. Nationalism, in this view, entails a certain view of human nature and political organization: not merely that we are naturally social and political animals, as Aristotle rightly said, but that we should seek to satisfy and fulfill our social, political,

---

[16]Reno, *Return of the Strong Gods*, 136-39, 152.
[17]Reno, *Return of the Strong Gods*, 144.
[18]Reno, *Return of the Strong Gods*, 155.

and even spiritual natures through our modern, extensive, impersonal, bureaucratic nation-states. It amounts to an effort to make modern nation-states fit the model of ancient Greek city-states in which civil society, religion, culture, and government were effectively merged into a single, all-encompassing locus of human life. Not all nationalists recognize or consciously embrace this view, but Reno is likely correct that it undergirds, tacitly or otherwise, the nationalist project because there are no stronger gods on which to base the nation's claim to moral legitimacy.

If this view of human nature is correct, governments have a moral duty to cultivate a sense of nationhood, cultural cohesion, and "solidarity." "Because the civic 'we' is not natural—that is, it is not simply a consequence of our shared humanity, or a biological dynamic of genetic connection—its particularity requires intentional effort to create, guide, and sustain," Reno argues. "In short, the 'we' does not just happen. . . . The civic realm needs to be defended; its history must be passed down, and the native language has to be taught." These are the imperatives of public policy, the rightful object of legislation. Reno believes that the jurisdiction or writ of the government justly encompasses engineering a thick sense of "we," defining who "we" are, and enshrining that definition in policy, law, symbols, and ceremonies. This is not merely a matter of drawing lines on a map, drafting a constitution, or naming a country or citizenship criteria. Reno envisions defining and imposing a religiously infused cultural solidarity on a people and calling them a "nation," as a state-sponsored, even state-enforced, pathway to human fulfillment and transcendent meaning. "The 'we' is an end in itself that asks us to do what is necessary to sustain and promote our shared loves, all of which harken to the call of strong gods. Governance, therefore, is integral to the 'we.'"[19] This is a rather explicit rejection of the classical liberal heritage and the old conservative emphasis on the limits of the government's writ.

Reno concludes with a call to "restore public life in the West by developing a language of love and a vision of the 'we' that befits our dignity and appeals to our reason as well as to our hearts," noting in passing that "the question of who we are must take biblical religion into account" because of its role historically defining who we Americans are. And Reno warns that if we do not do this, if we insist on resisting the religious claims in the public sphere, we will

---

[19]Reno, *Return of the Strong Gods*, 149-50.

not succeed in secularizing the nation; we will only leave ourselves susceptible to the dangerous forms of religious and political extremism. "We must attend to the strong gods who come from above and animate the best of our traditions. Only that kind of leadership will forestall the return of the dark gods who rise up from below."[20]

RICH LOWRY AND YORAM HAZONY

The previous authors demonstrate that nationalism predates Trump and has a serious intellectual pedigree. I want to note how contemporary nationalists in the Trump era use the same set of ideas to advocate for Anglo-Protestantism. A recent American example is in Rich Lowry's book *The Case for Nationalism*. Lowry, the editor of the conservative magazine *National Review*, echoes Biggar in emphasizing the importance of culture for national identity: "Contrary to the claims of anti-nationalists, it wasn't simply ideas that mattered in establishing the American project," he writes, arguing against creedalists who emphasize the importance of America's founding ideals. "Culture, and the people who embodied and delineated it, mattered as much or more. . . . Nations aren't mere intellectual constructs but accretions of history and culture."[21] Lowry believes there is a moral imperative to work for "the preservation of the American cultural nation," insisting that the "cultural nation" is not the same as the American creed. "The American creed is an important expression and pillar of this, our cultural nation. But that creed isn't the sum total of what makes us Americans. Mores, institutions, and ideals are all important."[22]

The particular cultural influence Lowry wants to preserve is that of the Bible and of "our English forerunner," to each of which he devotes its own chapter.[23] "Would America be the same if its people spoke Russian, the language of a country that has never effectively supported property rights, the rule of law, or limited government, rather than English? Would democracy have emerged if Americans read the Koran instead of the Bible?[24]" The country was established "by Englishmen, including their notions of liberty, which defined the American

---

[20]Reno, *Return of the Strong Gods*, 162, 157.
[21]Rich Lowry, *The Case for Nationalism: How It Made Us Rich, Powerful, and Free* (New York: Broadside, 2019), 101.
[22]Lowry, *Case for Nationalism*, 214, 217.
[23]Lowry, *Case for Nationalism*, chap. 5.
[24]Lowry, *Case for Nationalism*, 18.

experience at the outset."[25] Protestantism and the biblical heritage are a major part of this identity. "New England put an accent on three cultural attributes that took on an outsized significance in American national identity: a belief in our chosenness, the idea of the Covenant, and the King James Bible."[26] Similarly, "our rituals and holidays reflect the dominant culture. Christmas is a national holiday; Yom Kippur is not."[27]

As with Huntington, this would be unremarkable, if not very nuanced, if Lowry meant it only as a historical description of how America came to be. But Lowry intends more than that: to him, history is destiny. Because we came from Anglo-Protestant roots, we must remain true to those roots and preserve and protect our heritage. "The overarching priority of American nationalists has to be protecting and fostering the cultural nation, as a source of coherence and belonging and the foundation of our way of life."[28] Lowry is clear that he believes our culture is flexible and transmittable; one does not have to be physically descended from Britons or profess the Christian faith to be culturally Anglo-Protestant. He celebrates that there have been other influences on American culture, including from African Americans. He tries to argue that the American cultural nation (as he defines it) is not "White." Yet it is equally clear that he believes American culture should remain predominantly Anglo-Protestant. Protestant Englishmen founded the nation and stamped it with their likeness, and nationalism means using the government to preserve that inheritance for all Americans.

Non-American and non-Christian nationalists also see America as a nation defined by Christianity and its British heritage. Yoram Hazony, an Israeli scholar, advocate of nationalism, and organizer of the 2019 National Conservatism Conference in Washington, DC, wrote *The Virtue of Nationalism* in 2018. He argues that America constitutes a nation with a "common language, laws, religion, and history."[29] He writes, "The United States is held together by the bonds of mutual loyalty that unite the American nation, an English-speaking nation whose constitutional and religious traditions were originally rooted in the Bible, Protestantism, republicanism, and the common law of

---

[25]Lowry, *Case for Nationalism*, 18.
[26]Lowry, *Case for Nationalism*, 105.
[27]Lowry, *Case for Nationalism*, 18.
[28]Lowry, *Case for Nationalism*, 219.
[29]Yoram Hazony, *The Virtue of Nationalism* (London: Hachette, 2018), 148.

England."[30] Hazony means this as both description and prescription, an ethnographic account for how the American nation came to be (which is broadly accurate) and a recipe for how to hold the American nation together (which is the problem).

Hazony believes that because Anglo-American conservatism arose from British history and Protestant religion, it cannot be separated from its originating conditions: "Liberals have thus confused certain historical-empirical principles of the traditional Anglo-American constitution, painstakingly developed and inculcated over centuries . . . for universal truths that are equally accessible to all human beings, regardless of historical or cultural circumstances." Hazony distrusts purported universal truths, arguing instead in favor of "historical empiricism," the idea that we discovered truth "through the long historical experience of a given nation," and settled on traditions that are "refined through trial and error over many centuries, with repairs and improvements being introduced where necessary." Such empiricisms mean skepticism toward "the universal rights of man, or any other abstract, universal systems."[31]

That is why he believes the effort to sustain democracy without the Anglo-American roots is doomed to fail, citing past democratic failures in Germany, Mexico, France, and elsewhere (which is an odd argument considering that Germany and France are successful democracies today and Mexico freer than it was for most of the twentieth century). For Hazony, the distinction is so important as to constitute two different political traditions and two different regime types. "What is now called 'liberal democracy' refers not to the traditional Anglo-American Constitution but to a rationalist reconstruction of it that has been entirely detached from the Protestant religion and the Anglo-American nationalist tradition." (It is not entirely clear how Hazony distinguishes among universal claims: while he criticizes universal liberal rights, he also appeals to natural law, which is nothing if not a universal moral claim across boundaries of culture and nation. He also calls for national conservatism to be adopted by other countries, which seems to rest on a universal claim that all nations must be nationalist. This is in tension, at least, with his insistence that different nations travel different historical paths and arrive at different legitimate systems of government.)[32]

---

[30]Hazony, *The Virtue of Nationalism*, 159.
[31]Yoram Hazony, "What Is Conservative Democracy?," *First Things*, January 2019.
[32]Hazony, "What Is Conservative Democracy?"

Hazony's preferred alternative is "conservative democracy," rooted in "the Anglo-American tradition." This tradition, he says, "hearkens back to principles of a free and just national state—charting its own course without foreign interference—whose origin is in the Hebrew Bible." Because the Bible was formative of the Anglo-American tradition, Hazony argues, the government should recognize and give legal privilege to biblical religion. In a conservative democracy, "the state upholds and honors the biblical God and religious practices common to the nation. These are the centerpiece of the national heritage and indispensable for justice and public morals." Hazony calls for replacing public reason with "public religion," because "the only stable basis for national independence, justice, and public morals is a strong biblical tradition in government and public life." Similarly, he calls for recognizing and establishing the religious identity of the American people. "A republican government in America was, among other things, one that could see itself as reflecting and reinforcing the values of a 'Christian people,'" he says.[33] This amounts to "reject[ing] the doctrine of separation of church and state, instead advocating an integration of religion into public life that also offers broad toleration of diverse religious views."[34] Hazony recognizes the importance of religious freedom and does not argue that non-Christians must be forced to convert, only that Judaism and Christianity be given special status. He says that a nationalist, conservative democracy "is capable of embracing new members who declare that 'your people will be my people, and your God my God' (Ruth 1:16)."[35]

Lowry and Hazony have been two of the most outspoken and articulate defenders of nationalism in recent years. I'll return to both their works throughout this book to illustrate some of the main features—and problems—of the contemporary nationalist movement. But this brief survey should make clear that they believe preserving the United States' Anglo-Protestant culture should be a major focus of public policy, even if and when it conflicts with the tenets of classical liberalism, civic republicanism, and the American Constitution.

---

[33]Hazony, "What Is Conservative Democracy?"
[34]Ofir Haivry and Yoram Hazony, "What Is Conservatism?," *American Affairs* l, no. 2, Summer 2017.
[35]Hazony, "What Is Conservative Democracy?"

CONCLUSION

To summarize, nationalists believe the following: (1) Humanity is divisible into mutually distinct and internally coherent cultural units called "nations." (2) Each nation deserves its own state. Political and cultural boundaries should, ideally, align perfectly. (3) Governments have rightful jurisdiction over the cultural life of their nations. They have a responsibility to preserve and defend their national identity and cultural inheritance because: (a) national identity is intrinsically valuable and its preservation is part of the reason governments exist; (b) humans need a cohesive national community for fulfillment, flourishing, and meaning; and (c) every country requires a strong, cohesive, predominant culture to survive. Without a predominant culture to define the nation, it is likely to fragment or dissolve.

To this list, we can add the distinctive beliefs of Anglo-Protestant, or Christian, nationalists, as discussed in this chapter. Christian nationalists believe (4) America's predominant culture was, and substantially still is, Anglo-Protestant (or generically European and Christian). (5) We must sustain our Anglo-Protestant culture for the reasons listed above, and also because (a) our Anglo-Protestant culture was the essential precondition for the American experiment in liberty, and American democracy would become unsustainable without it; and (b) God blesses nations who honor him with symbolic gestures of reverence, and our Anglo-Protestant culture honors him. (This argument comes out more clearly in the work of pastors and theologians in the Christian Right, as I will show in chapter seven.)

Christian nationalism is not a catchall term for any kind of Christian political advocacy, and it is not the same thing as Christianity. Christians in America and elsewhere have been politically involved across a wide range of issues, in alliance with many different ideologies, including Christian republicanism (with a small *r*), Christian socialism, and Christian democracy. The unique feature of Christian nationalism is that it defines America as a Christian nation and it wants the government to promote a specific Anglo-Protestant cultural template as the official culture of the country. Some Christian nationalists in the past advocated for an amendment to the Constitution to recognize America's Christian heritage; others, to reinstitute prayer in public schools. Some work to enshrine a Christian nationalist interpretation of American history in school curricula. Others advocate for immigration restrictions specifically to prevent a change to American culture and preserve America's existing Anglo-Protestant demographic majority. Some want to empower the government to take stronger action to circumscribe behavior they believe violates Anglo-Protestant norms. And sometimes Christian nationalism is most evident not in its political agenda, but in the sort of attitude with which it is held: an unstated presumption that Christians are entitled to primacy of place in the public square because they are heirs of the true or essential heritage of American culture, that Christians have a presumptive right to define the meaning of the American experiment because they see themselves as America's architects, first citizens, and guardians.[36]

The strongest version of this argument emphasizes culture, not race and not doctrine, and so its stated beliefs are different from both White nationalism, White supremacy, and the alt-right, on the one hand, and Christian theocracy, on the other. Racial identitarian movements champion the supposed superiority of European ethnicity or ancestry; they define Western civilization and American identity as a function of European DNA. By contrast, Anglo-Protestant nationalists argue that anyone can assimilate to Anglo-Protestant *culture*, regardless of race or ethnicity. White nationalism is obviously racist and wrongheaded, and most people do not need a book-length refutation of it, and Anglo-Protestant nationalism is (at least in theory) distinct from it.

Similarly, the Anglo-Protestant nationalists emphasize the inherited norms, values, and habits of America's Christian heritage more than Christian theology. They avow support for democratic institutions and do not advocate granting theocratic power to the clergy, so (contrary to the claims of Katherine Stewart and Chris Hedges, among others) their argument is distinct from theonomists and Dominionists, who do advocate for a literal Christian theocracy. Christian nationalists do not believe non-Christians should be forced to convert or that other religions should be proscribed, and they do believe in the First Amendment (at least as it was interpreted prior to 1947). But they also believe that Christianity should keep its historic place as the unquestioned and dominant cultural framework in the United States, and that the government should actively construct and defend that cultural framework. A supermajority of Americans throughout history have been Christians and, Christian nationalists argue, they should have the right to define the nation's cultural

---

[36]Paul D. Miller, "What Is Christian Nationalism?," *Christianity Today*, February 3, 2021.

identity and to have it be recognized and affirmed by the government and the public. Like all nationalists, Christian nationalists demand recognition and prestige for their national identity; the boring details of policy are often secondary to symbolic gestures of recognition and affirmation.

I focus on cultural nationalism in this book, not racial or theocratic nationalism, because it is a stronger argument and a more popular kind of nationalism and deserves a more careful and sensitive treatment. But I also argue later that, despite the clear distinction between them in their stated beliefs, they often overlap in their embodied social and cultural practices. Today's Christian nationalists tend to overlook, deny, or downplay that overlap because they emphasize that they sincerely do not believe the same things that racists and theocrats believe. Nonetheless, in chapters eight and nine of this book, I focus on how the embodied social and cultural movement of Christian nationalism still has antidemocratic, illiberal tendencies, especially in how it treats ethnic and religious minorities.

The next three chapters are an argument against nationalism. In chapter four, I argue that humanity is not divisible into cultural units—making the belief that political and cultural boundaries should overlap essentially impossible. Together, these two errors undermine the cornerstones of nationalist dogma. I also show democracy does not depend on Anglo-Protestantism. In chapter five I argue against most of the claims lumped together under point number three above. I argue that the belief that government should have jurisdiction over culture is mistaken and dangerous, and I argue that nationalism undermines rather than creates national unity. I engage with arguments about the supposed biblical foundations of nationalist dogma in chapter six, showing that the Bible does not say what nationalists claim it says. The remaining tenets of nationalist theory are theological claims about the best paths to human and national flourishing. I take them up in chapter ten when I outline a theology of the nation.

THE CASE AGAINST NATIONALISM

4

Nationalists believe that humanity is divisible into mutually distinct cultural units called "nations," that these units merit sovereignty, that their governments have a responsibility to protect their respective national cultures, and that humans find fulfillment and meaning through national community. American Christian nationalists believe that the United States' rightfully predominant culture is Anglo-Protestantism and that the US government should promote and protect this cultural heritage. They believe a strong and predominant culture is necessary to sustain national unity and even national survival, and that Anglo-Protestantism in particular is necessary to sustain a democratic system of government and to secure God's blessing.

In the first part of this chapter I argue that humanity is not easily divisible into mutually distinct cultural units. Cultures overlap and their borders are fuzzy. That introduces a crucial flaw into the cornerstone of nationalist dogma. Since cultural units are fuzzy, they make a poor fit as the foundation for political order. Cultural identities are fluid and hard to draw boundaries around, but political boundaries are hard and semipermanent. Attempting to found political legitimacy on cultural likeness means political order will constantly be in danger of being felt as illegitimate by some group or other. The nationalist reaction to this predicament is predictable. The state's inevitable response is to try to manufacture or mandate cultural unity, even at the expense of liberty and cultural pluralism. Nationalism almost always turns out to be the enemy of free government.

NATIONS HAVE BLURRY BOUNDARIES

The cornerstone of nationalism is the belief that humanity is divisible into internally coherent, mutually distinct cultural units or blocs. In 1882 a famous nineteenth-century French scholar named Ernest Renan wrote, in one of the earliest inquiries into nationalism, that established nations are "individual historical units, the crucial pieces on a chequerboard whose squares will forever vary in importance and size but will never be wholly confused with each other."[1] But the map of the world's cultures is not a checkerboard; it is a Venn diagram—and the overlapping circles are blobs of irregular size and shape that fade imperceptibly into one another. Humanity is not easily divisible into neat cultural units or blocs. Different cultures certainly exist, but the boundaries between them are blurry. Cultures overlap. The nationalist vision depends on being able to draw clear and hard boundaries between cultures, to say *this* is Anglo-Protestantism and *that* is something else. That effort is essentially impossible, especially on the ground near the borders where cultures overlap and mingle. The difference between two cultures may be clear from respective cultural centers—say, Paris and Berlin. But take a walk to Alsace, a French region on the border between France and Germany, where the local dialect, architecture, and cuisine are closer to German than French but show influences from both. There is a hard political border that says Alsace is part of French territory (which has not always been the case), but drawing a hard *cultural* boundary and insisting that Alsace is part of French culture and not German would be silly. Politically, the inclusion of Alsace in France has nothing to do with its *Frenchness* and does not depend on cultural affinity with the political center.

The same is true virtually everywhere in the world where two cultures abut one another—which is to say, virtually everywhere in the world. The border between India and Pakistan was drawn ostensibly to divide the subcontinent between Muslims and Indians, yet two hundred million Muslims live in India today, while Punjabis on either side of the border share more in common with each other than Indian Punjabis have with Indian Tamils far to the south or than Pakistani Punjabis have with Pakistani Pashtuns in the far west—who in turn share more in common with Afghan Pashtuns across the Durand Line.

[1] Ernest Renan, "What Is a Nation?," in *Becoming National: A Reader*, ed. Geoff Eley and Ronald Grigor Suny (New York: Oxford University Press, 1996), 43.

There is no obvious cultural reason why the Spanish-speaking countries of Central and South America, who all share a Roman Catholic heritage and a mixture of Spanish and native ethnicity, should be considered different units or divided up the way they are. The boundaries of Russia correspond in almost no way to the cultural boundaries of Russian-speaking people, who are spread out across Eastern Europe, the Caucasus, and Central Asia, while some two hundred other ethnic groups live within the Russian Federation. In 1998, while backpacking through Europe, I shared a train car with a group of young men who turned out to be Pomaks: Bulgarian-speaking Muslim citizens of Greece. They lived on the wrong side of the border to be considered Bulgarian, they spoke the wrong language and professed the wrong religion to be considered truly Greek, and they shared nothing in common with their neighboring Turks except religion. To which "nation" did they belong? The nationalists' belief that international borders should correspond to cultural boundaries is simply impossible on its face.

The same is also true among levels of culture. A critic might respond to the previous paragraphs by arguing that Alsatians or Pomaks, for example, are simply subcultures, and that we can still draw hard boundaries between all subcultures in the world and lump them together by broad similarities if we could just account for them all. But we cannot. There is no downward boundary on how small a subculture could be: there could be, in principle, an infinite proliferation of subcultures within subcultures until there are as many subcultures as there are individual humans who each constitute their own distinct nation. (Which is, incidentally, not a bad description of identity politics.) There is also no upward boundary on generalization. Both France and Germany participate in something broader called European culture, or maybe Western civilization, which in turn is part of a planetary human culture. We inhabit a milieu of cultural identities above, below, and around us. The blurriness of cultural boundaries is three-dimensional.

And cultures change. Not only are their borders fuzzy; they are fluid. The culture of a certain place or a given population in one decade may be drastically different from its culture ten years before or afterward. The Americans of the 1790s were markedly less religious than they would be two decades later in the throes of the Second Great Awakening. The Jacksonian era brought a new cultural emphasis on the social implications of democracy and on the leveling influence of equality (among White men) that would have been foreign to the

Americans of the mid-eighteenth century. The culture of France changed dras-tically from 1780 to 1800 through war, revolution, and regime change. And—crucial for my argument—the pace of change is not evenly spread around a nation. Events unfold rapidly in urban centers and only gradually percolate out to rural areas. That is why city dwellers universally look on rural folk as backward bumpkins, while rural folk everywhere pride themselves as the true bastion of stalwart tradition against the heedless licentiousness of city ways. Whatever boundaries are drawn around city and country are obviously arti-ficial and certain to be out of date as soon as the next wave of change arrives. In the face of cultural change, upheavals, wars, revolutions, religious revivals, urbanization, the spread or contraction of literacy, and other engines of cul-tural dynamism, it is unclear how we are supposed to draw static boundaries around one culture to separate it from others.

While different cultures exist, they are neither mutually distinct nor inter-nally coherent—at least not to the degree required for nationalism to work. They overlap with each other and they overlap with internal subcultures, which in turn overlap with other subcultures and sometimes even bleed across inter-cultural lines and act as cultural bridges. And different aspects of culture do not line up with other aspects: a map of the world's religions does not line up with the map of its languages, for example, and neither line up with the map of ethnicities or races. In the face of these realities, there is no objective or rational decision principle to help us draw hard boundaries and to say that *this particular* boundary is the most important one, the longest lasting, the stur-diest, the most relevant, the one on which political borders should depend. The nationalist belief in the easy divisibility of humanity into distinct cultural units is nonsense, and its use of these units as the basis for large claims about po-litical order, morality, justice, and human life lacks any basis in reason, nature, truth, or justice.

This is hardly a novel insight: Max Weber noted a century ago that a nation cannot be defined "in terms of empirical qualities common to those who count as members of the nation," and that "there is no agreement on how these groups should be delimited."[2] In the 1940s Hans Kohn dismissed the essential-izing pretension of nationalism as rooted in "mythical prehistorical

---

[2]Max Weber, "The Nation," in *Readings and Commentary on Modernity*, ed. Stephen Kalberg (Ox-ford: Blackwell, 2005).

pseudo-realities."[3] Benedict Anderson, author of one of the classic studies of nationalism, remarked on the "philosophical poverty" of nationalist movements.[4] Anthony Smith similarly wrote that "the doctrine of nationalism is vague, illogical, incomplete, and sketchy," and he judged that "the indeterminacy of national criteria and their vague, shifting, often arbitrary character in the writings of nationalists have undermined the ideology's credibility."[5] Another scholar wrote that "it is one of the most ambiguous concepts in the present-day vocabulary of political and analytical thought," and that it "conceals within itself extreme opposites and contradictions."[6] It is commonplace among scholars to recognize that nationalism is frustratingly vague and evasive about its own meaning.

To pin it down, let us ask an obvious question: If nationalism rests on a claim that there are things called "nations," which we can identify on the basis of a shared trait, which trait counts? Language, culture, religion, race, ethnicity, history, heritage, and land have all been proposed as candidates by different nationalists, but they never seem to agree on which one matters. Of course we share traits in common with others, but nationalists want to elevate one trait above others and make it the basis of our political community. That requires drawing hard boundaries and writing exact definitions. Hazony, for example, says nations are defined by a common "language or religion." But which is it: language or religion? And who gets to say? These are precisely the questions around which countless wars have been fought.

Under Hazony's definition, one could argue that the United States, United Kingdom, Canada, Australia, and New Zealand are (or were) arguably one "nation," because of our shared British, Protestant, English-speaking heritage—which, if true, means it was illegitimate for any of the colonies to seek independence from the British Empire. If nations and states should overlap, then English-speaking Protestants in the colonies should never have sought to form their own governments apart from Westminster. Put to its logical conclusion, it would mean that government is legitimate if the governors speak the same

---

[3]Hans Kohn, *The Idea of Nationalism: A Study of the Origins and Background* (New York: Macmillan, 1944), 13.
[4]Benedict Anderson, *Imagined Communities: Reflections on the Origin and Spread of Nationalism* (New York: Verso, 2006), 5.
[5]Anthony Smith, *Nationalism: Theory, Ideology, History*, 2nd ed. (Cambridge: Polity, 2010), 11; *National Identity* (Reno: University of Nevada Press, 1991), 17.
[6]Peter Alter, *Nationalism*, 2nd ed. (New York: Hodder Education, 1994), 1, 2.

language or worship the same God as the governed, *regardless of what the government actually does*. Nationalism is often a convenient fig leaf for authoritarian governments to hide behind. The Nazi government of Germany was commendably nationalist, sharing the German language with its subjects, but few would argue that it was therefore just.

The power to define who "we" are is one of the central questions of politics. Nationalism tries to resolve the debate by fiat, simply announcing a principle that we should all rally around a common language, religion, ethnicity, or culture. This answer is so arbitrary, vague, and contestable that instead of resolving the debate it simply creates new lines over which to fight. In our lived experience, we are members of a multiplicity of groups who have crosscutting traits that overlap and diverge in no discernible pattern. Nationalists want us to feel a special moral obligation to define ourselves by their preferred trait, but why should we—especially when the traits they suggest are either vague, exclusionary, or both?

Religion cannot be the unifying principle. Most Middle Eastern states declare that Islam is the state religion, but many of them have substantial Christian minorities (and they used to have millennia-old Jewish communities too). Religion cannot serve as the basis of national identity even in America: while some three-quarters of Americans profess Christianity, that includes hundreds of variants and versions of Christianity. Any effort to settle on one national, official version of Christianity as the basis for American identity would be completely unworkable (besides violating the disestablishment of religion). India might be a candidate for a religiously defined nation because it is a majority-Hindu state—but it is also the founding home of Sikhism and home to one of the largest Muslim populations, largest Buddhist populations, and largest Zoroastrian populations in the world (and Hinduism itself is hardly monolithic).

"Race" cannot fill the gap and define national identity because, obviously, that would be incompatible with core American values. Many Americans did define American identity in racial terms for much of American history, which is how we got slavery, civil war, and Jim Crow. The story of American history is the story of overcoming that view and declaring it to be, in a real sense, un-American. More to the point, race is an invented, unscientific category with little basis in biology.[7] Culture, ethnicity, and heritage are better concepts, but

---

[7]Glenn C. Loury, *Anatomy of Racial Inequality* (Cambridge, MA: Harvard University Press, 2009), chap. 2.

they are amorphous, fluid, and changeable; highly important, but malleable, hard to define, and unfit to serve as the basis of a fixed political system.

The only category of national identity that might come close to being objective and meaningful is language. Language comes close to truly dividing humanity with deep boundaries: language shapes our conceptual and epistemological possibilities such that, at the extreme, native French speakers *think differently* than English speakers, for example. And language is saturated with history: when Americans hear "mystic chords of memory" or "freedom from fear," the words immediately evoke shared stories and historical meaning. When language and history overlap, the sense of shared community and group identity is extraordinarily powerful. Does that mean language should be the exclusive basis of political boundaries?

Possibly, but even so we should recognize that it will not solve our problems because language shows the same fuzziness as other categories of culture and group identity through regional dialects and linguistic borrowing. For example, if a Frenchman is one who speaks French, do the speakers of regional dialects, like Picard, Gascon, Limousin, Franco-Provençal, and Occitan, count? What about French-born Francophone Arabs whose ancestors immigrated from Algeria, or citizens of the twenty-one African nations where French is the official language? Are the Welsh and Scottish, who each have their own language but have adopted English as their standard, part of the English nation, or are they, together with the English, part of a broader British nation? The Kurds are often said to be the world's largest stateless nation—yet the northern Kurdish (Kurmanji) spoken in Turkey differs substantially from the southern Kurdish of Iran. Hindi and Urdu are nearly the same language, only separated by the partition line drawn between India and Pakistan in 1947, and the Farsi and Dari spoken in Iran, Tajikistan, and Afghanistan are only a little more distant from each other. Standard American English—the kind of bland, unaccented English used by TV news anchors—has as much in common with some dialects of British English as with the English spoken in the Appalachians, in Boston, or in New Orleans. American English has a range of dialects and accents that seem to grow further apart, not closer together, as social media allow subcultures to flourish. The boundaries between languages are not as easy to draw as one might expect.

Additionally, there are simply too many languages in the world for linguistic nationalism to work. With some sixty-five hundred languages in use around the world today, carving up the world into political units defined by language creates as many problems as it solves. Middle Eastern states are not uniformly Arabic in language, culture, or ethnicity, as Turks, Persians, Kurds, and others are marbled across the region. India has twenty-two official languages and another hundred major languages in widespread use; the number of ethnic, cultural, linguistic, and tribal groups is beyond count. The reality of cultural and religious pluralism is widespread around the world: almost a quarter of Russian citizens are not ethnically Russian and 15 percent do not speak the Russian language as their mother tongue. What if a smaller language group— like the Chechens of Russia, the Basques or Catalans of Spain, or the Québécois of Canada—decides it no longer wants to belong to the broader nation of which it is unwillingly a part? Even the United States today is effectively a bilingual country. The idea of linguistically defined "nations" becomes laughable when one glances at the map of Africa or Indonesia.

I am not denying that we have traits that we share with others and that we often feel a sense of group solidarity with them. But it is important to keep in mind several things about our group affinities that make them ill-suited to serve as the basis of government. The groups we are part of—our *peoples, cultures,* or *heritage*—are fluid and malleable; we create and refashion them with our participation; cultures overlap; the boundaries between them are fuzzy and indistinct; and we can, over the course of our lifetimes, pick and choose which traditions and cultures to recognize and cultivate as central to our lives and our families. We can, for example, learn new languages, convert to a different religion, or immerse ourselves in a different culture. The ability to do so is an important part of enjoying the diversity and plurality of the world. Such identities are not primordial, fixed in nature, or given once for all time.[8] I have no expectation that the way I combine a certain set of traits—speaking English, being a Christian, being of European (Swiss German) descent— should exactly line up with every other English speaker, every other Christian, and every other American of European or German ancestry. Some Christians are African American; some Americans speak Spanish; and some English speakers are Indian. Our various traits don't line up—and whether they do or not is immaterial to our ability to live together under one Constitution.

---

[8]See Smith, *National Identity*, chap. 2, for an excellent overview of the primordialist vs. instrumentalist debate about ethnic and national identity.

Nationalists insist that a politician or government official has the right to tell us which trait—language, religion, ethnicity, and so on—is supposed to command our overriding loyalty; that one of these shared traits must be the basis of my political community; or that all my traits must line up the same way as everyone else's in the nation. Nationalism is a political program, "a theory of political legitimacy, which requires that ethnic boundaries"—or the boundaries of whatever trait of commonality the nation unifies around— "should not cut across political ones."[9] Once you insist on that, you have to draw boundaries, define the nation, and choose which trait will be the basis of our nationhood. *Nations*, in the thick sense, aspire to be fixed, monolithic, and discrete; to have hard borders; they *need* to have clear distinctions between "us" and "them"; nations insist that we cultivate loyalty to one nation at a time; they ask us to believe propaganda about their antiquity and primordial character; and they often muffle or discourage political, cultural, or religious dissent or difference. That is where the trouble begins. Group feeling within a subculture is a simple fact; turning cultural solidarity into a political program is something else entirely.[10]

The nationalist vision is strikingly premodern, relying on an oversimplified cosmology. The idea of discrete, nonoverlapping cultural units smacks of nostalgia for an imagined past of cultural simplicity when everyone supposedly knew who "we" and who "they" were, a transplantation of simple tribalism to the era of large, impersonal, geographically extensive states. Even long ago in an era of much lower population density and before the age of mass transportation no such society existed; pluralism and cultural mingling was not invented with the dawn of the industrial revolution. But globalization, the intermingling of peoples, and the spread of liberty over the past three centuries has almost certainly accelerated pluralism by creating new minorities, subgroups, and cultural identities all around the world such that it is even less meaningful to speak of cultural units which either have a strong consensus around one shared trait or in which all the traits that are supposed to make up a national

---

[9]Ernst Gellner, *Nations and Nationalism* (Ithaca, NY: Cornell University Press, 2008), 1. I am following Smith, who insists nationalism is "an ideological movement for the attainment and maintenance of autonomy and individuality for a social group" (*Nationalism*, 26).

[10]Scholars will recognize the distinction I am drawing parallels Friedrich Meinecke's distinction between a "cultural" nation and a "political" nation. It also parallels Hans Kohn's "objective" vs. "subjective" nations. That we have shared traits is a simple fact. Our choice to politicize those traits is what creates nationalism as a political program.

group overlap—which means the political program of making cultural nations the basis of political organization is not viable.

There are effectively no true nation-states in the world today. Virtually every state in the world is a pluralistic, multiethnic, multilingual polity in which questions of who or what defines the polity are live debates. Perhaps only microsovereignties—tiny states with populations under one million— have the strong sense of oneness and a cultural consensus that nationalists say defines nations. Most states today are more akin to the multiethnic empires of the past than the culturally homogenous units of the nineteenth century's aspirations. Nationalism is a yearning for prehistorical tribalism, a world in which language groups only interacted on the margins for trade, commerce, or war, and adherents of different faiths lived in separate and discrete territories—a world in which racial, ethnic, and cultural segregation was an international principle. Such a world no longer exists, if it ever did, and to re-create it would be impossible.

NATIONALISM IS ILLIBERAL

Nationalism—the correspondence between cultural units and governments— has always been more aspiration than reality, in part because of the ambiguity surrounding what a "nation" is.[11] Eric Hobsbawm famously quipped that "nationalism requires too much belief in what is patently not so."[12] Nations are fabrications, but people fervently believe in them. In that sense, nations are real because people experience them as real. Michael Billig argued that "because of [its] imaginary element, nationalism contains a strong social psychological dimension."[13] Hans Kohn wrote that "nationalism is first and foremost a state of mind, an act of consciousness,"[14] or, put another way, "nationality is formed by the decision to form a nationality."[15] John Mearsheimer, an international relations scholar and an advocate of nationalism, admits as much: "The real basis of nationhood is psychological. . . . A nation exists when a large

---

[11]Much of this section is drawn from Paul D. Miller, "The Vice of Nationalism," *Orbis* 63, no. 2 (2019): 291-97; and Paul D. Miller, "The Unreality of Realism," H-DIPLO/ISSF, October 2, 2019.

[12]Eric J. Hobsbawm, *Nations and Nationalism Since 1780: Programme, Myth, Reality* (Cambridge: Cambridge University Press, 2012), 12.

[13]Michael Billig, *Banal Nationalism* (London: Sage, 1995), 10.

[14]Kohn, *Idea of Nationalism*, 10.

[15]Kohn, *Idea of Nationalism*, 15.

number of people think of themselves as members of the same unique social group with a distinct culture. In other words, a nation is a large group that considers itself a nation." Smith described the nation as "a construct of the mind," which is why "every nationalism aspires to its nation."[16] Once you become a nationalist, you have to set about creating your nation, making real the nation of your imagination. That is why, despite the arbitrariness of nationalism as an idea, nationalism has proven itself to have tremendous political force in history.

When nationalists go about constructing their nation, they have to define who is, and who is not, part of the nation. But because there are no rational or objective bases for doing so, nationalists can never have moral authority to persuade those who are hesitant to join the nationalist bandwagon—and there are *always* dissidents and minorities who do not, or cannot, conform to the nationalists' preferred cultural template. In the absence of moral authority, nations can only establish themselves by force. The nationalist emperor has no clothes, but he can order the execution of anyone who says so. Or, to switch metaphors, nations are the wizard of Oz, with all the appearance of power and reality—but nationalists are the propagandists behind the curtain furiously insisting that we pay him no attention for "the Great Oz has spoken!" The second problem with nationalism is that it is illiberal—that is, opposed to the classically liberal principles of liberty and equality. Nationalism is usually authoritarian in spirit and violent in practice, founded on the raw assertion of power.

Scholars are unanimous about the troubling historical record of nationalism in this respect, but even the apologists and defenders of nationalism are aware of the problem. "The fact is that there is no way to place a downward boundary on what may be reasonably called a nation," in Hazony's words.[17] Each constituent clan or tribe might aspire to be its own nation, especially if it is an ethnic or religious minority, as has happened with the Québécois of Canada, the Basques of Spain, all across the Balkans, and in countless other states. Hazony announces his solution by fiat: nations deserve independence

---

[16]Smith, *Nationalism*, 26. In a sense, every nationalism is effectively what he calls a "territorial" nationalism, one not based on an actual, existing commonality, but on an aspiration for such cultural unity that is felt to be missed. Smith contrasts this with "ethnic" nationalism based on an existing cultural unity; that kind of nationalism, it seems to me, is exceedingly rare in practice.

[17]Yoram Hazony, *The Virtue of Nationalism* (London: Hachette, 2018), 169.

if they "are cohesive and strong enough to secure it."[18] Philpott's subjective criteria—a group is a group if they feel they are a group and act like one on the world stage—has the same problem.[19] If a group can amass enough power to convince others that it counts as a nation, then it does; if not, then it does not. In other words, for nationalists, *might makes right*. Advocates of nationalism argue this allows for organic, bottom-up expressions of authentic local identity; in practice, it has usually been occasion for a fabricated, top-down imposition of national identity by warlords, demagogues, and populists. That applies at home as well as abroad. Nationalists often have to use force against their own countrymen to get them to recognize or believe in the idea of whatever nation they are trying to build. As Lowry rightly notes about France, "It undertook an intensive, far-reaching campaign to wipe out distinctive regional cultures and dialects to forge the common national culture,"[20] of France—though it is baffling why Lowry thinks this is an argument in his favor.

The problem starts innocuously enough. Nations weave myths about their naturalness, antiquity, and rootedness in smaller and more natural forms of affiliation. In the nationalist vision, humans live in nested relationships of family, clan, tribe, and nation, each layer representing a larger amalgamation of the previous. That is true as far as it goes, but nationalists conceive of the nation as a family writ large. The nation exists "due to the family like bonds of mutual loyalty that persist among" the individuals, clans, and tribes, in Hazony's words. It is "an extended family with one national character."[21] Billig says the same thing, though from a critical perspective: in national consciousness, "nations, national identities and national homelands appear as 'natural.' Most crucially, the 'world of nations' is represented as a 'natural,' moral order."[22] In this myth, the family, tribe, and nation are simply different versions of each other at different scales. Nationalists want us to feel that we owe to our fellow nationals the same familial devotion, attachment, and loyalty we owe to our siblings and parents.

---

[18]Hazony, *Virtue of Nationalism*, 176.

[19]Daniel Philpott, "In Defense of Self-Determination," *Ethics* 105, no. 2 (1995): 352-385.

[20]Rich Lowry, *The Case for Nationalism: How It Made Us Rich, Powerful, and Free* (New York: Broadside, 2019), 18.

[21]Hazony, *Virtue of Nationalism*, 89, 112.

[22]Billig, *Banal Nationalism*, 10.

One problem with this view is that families are dictatorships: children are subjects, not citizens. When we treat the nation as a large family, the president or head of state is a patriarch and we, his children: the template is not conducive to equality under law or to democratic accountability. That is why nationalism usually comes with illiberal tendencies at home. Whoever gets to define the nation—typically, the majority tribe acting through the government—also gets to define who isn't part of the nation and therefore who doesn't count as a full citizen. That was the reasoning behind slavery, the Indian removal policy, the system of segregation across the American South, and legalized abortion. Because Native Americans and enslaved Africans did not count as members of the American nation, Americans could justify doing whatever they wanted to them. Even today, Lowry acknowledges the wrongs of "brutality and duplicity in our dealings with the Indians and Mexicans" but responds with a shrug. "Does anyone believe that Texas and California would be better governed, freer, or more prosperous under the suzerainty of Mexico?"[23] He seems to think the question is rhetorical and not worth serious discussion. But African Americans would certainly have been better off if given the chance to live under Mexican law, where slavery had been abolished in 1829, than in Texas or the southern United States of the 1840s. Lowry nonetheless insists, "We should always remember the bottom line of our expansion: it was a stupendous boon to our nation, to our people, to our interests, and to our power."[24] Lowry believes that American power is self-justifying: "If we had remained the coastal country we were in the eighteenth century, we would have been a significant, but not a world-historical, nation. Size matters. The Swiss have ideals. Does anyone give a damn?"[25] Such a statement from a supposed public intellectual is appalling. This is not a serious argument, and it is certainly not a Christian argument; it is, in fact, no argument at all, but simply the raw assertion of power for its own sake, praising America for doing whatever was necessary to become a "world-historical" nation. What makes America world-historical is its universally admired creed, and if America holds itself up as an example of liberty and justice for all, then Lowry's praise of self-legitimating power is, ironically, un-American.

---

[23]Lowry, *Case for Nationalism*, 25.
[24]Lowry, *Case for Nationalism*, 136.
[25]Lowry, *Case for Nationalism*, 26.

A bigger problem with the nation-as-family argument is that, of course, the entire story is untrue. We are not all related to each other, and pretending that we are is unhelpful. A nation is not simply a large family or tribe; it is more accurately the conquest by one tribe over other tribes and their assimilation—usually coerced—into a larger unit. As a nation's definition gains specificity—as it settles on a particular ethnicity, language, culture, or religion—it necessarily excludes those who do not share the nation's identity. Acting like we are supposed to be one big family gives permission for the patriarch—the government—to punish those who do not fit in. Smith argued that "the goal of every nationalist is therefore autonomy or a return of self and community to its genuine and uncontaminated state"—uncontaminated, that is, by outsiders and cultural dissidents—and it "signifies the awakening of the nation to its oppression and a struggle for liberation *from alien traits.*"[26] The presence of *traits* deemed to be outside the national norm is, for the nationalist, a form of oppression, disloyalty, or subversion, the answer to which is to purge or subordinate the alien element.

Nationalism amounts to Jim Crow on a global scale, an insistence that cultural majorities have a presumptive right to defend their culture with the power of the state, a right cultural minorities lack for no other reason than being in a minority. Though it can sometimes wear a more benign face and speak a language of tolerance, at heart nationalism is *internal imperialism*: the rule by a cultural majority over cultural minorities under the ruling group's predominant language, culture, or religion. It is the effort by the largest or most powerful group to establish itself as the dominant group whose identity defines the nation. Hazony admits as much (and remember Hazony is an advocate for nationalism, who thinks it is a good thing worth pursuing): "What is needed for the establishment of a stable and free state is a majority nation whose cultural dominance is plain and unquestioned."[27] One tradition, religion, or subculture should have title to define the nation's identity. Lowry acknowledges the same: "Almost every nation rests on an ethnic core and consequently a deep sense of natural, unchosen ties, like those of family."[28]

---

[26]Anthony Smith, *Nationalism: Theory, Ideology, History*, 2nd ed. (Cambridge: Polity, 2010), 11, emphasis added.
[27]Hazony, *Virtue of Nationalism*, 165.
[28]Lowry, *Case for Nationalism*, 33.

Hazony recognizes that often this kind of nation building requires crushing internal diversity. Citing the same example as Lowry, he notes that in pursuit of national cohesion, "The French have a long history of expressing their national freedom through the suppression of languages and religious practices they find offensive," he writes, with no apparent discomfort. More broadly, in some cases of internal dissent, "there is no choice but for the national state to apply more rigorous measures to deprive imperialist and anarchic elements of their aspirations by force."[29] Hazony, bafflingly, seems to approve. Smith does not: "The nationalist ideal of unity has had profound consequences . . . it has encouraged the idea of the indivisibility of the nation and justified the eradication, often by force, of all intermediate bodies and local differences in the interests of cultural and political homogeneity."[30] Hazony clearly recognizes, and endorses, the idea that the dominant cultural group should use force against those who dissent. This by itself should cast doubt on his claim that nationalism is the one reliable route to safeguarding individual liberties. Nationalist governments are, in practice, notorious for their oppression of religious, ethnic, and cultural minorities.[31] Mearsheimer, similarly, recommends the solution used by absolutists, autocrats, and nation builders throughout history: "The key to success is to eliminate heterogeneity," such as by enforcing a single national language. There are, of course, less savory ways of eliminating heterogeneity.

The problem with nationalism is that plenty of people do not want to be part of whatever culture the state tries to enforce as the national model, and the nation can only enforce cultural uniformity through coercion. If nationalism is much like a religion, it does not admit room for heresy. Eliminating heterogeneity may be pragmatic, but it violates human liberty and equality. It almost always requires coercion to sustain one's avowed traditions, heritage, and identity in the face of change and cultural pluralism. And it is typically the group of dominant rich men who work the hardest to resist such change because it would threaten their power. Another word for tribalism is patriarchy; yet another, oligarchy.

That is why everywhere nationalism has actually been tried, it has rarely resulted in states that are at peace with themselves and their neighbors. The

---

[29]Hazony, *Virtue of Nationalism*, 136, 183.

[30]Anthony Smith, *National Identity* (Reno: University of Nevada Press, 1991), 76.

[31]The relationship between nationalism and racism is complex. Anderson, for one, traces racism to class, not to nation (*Imagined Communities*, chap. 8).

most common criticism of nationalism is also the one that rings most true: "In the name of 'national identity' people have . . . been prepared to trample on the civil and religious rights of ethnic, racial and religious minorities,"[32] as Smith rightly argues. Nationalism is virtually always contested: once citizens come to believe that their affinity group and their government should embody something called a "nation" (in the thick sense), people immediately begin to fight over what that nation is and who counts as a member. Historically, nationalism has an unsettling tendency to attract racist, xenophobic, and sectarian fellow travelers. The age of nationalism is the age of civil wars, insurgencies, terrorism, and national liberation movements, to say nothing of international competition and war.

ANGLO-PROTESTANTISM
IS NOT NECESSARY FOR DEMOCRACY

My argument so far amounts to a plea for more genuine tolerance for cultural pluralism and difference. Nationalists insist on promoting an overarching cultural template to which everyone is expected to assimilate. I've argued the effort is basically impossible, given cultural fuzziness, and bound to deteriorate into illiberalism. I want to add another argument. Some Christian nationalists argue that we need to sustain Anglo-Protestant culture because it is the necessary precondition for democracy. In this section I argue that we do not need Anglo-Protestant culture to sustain the ideals of the American experiment.[33]

The ideals of the Constitution and Declaration can exist and thrive outside the cultural context of Anglo-Protestantism. Anglo-Protestantism was the *originating condition* of modern democracy and individual rights.[34] That does not mean it is the *necessary precondition* for these liberal institutions in the future. Liberal democracy has spread and thrived all around the world over the past two centuries, having taken root in non-Western cultures, such as Japan and India, without an Anglo-Protestant influence, proving democracy and Anglo-Protestantism are separable. Indeed, American and European

---

[32]Smith, *National Identity*, 17.

[33]This section draws from Paul D. Miller, "Non-'Western' Liberalism and the Resilience of the Liberal International Order," *The Washington Quarterly* 41, no. 2 (Summer 2018): 137-53; and Paul D. Miller, "Against 'Conservative Democracy,'" *Providence Magazine*, June 19, 2019.

[34]Daniel Hannan, *Inventing Freedom: How the English-Speaking Peoples Made the Modern World* (New York: Harper Collins, 2013).

cultures have profoundly shifted over 250 years, departing in dramatic ways from Anglo-Protestantism, yet democracy still lives in its original home.

Scholars have never come to consensus about the essential preconditions for democracy and human rights. Some have suggested that democracy is easier in wealthy societies—which is obviously true because wealth makes everything easier. I imagine authoritarians find it easier to sustain tyranny when they are rich than when they are poor. Other scholars have suggested that democracy requires a certain level of literacy, industrialization, or urbanization, which cannot account for democracy in India and the democracies of Africa. Still others point to cultural or historical factors, such as a European heritage, Protestantism, individualism, the experience of the Renaissance or Enlightenment, or similar historical experiences. As we saw in chapter three, this is the heart of the nationalist argument: they argue there are specific cultural preconditions for democracy, alternatively described as Western, European, British, Christian, Protestant, Anglo-Protestant, or Judeo-Christian. One scholar has termed this "Judeo-Christian exceptionalism," or the idea that "the Judeo-Christian tradition [is] the essence of both American democracy and Western civilization."[35] Oliver O'Donovan argues there is a necessary, underlying theological logic binding Christianity to liberal democracy: "to display the liberal achievement correctly, we have to show it as the victory won by Christ over the nations' rulers."[36]

This argument has an intuitive appeal to it because we know, as a matter of history, that the ideas of democracy and republicanism were first articulated by Europeans (ancient Greeks) and rediscovered by other Europeans (Renaissance Italian and English civic republicans), and that modern democracy and individual rights first emerged in the early modern United Kingdom, France, and the United States. There are obvious, clear, and strong historical and cultural links between Christianity and the ideas and institutions of classical liberalism and civic republicanism. In my book about just war theory, I suggested liberalism is best understood as the political theology of secularized Christendom, which I take to be roughly similar to O'Donovan's point. Liberalism, democracy, and republicanism all arose in Christian Europe, from Christian

---

[35]Healan K. Gaston, *Imagining Judeo-Christian America: Religion, Secularism, and the Redefinition of Democracy* (Chicago: University of Chicago Press, 2019), 11.
[36]Oliver O'Donovan, *The Desire of the Nations: Rediscovering the Roots of Political Theology* (Cambridge: Cambridge University Press, 1999), 229.

European thinkers, and were embodied in Christian and European traditions, institutions, and mores.

But the history of the relationship between democracy and Christendom is just that—history.[37] It is not a deterministic blueprint for the future of democracy or its prospects outside of the West. Non-Western democracy exists: it is demonstrably possible to have a democracy in a place that did not experience Western history or have a Christian culture or produce Enlightenment philosophers, which proves that Western culture and political liberty are separable. Japan, India, and South Korea are the most obvious examples of thriving, prosperous, and stable non-Western democracies and have been for decades. Botswana, the Philippines, and South Africa are further examples of democracy at varying times and varying levels of stability and prosperity. They are a small sample of sixty-four non-Western states that Freedom House ranked "free" (twenty-four states) or "partly free" (forty states) in 2017.[38] Of all the states in the world, about a third were free or partly free non-Western states; 43 percent of all fully or partially free states are non-Western; and 27 percent of all free states are non-Western.

Table 4.1. Freedom status of states

	Not Free	Partly Free	Free	Total
Western	5	19	63	87
Non-Western	44	40	24	108
Total	49	59	87	195

Source: Freedom House, "Freedom in the World," 2017

This is only a snapshot in time, however, one taken after more than a decade of democratic decline across the world.[39] To get a better sense of the history of non-Western democracy, we can look at a dataset of almost every

---

[37]For the sake of brevity, in this section I am using *democracy* and *liberalism* interchangeably as shorthand for all the ideas and institutions of an open society. I hope to address the differences between these ideas in a subsequent volume.

[38]Freedom House, "Freedom in the World," Washington, DC, 2017, https://freedomhouse.org /sites/default/files/FH_FIW_2017_Report_Final.pdf.

[39]Larry Diamond, "The Democratic Rollback: The Resurgence of the Predatory State," *Foreign Affairs* 87, no. 2 (March/April 2008): 36-48. Arch Puddington, "The Erosion Accelerates," *The Journal of Democracy* 21, no. 2 (April 2010): 136-50.

state in the world and its level of freedom every year since 1800. According to this body of evidence, seventy non-Western states have been "partly free" at some point over the past two centuries, including fifty-two that have been "free." This includes many states that had a prior experience of full or partial democracy but are no longer democracies today, such as Ethiopia (between 1855 and 1929), Laos (1956–1959), Burma (1948–1961), Singapore (1959–1962), Sudan (short stints in the 1950s, 1960s, and 1980s), the Gambia (1965–1993), Uganda (1962–1965), and even Syria (1944–1957). All told, non-Western states have experienced 1,677 country-years of full or partial democracy since 1800.[40]

Modern democracy arose with the context of eighteenth-century Protestant Britain. That does not mean it only works under the conditions of eighteenth-century Protestant Britain. This simple distinction is somehow lost on nationalist scholars, activists, and pundits. What nationalists fail to appreciate is that ideas can migrate and adapt to new conditions. For any new idea, invention, or concept, there is a difference between the pristine or original case and subsequent imitations of it. It is obviously difficult to invent something anew. The first time a new thing comes along, its arrival is contingent, accidental, and dependent on a lot of things that could have happened otherwise. It is often possible only with herculean effort, genius intellect, and visionary insight about how things could be different. But once a new thing is invented or a new idea discovered so that other people can see it—like the institutions of democracy and civil liberties—others can emulate it with far less hassle and effort. Galileo was persecuted and mocked for his heliocentrism; a few brief years later, anyone who was not a heliocentrist was mocked for stupidity and ignorance. It took centuries of study to discover the art of latitudinal navigation; now a Boy Scout can do it with a map, a compass, and a few short lessons. The first iPhone was a work of genius. Now you can get a cheap knock-off at any corner market for cut-rate prices.

As Jonah Goldberg argued, the institutional arrangements of capitalism and democracy are a unique "miracle" that depended on the weird tribal habits of Angles, Saxons, and Normans that developed, *sui generis*, over centuries.[41] They

[40]Monty G. Marshall, "Polity IV Project: Political Regime Characteristics and Transitions, 1800-2016," Dataset, Center for Systemic Peace, 2016.

[41]Jonah Goldberg, *Suicide of the West How the Rebirth of Tribalism, Nationalism, and Socialism Is Destroying American Democracy* (New York: Crown Forum, 2020).

did not drop from the heavens as a revelation in the brain of John Locke, Thomas Jefferson, or John Rawls (the philosophers explained, they did not invent, classical liberalism and republicanism). It is probably true that the uniquely modern form of representative, small-*r* republican, liberal democracy was highly likely to be invented first in the Anglo-Protestant cultural context given its predisposition in favor of individualism, limited authority, the rights of conscience, and more. But we should also remember that the basic idea of electoral democracy was invented by pagan Greeks, not British Christians, suggesting that we should not give Anglo-Protestants too much credit. Regardless, as Francis Fukuyama rightly pointed out, history has delivered a verdict: these institutions have proven the most effective in world history, and so nations around the world have scrambled to copy them.[42] The force of competition compels other nations to adapt. The ideas of liberalism, capitalism, and democracy simply *work*, and so other societies must copy them or get left behind.[43]

Critics may respond that democracy in non-Western nations is not organically connected to their cultures and therefore has shallower roots. The present quality and future persistence of these non-Western democracies is thus in doubt simply by fact of being non-Western. They argue that non-Western democracy is a result of Western imperialism or cultural transplantation and they point to the higher levels of corruption and frequency of military coups in non-Western democracies as proof. O'Donovan, for example, argues that there is a strong and inextricable tie between Western history and liberal politics. He suggests that to demand societies "which do not have the historical experience of Christendom behind them" adopt democracy is a form of "cultural imperialism," especially "when those practices are expensive and the societies are poor." This idea stems from his notion that "political authority arises when power, the execution of right and the perpetuation of tradition are issued together." Since non-Western nations do not have the traditions of Christendom, the forms of democracy are alien to them and do not express any authentic, local form of rule or convey any legitimate sense of authority within those cultures.[44]

---

[42]Francis Fukuyama, "The End of History?"

[43]See also Walter Russell Mead, *God and Gold: Britain, America, and the Making of the Modern World* (Vintage, 2008), for a discussion about how competitive forces compel other countries to adapt to liberalism or risk being left behind.

[44]O'Donovan, *Desire of the Nations*, 230, 46.

If so, it appears to be a form of imperial yoke that much of the world has willingly placed upon itself. The case against non-Western democracy is clearly an example of motivated reasoning. Such critics begin with the presumption that democracy and Western culture have to go together, work backward to conclude that the actual cases of democracy in non-Western nations must be somehow less real or subpar compared to their Western counterparts, and cherry-pick historical evidence to fit their case. This is intellectually dishonest and, insofar as it implicitly assumes non-Westerners are not "fit" for freedom, quite troubling. It is the height of "Orientalism" to claim, *prima facie*, that non-Western democracies are necessarily less real than their Western counterparts simply by virtue of not being Western. It is tautological reasoning, smuggling the conclusion into the premise of one's argument such that non-Western democracy is automatically suspect because of its being non-Western. Anecdotally, I have found this view about the relationship between Western history and democracy most popular among theologians and political theorists, who tend to exaggerate the importance and agency of ideas in history, and less so among historians and political scientists, who recognize that ideas are one among many factors that drive political phenomena and who simply look at the data and recognize that democracy exists outside the West.

Only a quarter of non-Western democracies plausibly came about from Western imperialism (such as Japan, India, and several South Pacific island states) and three-quarters did not, suggesting that non-Western democracy has indigenous origins in the non-Western world and should not be credited to Western imperial influence. It was not Western imperialism or Western heritage that led Malawians to vote in an open 1993 referendum to reject single-party dictatorship in favor of multiparty democracy, or that led millions of South Koreans into the streets in 1988 to protest their military regime, or that inspired the African National Congress to dismantle apartheid and introduce multiracial democracy in South Africa in 1994, or that inspired millions of Arabs to protest for more accountable governance in 2011. It is true that non-Western democracies have higher rates of corruption and coups, likely because Western democracies have been around longer, giving them time to harden norms about corruption and civilian control of the military. Newer democracies in Africa, Asia, and Latin America are still grappling with the institutional legacies of past authoritarian and imperial regimes, naturally making them more institutionally fragile.[45]

For that matter, European democracies did not arise from an Anglo-Protestant heritage either; nationalists sometimes conflate "British" with "Western" and "European," but that ignores the very large differences between Britain and the Continent and the very different paths to democracy taken by, for example, France, the Netherlands, and Germany. And the state of democracy in the United States today should suggest that having a Western heritage is not guarantee of the survival of democracy. Europe and America got there first, but plenty of others followed. The institutions of political liberty are separable from Western history, Western heritage, and Western political philosophy. Irrefutably, there is a widespread, grassroots, indigenous desire for accountable, representative government around the world as repeatedly demonstrated by referenda, protests, demonstrations, people's movements, uprisings, and revolutions, especially by women and ethnic and religious minorities—to say nothing of successful elections and peaceful transfers of power. As President Ronald Reagan said in 1982, "Freedom is not the sole prerogative of a lucky few, but the inalienable and universal right of all human beings."[46] There is nothing uniquely Western about not wanting to be oppressed. Anglo-Protestantism is not necessary for the preservation of political liberty.

I have emphasized the empirical record to disprove the alleged dependence of democracy on Anglo-Protestantism. I want to add an argument against the logic that some nationalists claim links the two. Some argue that Anglo-Protestantism is the essential foundation of civic virtue required to sustain democracy. Civic virtue includes things like honesty, lawfulness, public spiritedness, patriotism, loyalty, selflessness, and more. American nationalists claim that Christianity uniquely inculcates these virtues and thus that democracy cannot function without it.

But Anglo-Protestantism is not the same thing as civic virtue, and Christianity is not the only source of it. Christian nationalists have an impoverished view of the doctrine of God's common grace, an overemphasis on the uniqueness of Christianity's moral code, and sometimes a chauvinistic attitude

---

[45]See Paul D. Miller, "Non-'Western' Liberalism and the Resilience of the Liberal International Order," *The Washington Quarterly* 41, no. 2 (2018): 137-53, for the longer argument.

[46]Ronald Reagan, "Address to Members of the British Parliament," June 8, 1982, www.heritage.org /europe/report/20-years-later-reagans-westminster-speech.

that Christians are the best at everything just because we believe the Bible. Just as God's common grace brings the rain to fall on the righteous and the unrighteous alike, so too has he throughout history allowed and enabled non-Christian and non-Protestant people to discover and practice virtues— including the virtues of political liberty. We might benefit by recovering the practice of prior generations of Christians who spoke with respect about the "virtuous pagans," like Socrates and the Romans, whose moral example they hoped to emulate, despite the pagans' ignorance of Christ. Again, pagan Greeks and Renaissance Italian Catholics practiced forms of democracy and republicanism without Anglo-Protestant culture. In fact, in earlier centuries, Christian thinkers and republican theorists generally agreed that Christianity *undermined* republicanism because Christianity emphasized otherworldly piety while republicanism emphasized this-worldly loyalties and affairs.[47] The American revolutionary generation was essentially the first in history to suggest that Christianity and republicanism go together. As it happens, I think that they were right, but I also think that Christianity is not the only possible fount of civic virtue and thus not the only possible foundation for republicanism or democracy.

One final implication: Christian nationalists—those who believe that Anglo-Protestantism is essential for political liberty—emphasize culture over ideas, which contradicts what the founders believed about their ideas. Christian nationalists contend that the founders' Christian values were essential to the Constitution they set up. In effect, Christian nationalists do not really believe in the disestablishment of religion. They contend that formal disestablishment is only sustainable so long as the United States remains culturally homogenous and Christian. Formal disestablishment is a sort of pretense; the *government* may not set up a national church, but the culture did—as reflected in Protestant public schools and a Protestant public culture in the eighteenth and nineteenth centuries—and cultural pressure made government enforcement unnecessary. Without cultural consensus, they believe, disestablishment would lead to social fragmentation and the disappearance of support for the Constitution and the American experiment altogether. But if that is true, if the culture is doing all the work, how important are the ideals?

---

[47]Mark A. Noll, *America's God: From Jonathan Edwards to Abraham Lincoln* (New York: Oxford University Press, 2002).

Nationalist political theory minimizes the importance of ideas by treating them as byproducts of cultural practices. For them, political liberty is downstream from Christian culture. What, then, do Christian nationalists really believe in: Christian culture or political liberty? Defending Christendom or achieving justice? Christian power or Christian principle? In nationalism, Christian culture does all the work. It is the independent variable that effects all the meaningful social and political outcomes they value, while political liberty is epiphenomenal, a secondary thing wholly determined and caused by a prior, more important thing.

Nationalism is a form of cultural determinism, and it trivializes the ideals for which the founders fought, sacrificed, and died. The founders certainly believed that their political ideals were important because they wrote about the ideals at length and risked their lives and fortunes to secure them. Independence from Britain was hardly necessary to preserve a Christian culture, which was not threatened by the Christian monarch of Protestant England. They sought to gain independence for one Christian people (America) from another (Britain) because they valued political liberty enough to fight and die for it. Christian nationalism has the perverse implication of insulting the founders by minimizing the importance of the ideals for which they fought.

The reality of democracy around the world demonstrates that political liberty and Anglo-Protestant culture are separable. Since that is the case, we can be confident that democracy can survive in the United States even as American culture changes and even if Anglo-Protestantism is no longer our predominant culture. By the same token, we do not need to fear immigrants to our country from around the world; there is no necessary reason why non-Anglo or non-Christian immigrants cannot or would not be capable of assimilating to the norms of the US Constitution and Declaration of Independence. More often, immigrants come to the United States *because of* our long tradition of liberty and opportunity; they would hardly make its destruction their first priority upon gaining citizenship. In particular, Huntington's fear that Hispanic immigration will undermine American democracy is bizarre considering almost every nation in Latin America today is a democracy, suggesting there is no tension between Hispanic culture and political liberty. Indeed, some Hispanic immigrants are refugees fleeing the few remaining islands of authoritarianism in the Western Hemisphere (Cuba and Venezuela)—which again is testament to their strong desire for freedom. To the extent that there are antidemocratic tendencies in American politics that might undermine the American experiment in democracy, they come from movements—progressivism and nationalism—that originated in Anglo-Protestantism itself, not from immigrants or by people unfamiliar with Western civilization. It is true that the United States is gradually becoming less culturally Western, less British, and less Christian. That says nothing at all about the prospects of democracy in America.

5

NATIONALISM, CULTURAL PLURALISM, AND IDENTITY POLITICS

IN THE LAST CHAPTER I ARGUED against three key nationalist beliefs: that humanity is divisible into cultural units, that cultural units should be the foundation of political order, and that Anglo-Protestantism is essential for democracy. In this chapter I argue that nationalism does not produce national unity but its opposite.

Nationalists typically argue that nations need strong, unified cultures as a precondition for their political survival, coherence, or unity. They are probably correct that cultural unity makes governance easier and less costly: absolutist monarchs and nation builders in the early modern era wanted to enforce a sameness of culture, especially language, to make their nations easier to tax, their populations easier to conscript, and their laws easier to apply. But that does not mean nationalism is *just*. Nationalism amounts to a claim that we, as individual citizens, owe a presumptive duty to make ourselves more easily governable for the government's ease, convenience, and efficiency; that we ought to subordinate our cultural identities to the majority's social norms so that society does not have to put up with the hassle and cost of governing a diverse rabble; that governmental efficiency trumps individual freedom. That is hardly consistent with the ideals of the US Constitution.

More to the point, it is divisive. Nationalists claim they are deeply concerned about strengthening the nation through cultural unity, yet their efforts do not create unity. Because cultures have blurry boundaries, they are a poor candidate to serve as the basis for our political boundaries. When governments try to make those boundaries align anyway, they end up having to police culture, to say which culture is "ours" and which is not, what counts as an authentic expression of the nation and what does not—all of which is divisive, not unifying. It incentivizes a never-ending culture war to capture the state and use it to enforce one or another version of national identity. Nationalists embrace this as a legitimate function of government, despite the obvious problems and complications it involves. Policing culture violates the norms of cultural pluralism and divides, rather than unifies, a nation.

Republicanism (with a small *r*) argues for a different relationship between government and culture (one that I think has roots in Augustinian thought). The First Amendment to the US Constitution bars the government from prohibiting speech or the exercise of religion. We are allowed to say, print, believe, and worship whatever we want with very few exceptions. The Supreme Court has interpreted this to mean that the government cannot privilege or persecute anyone on the basis of their words or their beliefs. While the government treats different people differently, those differences cannot arise from the fact of different beliefs. The Supreme Court has enshrined this in a Constitution doctrine called viewpoint neutrality. Viewpoint neutrality is the idea that the government should not endorse a specific ideology, belief system, or way of viewing the world. While the language of "neutrality" is not the best way to think of the issue, I want to treat viewpoint neutrality as the legal corollary to a broader idea: if the government cannot police words, beliefs, or religious practices, it is just a half step further to say it should not (or should rarely) police culture, the "pattern of meanings," "inherited conceptions," and "webs of significance" that are embodied in a particular way of living, in literature, religious practice, forms of community, education, public symbols, social habit, mores, customs, and more. With some exceptions, the government should respect the existence of plural cultures; it should tolerate cultural pluralism and it should not seek to enforce cultural uniformity on the nation. Free speech and free religion imply a doctrine of "free culture," the exact opposite of nationalism.

This argument requires a fine distinction between culture, on the one hand, and universal values, morals, or objective standards of justice, on the other. Nationalists often argue that the government must intervene in culture to promote virtue. Not all cultures are made equal; some are superior to others, and the government has a rightful interest in promoting the better sort, they say. Political scientists, like Samuel Huntington, might cast this in the idiom of republicanism and say the government should promote civic virtue. Theologians like Nigel Biggar, R. R. Reno, and others cast this in a theological idiom and argue that governments have a biblical obligation to "punish those who do evil and to praise those who do good" (1 Peter 2:14) because "righteousness exalts a nation, but sin is a reproach to any people" (Proverbs 14:34). In either case, they say, the government should not be neutral between competing conceptions of morality. In fact, we are incapable of true neutrality: the government inevitably picks sides because all lawmaking is implicitly premised on underlying morality, in which case we should give up on the effort to stay neutral between competing cultures and simply try to make the government promote the right kind.

I affirm, theologically, that government should punish evil and praise good and also that it should promote civic virtue. However, I think in practice this looks very different from the nationalists' idea of cultural engineering. In practice, the best and truest ways to do this end up looking much like republicanism and the doctrine of "free culture." Why? There is a difference between *cultural* neutrality and *moral* neutrality; I affirm the first and reject the second. While government should punish evil and praise good, it should draw its understanding of good and evil from natural law, not from the particularistic embodiments of it in any specific cultural expression. Natural law is the objective and universal moral code inherent in the created order accessible to the rightly formed intellect and applicable across boundaries of time and culture. It should rightly guide legislation. (Protestants historically have been skeptical of natural law because they rightly argue our fallen and sinful minds cannot grasp the natural law perfectly. That, however, does not mean natural law does not exist, nor that we should not aspire to understand it.) Importantly, natural law is distinct from any one culture's understanding of it. If we must repress an immoral cultural practice, we do so because it is immoral, not because it is culturally alien.

The nationalist argument boils down to an assertion that, in order to promote virtue, we should promote Anglo-Protestantism or "Christian values," usually with an unstated understanding that Anglo-Protestant culture is the true or best embodiment of natural law, which is both culturally chauvinistic and historically ignorant. Treating one culture as the embodiment of virtue and giving it government sponsorship ends up rigidifying cultural practices and places emphasis on the wrong thing—on the culture rather than the virtues it supposedly embodies. It turns into a kind of ancestor worship in which we revere and try to emulate or "get back to" the practices of previous generations under the assumption that because their ways set down the template we inherited, they must be closer to true, unspoiled virtue. Worst of all, this approach treats other cultural embodiments as inherently less valuable and intrinsically less capable of virtue, which treats the people of other cultures as second-class citizens while simultaneously cutting us off from new cultural resources from which we might grow and learn. Instead, government should permit and even encourage cultural openness and change so as to better discover natural law and guard against the confusion of natural law with a particular culture.

THE ARGUMENT AGAINST GOVERNMENT NEUTRALITY AND CULTURAL PLURALISM

The idea of "free culture" has come in for criticism by the post-liberal right in recent years because they recognize these ideas pose a threat to their desire to police culture and enforce their nationalist blueprint. The dispute was dramatized in the summer of 2019 when Sohrab Ahmari, an American Catholic writer and advocate for nationalism, took umbrage at a group called Drag Queen Story Hour and its activities at a public library. He argued the government should be empowered to deny Drag Queen Story Hour access to the public library because of its potential to influence children. He criticized the idea that there could be "neutral zones that should, in theory, accommodate both traditional Christianity and the libertine ways and paganized ideology of the other side." He argued that, instead of taking refuge in the state's failed attempt at neutrality and pluralism, Christians had an obligation "to fight the culture war with the aim of defeating the enemy and enjoying the spoils in the form of a public square re-ordered to the common good and ultimately the Highest Good."[1] Neutrality has proven to be a sham, a procedural trick by which progressives box Christians into a corner and prevent us from advocating for our view of the good while doing so themselves. Neutrality, to Ahmari, is a Trojan horse in which progressive

---

[1]Sohrab Ahmari, "Against David French-ism," *First Things*, May 29, 2019, www.firstthings.com /web-exclusives/2019/05/against-david-french-ism.

secularism is hiding. Progressives have defined what counts as acceptable public discourse. If we play by their rules, we end up cutting ourselves off from our best and truest resources.

Adrian Vermeule, a professor of constitutional law at Harvard Law School and another Catholic advocate of nationalism, has given this argument a deeper grounding and outlined what a nationalist jurisprudence might look like. Vermeule criticizes the conservative doctrine of "originalism"—interpreting the Constitution by divining the original intent of the founders—and advocates instead for using the constitutional order to direct citizens toward the correct vision of the good life. "Such an approach—one might call it 'common-good constitutionalism'—should be based on the principles that government helps direct persons, associations, and society generally toward the common good, and that strong rule in the interest of attaining the common good is entirely legitimate." There is no room in common-good constitutionalism for viewpoint neutrality or cultural pluralism. Instead, the government should operate under "a substantive moral constitutionalism," what Vermeule frankly labels an "illiberal legalism," "to ensure that the ruler has the power needed to rule well." He explicitly calls for the repeal of "the libertarian assumptions central to free-speech law and free-speech ideology—that government is forbidden to judge the quality and moral worth of public speech," and more.[2] Ahmari, Vermeule, Hazony, and others believe the public square is not neutral and has not been for a century, and so we should drop the pretense, fight back, and try to impose our vision of the common good.

Patrick Deneen, a professor of political theory at Notre Dame, agrees. "In contrast to its crueler competitor ideologies, liberalism is more insidious: as an ideology, it pretends to neutrality, claiming no preference and denying any intention of shaping the souls under its rule."[3] No regime can be neutral because all law has an educative effect and a moral basis: if it is illegal to drive a certain speed, the state is habituating people to believe it is *wrong* to do so premised on a moral vision that human life is worth preserving and the state should regulate car speed to protect humans from car accidents. Liberalism's unique vision of the good is most visible in its idea of human nature and human relationships. Abstractly put, "Liberal theory sought to educate people

---

[2]Adrian Vermeule, "Beyond Originalism," *The Atlantic*, March 31, 2020.
[3]Patrick J. Deneen, *Why Liberalism Failed* (New Haven, CT: Yale University Press, 2019), 5.

to think differently about themselves and their relationships," emphasizing individualism and free choice over against group identity and unchosen obligations. Liberalism is "premised upon the fiction of radically autonomous humans in the State of Nature," rather than the reality of humans in families, communities, tribes, and nations. Liberalism cloaks this individualism in the language of neutrality. "Liberalism often claims neutrality about the choices people make in liberal society; it is the defender of 'Right,' not any particular conception of the 'Good.' Yet it is not neutral about the basis on which people make their decisions. . . . liberalism teaches a people to hedge commitments and adopt flexible relationships and bonds. . . . Liberalism encourages loose connections." Additionally, liberalism is not neutral toward any cultural practice it deems to be in tension with liberalism itself. "The powers of the liberal state are increasingly focused on dislocating those remaining cultural institutions that were responsible for governance of consumer and sexual appetite—purportedly in the name of freedom and equality." It exhibits "hostility towards local customs" and is "impatient with local variety." In short, "Liberalism has always been animated by a vision of how humans 'ought' to live, but it masked these normative commitments in the guise of neutrality."[4]

Rod Dreher, a senior editor at *The American Conservative* and author of *The Benedict Option*, has driven the point home in his argument that Christians have lost the culture war, law increasingly is biased against traditional Christian beliefs, and Christians have little option left but to acknowledge their cultural defeat and seek to weather the coming storm. He argues that "Christians who hold to the biblical teaching about sex and marriage have the same status in culture, and increasingly in law, as racists," especially after the Supreme Court's 2015 ruling recognizing same-sex marriage. So far from having a neutral public square that respects cultural pluralism, "Hostile secular nihilism has won the day in our nation's government, and the culture has turned powerfully against traditional Christians." In his view, accepting the terms of contemporary society requires "abandoning objective moral standards; refusing to accept a religiously or culturally binding narrative . . . [and] distancing oneself from community," none of which even pretend to respect plural cultures.[5] To this debate Jonathan

---

[4]Deneen, *Why Liberalism Failed*, 33-34, 68, 80.
[5]Rod Dreher, *The Benedict Option: A Strategy for Christians in a Post-Christian Nation* (New York: Penguin, 2017), 3, 9, 16. See also Michael Hanby, "The Civic Project of American Christianity," *First Things*, February 2015, for similar explication.

Leeman, editorial director of the 9Marks parachurch ministry, has added a theological point: liberal neutrality is impossible if we approach it with Enlightenment or secular premises. "The public square is not neutral and god-free. We all have gods hiding inside our definitions of those shared terms, and we're all trying to win the vote for the sake of our gods." Leeman still believes "we don't want to give up on the institutions of liberal democracy just yet" but is cautious and skeptical about its claims and about the prospects for it to be hijacked and turned into the "subtler tools of a twenty-first century legal totalitarianism."[6]

CULTURAL NEUTRALITY, NOT MORAL NEUTRALITY: NATURAL LAW AND HUMAN FLOURISHING

Whether or not cultural neutrality is possible or desirable is extraordinarily complex. I do not have space to explore the philosophical debate with the detail it deserves. I want to note at the beginning that the principle of *cultural* neutrality can be, and has been, abused and misinterpreted by the left to mandate *moral* neutrality and state-sponsored secularism. But the abuse of a principle does not invalidate its proper use, and state secularism akin to the French ideal of *laïcité* is not the version of neutrality I will defend. I want to defend the idea that some degree of cultural neutrality is possible on most public policy issues, and, where possible, the state should aspire toward as much "free culture" on as many issues as it can.

But first, I want to acknowledge several areas in which the state either cannot or should not be neutral and should accept its role shaping the cultural and moral life of the nation. First, as I argued above, the state does have an obligation to punish evil and praise good; it should be *culturally* neutral, not *morally* neutral, which means it should promote a transcultural standard of justice: it should govern in accordance with natural law. Some readers may be nervous by the language of natural law and wonder how it can be consistent with democracy at all, and others might wonder how we can discern and adopt such a standard without establishing either an official culture or a religion. I respond that natural law is how we *save* democracy from relativism, on the one hand, and theocracy, on the other; natural law is how we ground politics in morality without grounding it in a specific sect.

---

[6]Jonathan Leeman, "Conservatives Clash on the Goal of Government," *Providence Magazine*, September 6, 2019.

There is, I think, a central organizing concept that can and should provide the standard of natural law: human flourishing. As philosopher Martha Nussbaum has argued in her work, human flourishing can be the universal standard by which to judge the superiority of some ways of living over others.[7] Choices that promote human flourishing are demonstrably superior to those that do not, and it does not require an explicit appeal to revelation to make that claim. Human life is not infinitely malleable. Not even the most hardened multiculturalist will claim, for example, that illiteracy is better than literacy, war better than peace, or poverty than prosperity. There are certain aspects of humanity that we recognize as intrinsically important to human nature across cultures—laughter, sex, abstract thought, family, physical health and wholeness, etc.—without which we would rightly say a life is less than it potentially could be (not less worthy or dignified, but less fulfilled or realized). Human flourishing is the fulfillment of humanity in all its dimensions, perhaps akin to the Hebrew idea of *shalom*. Some choices—basic education and physical health— are universally good because they help realize human potential, no matter what culture one lives in. With the normative framework provided by the *telos* of human flourishing, natural law can serve as the common language with which to talk about human life in a way that is comprehensible and legitimate across boundaries of religion, culture, and time. The government should not be neutral toward the protection or denigration of human life, human dignity, and human flourishing: all legislation and policy should seek to promote, not undermine, these foundational values.[8]

Grounding government in natural law, understood as human flourishing, is consistent with democracy, religious freedom, and free culture. My argument here is similar to J. S. Mill's famous argument in favor of free speech. Mill argued that free speech is vital because we can never be certain if we have the complete and untainted truth. Free speech is a sort of insurance policy against intellectual and cultural blindness. Free speech allows ideas to circulate that, in one age, might be despised and universally thought wrong but, as time passes and circumstances change, come to offer some needed wisdom. Similarly, a policy of "free culture" is a way of acknowledging, in principle, the

---

[7]Martha C. Nussbaum, "Human Functioning and Social Justice: In Defense of Aristotelian Essentialism," *Political Theory* 20, no. 2 (1992): 202-46.
[8]Paul D. Miller, "The Evidence for Virtue: Social Science, Natural Law, and Human Flourishing," *Public Discourse*, February 28, 2014.

finiteness and imperfection of our culture and the possibility that other cultures—even those most foreign and uncomfortable to us—might someday offer wisdom to our country in ways we ourselves cannot see and cannot anticipate (so long as they do not undermine human flourishing).

The second area in which the state should not be neutral is toward its own theory of justice. Biggar is right that free societies cannot be neutral toward values like liberty and equality (see chap. 3); they must privilege and protect democracy and human rights and hold them up as superior to the alternatives, like fascism, dictatorship, inherited aristocracy, monarchy, and so on. This is another way of making my earlier point that governments should promote justice. Liberal society has a legitimate interest in perpetuating itself, and thus has a valid responsibility to teach about the virtues of democracy and individual rights. This idea is sometimes abused under a mistaken notion of what is required to sustain democracy: Biggar and others argue that privileging democracy requires privileging Anglo-Protestant culture or establishing a religion, which is false. But setting that aside, there should be no obstacle to the state endorsing and privileging the ideals of the American experiment. The government can and should promote small-*r* republican and democratic norms without promoting Anglo-Protestant culture.

There is a gray area around whether or not the state can or should promote civic virtue. There are undoubtedly some habits and mores that make democracy work better, habits like honesty, literacy, lawfulness, public spiritedness, public participation, patriotism, the concept of a loyal opposition, and more. These habits are good and even necessary, but it is generally dangerous to make the government responsible for their development. Some of these habits might shade into a culturally specific form. And the national government is hardly the best suited to train citizens in virtue. I am most comfortable with locally defined and locally driven efforts to encourage civic virtue, which would ensure no single cultural embodiment of virtue is established nationwide.

Third, open societies should not be neutral toward their own history. When I say that government should not police culture, I have in mind the harder forms of cultural policing, like privileging one religion, ethnicity, or culture like Anglo-Protestantism, as well as more trivial forms of cultural policing, like subsidizing a national film industry, which is wasteful and discourages innovation. But liberal societies should nonetheless promote awareness of the best parts of their own histories and creeds, which involves more generic forms of state-sponsored cultural intervention, like creating national symbols, commemorating a national holiday, honoring an historical figure, recognizing an historical site, and requiring the teaching of history and civics. These kinds of cultural interventions are (usually) benign and helpful insofar as they educate the public about our history and help us cultivate emotional bonds to our country. But to stay benign, it is vitally important, in teaching our history, to leave it open to reinterpretation, reappropriation, and remixing with new cultural approaches. Even history itself can jump across cultural lines and take on a new light when appropriated and retold through new eyes and new cultures (e.g., the musical *Hamilton*). I will have much more to say about the importance of national history in chapter ten, but in short: I affirm the importance of knowing and telling our history but reject a government-sponsored official interpretation of it. There is a fine line between appreciating our history as the seed from which we sprang and entombing it like a dead relic we venerate.

Fourth, the state cannot be neutral between mutually exclusive, collectively exhaustive, non-divisible beliefs that have unavoidable implications in public policy. For example, neutrality between opposing conceptions of human personhood and human sexuality is impossible. The state cannot be neutral between the belief that human sexuality is fixed, objective, and set by nature, on the one hand, and the belief that sexuality is malleable and socially constructed, the expression of which is a fundamental human right which should not be hindered, on the other. The state cannot avoid the issue unless it tried to repeal all laws relating to family, marriage, childrearing, or sex, which it cannot do—which means the government has to have a position on what those things mean and on the definition of the roles people play in those relationships. There is no middle ground between the two views, no way to compromise or meet halfway. And there is no way to depoliticize the issue or avoid the government having to pick a side. There are few areas of public policy that require the state to adopt a substantive philosophical commitment, but they are vitally important, including the scope of religious freedom and civil rights, the meaning of the First Amendment, antidiscrimination policy, and (this is crucial) the purpose of the state itself. It cannot be neutral about the purpose for which it exists or the scope of its own jurisdiction. On these few issues, Leeman is right that the public square is a "battleground of the gods," in which we can do no other than to advocate for our own fundamental beliefs—with clarity, grace, and wit, not with despair, vindictiveness, or vengeance.

Finally, I am comfortable asserting that to the extent the state should discriminate, it should discriminate in favor of the poor, the historically oppressed, and the disenfranchised, not in favor of a preferred cultural group. There is a much longer conversation about how best to help the poor, oppressed, and marginalized; how to do so effectively while minimizing unintended consequences; and without setting up bad incentives, all of which should blunt left-wing enthusiasm for its various social programs. But leaving aside those practical concerns, the principle of using state power non-neutrally in favor of the poor is sound.

SOME DEGREE OF NEUTRALITY
IS POSSIBLE AND DESIRABLE

But, aside from these (very important) issues, there are very few public policy issues that require the state to take a side like this. Most public policy issues are not defined by two sides whose positions are mutually exclusive and nondivisible. Tax policy, for example, might feature one side that believes the government should tax 50 percent of your wealth and the other side that believes it should tax 10 percent of your wealth. They might even frame these beliefs as moral absolutes—but the government can safely ignore such claims and tax everyone at 30 percent. In that sense, the government can act neutrally toward rival conceptions of tax policy. And, more to the point, it can and should *use* tax policy neutrally and should not tax one group of Americans defined by a belief system more favorably than other groups: it grants tax-exempt status to all religious organizations, for example, not just Christian ones. Similarly, it must recognize religious freedom for Muslims and Hindus, not just Christians; the increase in one group's freedom does not diminish the others', and there is no conflict between them. The state cannot use zoning policy to make room for churches but turn around and use zoning policy to prevent the construction of mosques or temples.

Other issues might feature mutually exclusive beliefs, but they do not have unavoidable political implications, as is the case with most rival religious claims. Islam and Christianity teach diametrically opposing things about the person of Jesus: Muslims say he was a wise prophet, Christians say he is the living Son of God. This is an unavoidable conflict of a mutually exclusive and non-divisible truth claim. But it does not have to be political (in the normal, secular sense of the word): the state can and should be neutral in this dispute. There is no public need compelling the state to take a position on it because there is no area of law that punishes one belief and rewards the other. It need not (and should not) make theological pronouncements about Christology. (Recognizing that Jesus is king is a profoundly *political* belief, but not in the typical sense of that word.)

The problem with the postliberal right's critique of neutrality is that it has let the perfect be the enemy of the good. They argue that since perfect neutrality is not possible on every issue, no degree of neutrality is worth preserving on any issue. They take the exceptional cases which require the state to take a side—like family law—as normative for all public policy, a permission slip for the government to act with bias across the full scope of the law. The postliberals and nationalists—see especially Vermeule's argument above—seem to relish the opportunity to jettison neutrality and start using state power to do all sorts of cultural engineering in favor of their nationalist blueprint. They treat a narrow philosophical conclusion—perfect neutrality is impossible in all areas of policy—as an excuse to dramatically expand the jurisdiction of the state and to throw out the classical liberal heritage of neutrality entirely. Neutrality is impossible, they say, so we should go ahead and restrict immigration to certain cultural groups, beef up moral legislation to reflect our culturally particularistic understanding of moral values, declare an official cultural template of Anglo-Protestantism, rewrite public-school textbooks to emphasize our version of history, or recapture the public educational system and use it as an arm of nationalist cultural engineering.

The case against neutrality is that it is impossible because of human sin and the limits of our finite minds. Neutrality is impossible, critics say, because objectivity is impossible. We are inevitably biased about everything in life. We are not so much reasoning creatures as feeling creatures. Instead of abstract rationality, we engage in motivated reasoning; that is, we engage in ex post facto rationalization, working backward to find reasons that support what we already believe or what we know to be in our self-interest, rather than working forward, so to speak, from first principles to wherever pure logic leads. Work this out to its implications in the public square and you get a version of Leeman's argument: neutrality is impossible because public life is always and everywhere a battleground of the gods (not just on a few select issues). As Augustine might say, we are defined by our loves, and that means, for most of us, our idols. We live our lives pursuing this or that idol, and politics is largely all about which idol wins, or which idol gets recognition and funding from the state. Enlightenment philosophers were naive and arrogant in their presumption to have a "view from nowhere," and their pretensions to objectivity led to the philosophical cul-de-sac of postmodernity that we live in today.

This argument overstates the implications of human fallibility. I agree with the premise (we are imperfect, sinful, and often very stupid), but I don't think the *political* implications of this premise are as bad as critics seem to think. If we follow their argument all the way to its logical conclusion, they are actually arguing that the rule of law itself is impossible. Law is nothing if not an abstract rule that is supposed to be applied fairly, equally, and *neutrally* to all under its jurisdiction. Yet we live under a regime of workable, if imperfect, legal fairness, which suggests some degree of legal neutrality is possible. No matter how flawed our legal system (especially when it comes to impartial justice across racial and ethnic lines), I hope the critics would grant that we have one of the better legal environments in history. The success of the rule of law in much of the developed world (not just the Western world but also nations like Japan and South Korea) shows that it is *possible* to have a system of law that actually functions with some rough degree of acceptable fairness and neutrality.

For example, to return to Drag Queen Story Hour, if Ahmari and Vermeule are right, it would be *impossible* for a library administrator to effectively, impartially adjudicate the requirement to sustain "viewpoint neutrality" in deciding how to allocate library resources. But that seems absurd on its face. How hard is it to say both drag queens and fundamentalist Christians can both use the library and host events there? This isn't especially hard, no matter how deep original sin goes, no matter the noetic effects of the fall. And if it is possible, it is also desirable: drag queens are people too, and no matter our views on their sexuality, they are tax-paying citizens and deserve equal treatment under law and thus equal access to public resources. Denying them access to public facilities on the basis of their *beliefs* or identities would be simply unfair and unjust, a clear misapplication of government's duty to promote good and punish evil. (Libraries can of course regulate *conduct* once people are inside the building, which suggests a library administrator cannot preemptively ban drag queens from using library event space but can enforce a code of public decency once inside—again, so long as the code applies to everyone and is not specifically targeted at drag queens.)

Some degree of cultural neutrality is usually possible and desirable on most public policy issues, which means neutrality should be an aspiration where possible. The First Amendment affords important protections to everyone, including Christians. As David French has powerfully documented, Christians have made important gains protecting religious freedom through decades of court battles since the 1980s, even as we have lost cultural power and influence through dwindling numbers.[9] Though it may surprise many Christians to hear it, we are winning: not at imposing our view of the good on society, but at protecting the principle of liberty of conscience for everyone. And this is the right battle to wage. It is important to think beyond the next election. What will happen if the other side wins power and uses the government to impose their vision of the good on the rest of us (even more so than they already do) using the precedent we would set if we jettisoned liberal neutrality? I would not want to live in a country in which drag queens were barred by law from going to the library or hosting an event because that will obviously incentivize a drag queen to run for mayor and turn the ban around against fundamentalist Christians. The idea of *precedent* isn't terribly hard to grasp.

That is why it is important to *aspire* to neutrality in every policy area in which neutrality is feasible. We should not seek out excuses and opportunities to throw out neutrality and wield the law for a project of cultural engineering. The edifice of law holding together our pluralistic society was a remarkable achievement and is more fragile than we like to admit; we discard it at our peril. Neutrality may not be possible in a few areas like family law, but we should give up neutrality only by necessity, when forced to it, not seek out opportunities to preemptively throw it out.

Drawing the argument out to the rule of law itself helps us see why neutrality is not just possible but desirable, even mandatory. The United States aspires to "equal justice under law," as emblazoned on the front of the Supreme Court. Lady Justice is always portrayed in classical art blindfolded to symbolize that *justice is blind*: that is, it is blind to the person, ignorant of the particulars of his or her identity, background, or circumstances. If one renders

---

[9] David French, "Liberty Gained and Power Lost," *The Dispatch*, January 10, 2020.

judgment justly, one renders it neutrally among the contesting parties. Justice *requires* neutrality, at some level. Moses commanded judges not to be "partial in judgment" (Deuteronomy 1:17; or in the KJV, "ye shall not respect persons"), that is, to judge without regard for the particular characteristics of the people involved in the case. King David is praised in 2 Samuel 8:15 because he "administered justice and equity to all his people." God himself is said to judge with equity (Psalm 96:10). Proverbs exhorts us to seek "righteousness, justice, and equity" (1:3). Equity is fair dealing; it is synonymous with impartiality. The just judge—and as citizens in a democracy, we are all called to render judgment justly—does not discriminate against other citizens on the basis of who they are or what they believe; we render judgment based on the law and on the deeds at hand. Law itself aspires to be neutral; it is part of the very essence of what it is.

Neutrality sounds very complicated in theory but is rarely that hard in practice (again, with limited exceptions around family law and civil rights). The left sometimes abuses and distorts the law to discriminate against Christians by arguing that neutrality actually means a naked public square stripped of religion. The Supreme Court is not on their side. That is why conservative lawyers have been so successful suing universities and other places who violate neutrality by trying to deny Christians access to their resources. The solution isn't to give up on neutrality; it is to *strengthen* neutrality.

IS NATIONALISM POSSIBLE AND DESIRABLE?

I want to advance a counterargument. Nationalists assert that neutrality is impossible and undesirable, which is false, but they also assert—without evidence—that nationalism and its attendant effort to use the government to promote a specific vision of cultural life and moral good is both possible and desirable. In their view, state-sponsored cultural engineering to foster and protect the nation's cultural identity and moral values is realistic, desirable, and achievable. They want to use government to restore an idealized version of their national culture and, once they've arrived at some unspecified cultural apogee, to freeze the moment and prevent any further change. Victor Orban, the prime minister of Hungary who has been at the forefront of the nationalist surge around the world, said in a landmark 2015 speech, "I am convinced that Hungary has the right—and every nation has the right—to say that it does not want its country to change," specifically asserting that "a community has the right to decide if it wants to change its ethnic and cultural composition."[10]

This is a profoundly ridiculous claim. Whether or not nations have a *right* to stop change, they certainly lack the *competence* to do so. Cultural change is inevitable, ubiquitous, uncontrollable, and often quite good. Governments cannot stop cultural change; they lack the competence to orchestrate or control culture and make bad judges of what makes good culture. As Biggar rightly argued, "As historical, nations are mutable. Therefore, the patriot should be willing to contemplate changes in his or her nation—whether in its constitution or even its very definition—if that is what justice and prudence together require."[11] Biggar is too cautious: not only should we embrace change when justice and prudence require, but we should embrace change simply because we can neither stop it nor control it with any precision—and the blunt instrument of government is especially ill-equipped for the task. Nationalism is impractical and kind of silly in its pretensions. Put another way, it is unlikely that the US government is competent to sustain, create, or orchestrate a common national cultural template for a nation of 320 million people when it can barely deliver the mail.

I earlier suggested that subsidizing a national film industry would be a bad idea because it is wasteful and discourages innovation. Rich Lowry tries to defend nationalism in a related field of artistic endeavor. Recall that Lowry argued the government should "preserve the cultural nation" (see chap. 3). Yet in the process of explaining why his argument is racially tolerant and is distinct from White nationalism, Lowry offers an example of non-White cultural influences that only serves to undermine his argument about the importance of preserving culture. He recounts the origin of the blues and jazz in the musical heritage of African Americans and celebrates how "the cultural context that gave us the blues was the rich, racially mixed musical tapestry of the American South."[12] It is unclear how this serves Lowry's argument. The blues and jazz, as Lowry rightly recognizes, were not invented by Englishmen or by British Americans. For all their virtues, Anglo-Protestants, I feel confident in saying,

---

[10]Quoted in Brian Pascus, "Who Is Victor Orban?," CBSNews.com, May 13, 2019.

[11]Nigel Biggar, *Between Kin and Cosmopolis: An Ethic of the Nation* (Eugene, OR: Wipf and Stock, 2014), 19.

[12]Rich Lowry, *The Case for Nationalism: How It Made Us Rich, Powerful, and Free* (New York: Broadside, 2019), loc. 3848, Kindle.

would not have invented jazz in a thousand years. But that means a government dedicated to preserving the American cultural nation as it existed in 1900—if there had been a Bureau of American Music that subsidized European music and American folk songs—would never have invented jazz and probably would have sought to suppress it. White critics in the early twentieth century wrote articles titled, "Why Jazz Sends Us Back to the Jungle," explained "that jazz was dangerous, unhealthy, or, even worse, a form of bayou voodoo," and worried about the "harmful effects jazz has on the learning capabilities of White students," according to one scholar.[13]

If the government at the time had wanted to "preserve the cultural nation," it would have deemed jazz to be "un-American" and sought to suppress it in favor of traditional European music. The great musical innovations of early twentieth-century America were an example of cultural *change*, mingling, and appropriation at its best, not of preserving a fixed cultural nation. Jazz emerged precisely because of the blurriness and fluidity of cultural boundaries—fluidity which nationalism seeks to eliminate. The sort of nationalist agenda Lowry calls for—"protecting and fostering the cultural nation"—would be inimical to the kind of cultural fluidity, intermingling, and change that was the essential precondition for jazz. If the government assumed jurisdiction over the nation's cultural identity, including its music, the world would not have known the creativity and genius of jazz music. Lowry celebrates jazz, claiming it for his argument about American nationhood, without recognizing the inconsistency between his celebration of a product of cultural intermingling and innovation, on the one hand, and his call for cultural preservation and traditionalism, on the other. Again, consider the musical *Hamilton*, quintessentially a product of cultural intermingling and change, and also a quintessentially patriotic celebration of all that makes America great.

To the extent Lowry is simply celebrating America's tradition of cultural appropriation, adaptation, and reinvention, he is entirely correct—but that makes his call to "preserve the cultural nation" nonsensical. At no point has America's culture been defined by its concern to "preserve" anything, but rather to constantly reinvent everything. Nationalism, as Orban explicitly said, is an effort to freeze-frame culture at one particular moment, to stop cultural

---

[13]Maureen Anderson, "White Reception of Jazz in America," *African American Review* 38, no. 1 (2004): 135, 136, 144.

change, to designate a specific snapshot in time as the ideal expression of a given people, and to prevent departures from it. There is little evidence such an effort is possible—nor is it clear our lives would be richer and more fulfilling if it were. Nationalism is a form of cultural traditionalism and cultural essentialism, in response to which the idea of free culture refuses to take sides or to declare one form of culture to be the nation's official template: it is an expression in law of our openness to cultural change, innovation, and invention—the very essence of the American experience. Imagine a world in which American culture is forever defined by the musical traditions of European classicism, a world in which jazz does not exist. Who wants to live in that world? Among its many other faults, nationalism is boring.

NATIONALISM DOES NOT FOSTER NATIONAL UNITY: IDENTITY POLITICS AND NATIONALISM

I want to offer a second counterargument.[14] Nationalists argue that governments need to promote and privilege one culture over others because they believe nations require a strong, unified, cohesive, predominant culture to survive. They are right that cultural affinity makes governance easier and facilitates unforced bonds of trust in civil society at the local level. But nationalism, trying to force that cultural affinity on to an entire nation, does not foster national unity; it does the opposite. Because nationalism is arbitrary and relies on coercion and exclusion to fabricate a national identity, it fosters division, not cohesion; fragmentation, not unity. Nationalism undermines its own goals. It is a counterproductive political program that inevitably provokes a backlash whenever it is tried. Throughout American history the official or elite effort to dictate to us who we are has always produced dissidents, activists, nonconformists, and others dedicated to resisting the official narrative. That tradition of dissent too is part of American identity. The harder nationalists try to tell us that we have to assimilate to Anglo-Protestant culture, the more non-Anglos, non-Christians, and secular multiculturalists will flock to identity politics and tell us that we should define ourselves by some trait *other* than Anglo-Protestant nationality. Nationalism does not produce unity; it throws fuel on the fire of our never-ending culture war.

---

[14]Drawn from Paul D. Miller, "The Jedi Are Selfless: Nationalism, Identity, the Humanities, and Liberalism," *Mere Orthodoxy,* May 8, 2019.

To understand why this is the case, it is helpful to recognize that nationalism is another form of identity politics. As Francis Fukuyama argued in his masterful book *Identity: The Search for Recognition and the Politics of Resentment*, human beings seek to find and express an identity, and in our contemporary era we look for recognition and validation of our identities in the public square. As Fukuyama says, "The modern concept of identity places a supreme value on authenticity, on the validation of that inner being that is not being allowed to express itself."[15] Our drive for recognition is not limited to relationships among the family or tribe. We take it into the public square. Fukuyama argues, "Because human beings naturally crave recognition, the modern sense of identity evolves quickly into identity politics, in which individuals demand public recognition of their worth."[16] Mark Lilla, a left-leaning political scientist at Columbia University, suggested in his 2017 critique of identity politics that identity groups "wanted to feel at one with political movements that mirrored how they understood and defined themselves as individuals. And they wanted their self-definition to be recognized."[17] When minority groups do this, we call it identity politics. When majority groups do the same thing, we call it nationalism. (When Muslims do it, we call it Islamism, etc.) Nationalism is the identity politics of the majority tribe; identity politics is the nationalism of small groups. In each case, groups of people defined by some shared identity trait look to the public square for status, spoils, recognition, and power.

Viewing American nationalism as the identity politics of White Christians is another way of saying that "White Christian" or "Anglo-Protestant" or "White evangelical" has come to denote a distinct ethnoreligious sect, a tribe marked more by cultural particularity than by theological universality. Ethnoreligious groups are common throughout the world, including the Sikhs of India, the Druze of Lebanon and Syria, the Copts of Egypt, and the Uighurs of China. Ethnoreligious groups equate their ethnic and religious identities such that to affirm one is to affirm the other, and to betray one is to apostatize from the other. Crucially, an ethnoreligious identity is inherited, not chosen;

---

[15]Francis Fukuyama, *Identity: The Demand for Dignity and the Politics of Resentment* (New York: Farrar, Straus and Giroux, 2018), chap. 3.

[16]Fukuyama, *Identity*, chap. 1.

[17]Mark Lilla, *The Once and Future Liberal: After Identity Politics* (New York: Oxford University Press, 2018), 76.

religion is treated like an ethnicity, passed from parents to children like blood (an idea which should be appalling to Christians). Ethnoreligious groups are typically minority communities because it becomes more difficult to enforce in-group conformity as the group grows larger, especially if it becomes a majority and no longer faces the common threat of being overwhelmed by some larger faction.

Scholars have not yet widely applied the concept of ethnoreligious identity to White American evangelicals, but they likely will in coming years, perhaps as a subset of "Whiteness" studies. That White American evangelicals are increasingly acting like an ethnoreligious sect means that they feel they are, or will soon be, a minority; that in-group cohesion is more important than out-group persuasion; that they face a common threat from fellow citizens who are not in their group; and that their agenda should prioritize group survival and group power over the common good. Recognizing the particularity of Anglo-Protestantism is important because it helps us recognize that it is not coterminous with Christianity, not the sole, final, or perfect expression of the true faith for all time. It can help us be attentive to the ways in which its cultural and historical particularity may distort its vision and its interpretation of the faith. And it can help us recognize that there are other legitimate cultural embodiments of Christianity. I'll return to this idea in chapter eight.

How governments relate to ethnoreligious groups is an important question. Oppressive governments typically try to crush or eradicate ethnoreligious groups, as China has the Uighurs, because they are an extraordinarily resilient and independent source of power outside the state's control who often command stronger loyalty from citizens than the state itself. Democracies take different approaches. Some try to ignore group identities and treat everyone as an individual under law. Others take the "consociational" approach, governing with and through the informal governance structures provided by ethnic and religious communities, often by explicitly adopting racial, ethnic, or religious quotas, as has sometimes been the case in Lebanon and Belgium. Some ethnoreligious communities around the world may have no other choice or option, and I do not mean to criticize, for example, the Sikhs for their political choices. But insofar as White evangelicals are acting like an ethnoreligious sect, to that extent they are giving up on what Michael Hanby has called the civic project of American Christianity[18]—the reconciliation of the Christian faith with principles of American democracy—and instead seeking to ensure their group survival through a consociational compromise. Such a stance goes under the label of nationalism, but in an important respect it is *antinational,* in the sense that it represents American Christians giving up on the American nation if they do not get to define its meaning or enjoy a preeminent place in it. Put another way, the nationalist project of insisting that America is a Christian nation feeds off a despairing belief that America would not survive if defined any other way. Christian nationalism insists on unifying the nation on its terms or not at all.

Nationalism and identity politics feed off one another, and both undermine true national unity. When nationalists advocate for their preferred "national" identity, those who fall outside that identity are forced to close ranks and advocate for the interests of their identity group as a defensive measure. When Anglo-Protestants used their cultural and political dominance to entrench their power amid rising pluralism, ethnic and religious minorities understandably responded by advocating for their interests, centered around their identities. But as identities splinter and proliferate and various minority groups demand recognition, the majority feels threatened that their polity is disintegrating. That makes the majority even more keen to reaffirm their sense of identity as an antidote to the perceived fragmentation around them. In that way, the success of identity politics for minorities leads to Anglo-Protestants doubling down on their group identity and insisting all the more that their group should define the nation. As Fukuyama says, "This crisis of identity leads . . . to the search for a common identity that will rebind the individual to a social group and reestablish a clear moral horizon. This psychological fact lays the groundwork for nationalism." Nationalism is "based on an intense nostalgia for an imagined past of strong community in which the division and confusions of a pluralist modern society did not exist."[19]

In this way, the more each group advances their identity claims, the more the other feels threatened and responds in kind. Rival identity claims take the form of an arms race or a spiraling conflict. We call this clash of identities the culture war. The culture war in the United States stems from Americans' felt

---

[18]Michael Hanby, "Civic Project of American Christianity," *First Things,* February 2015.
[19]Fukuyama, *Identity,* chaps. 6-7.

need to seek validation and affirmation of their identities from the public square. Culture war is only possible when Americans look to their government to establish a cultural template for the nation but disagree about what that template should look like. Another way of putting it: culture war is the natural consequence of nationalism because people will inevitably fight over the definition of the "nation," especially over who counts as a member of the nation. There is a reason why every culture war witch-hunt in the past seven decades has been dubbed a new form of "McCarthyism." Joseph McCarthy was an expert culture warrior.

The story of how democracy devolved into a never-ending fight between warring tribes is a complex one. Part of what happened is that democracies professed equality but in practice governed in the interest of the majority tribe. Democracy in America claimed to represent all people equally but empowered only White men for much of American history. Minority groups justifiably demanded that America live up to its creed and give them equal treatment. But in the process of rectifying historical wrongs, we introduced new pathologies into our body politic in the form of identity politics. Instead of adhering to the principle of equal representation for every individual, we have a hodgepodge legal regime that combines some features of individual representation and some features of consociational democracy with implicit, subjective racial and ethnic quotas.

Nationalist thinkers routinely—and rightly—inveigh against the dangers of identity politics. But nationalism does not solve the problem: it exacerbates it. Because nationalism is simply another form of identity politics, it perpetuates the cycle of political warfare between nationalist majorities and identity-group minorities, each side approaching politics as nothing more than an extended exercise in special pleading, trying to seize state power and milk it for perks for their tribe until the next election, driven by the inexorable logic that if they do not, the other side will. Identity politics and nationalism have a corrosive, centrifugal force on the culture of democracy. As Fukuyama argued, "The rise of identity politics in modern liberal democracies is one of the chief threats that they face, and unless we can work our way back to more universal understandings of human dignity, we will doom ourselves to continuing conflict."[20] Identity politics and nationalism undermine democracy by

---

[20]Fukuyama, *Identity*, preface.

fragmenting the electorate, eroding a sense of shared citizenship, and pitting groups against one another in a competition for prestige rather than a pursuit of equal justice for all.

CONCLUSION

In light of these realities, it would be easier and better for us to recognize a simple truth: "nation-states" in the thick sense—separate and discrete sovereign cultural units with hard boundaries between them—do not exist apart from our construction of them, and every effort to make them real is dangerous and antidemocratic. Imagined communities are just that: imagined. They are fabrications invented by political entrepreneurs and demagogues looking for an easy way to harness and manipulate mass sentiment. The "nation" in the sense of a shared culture united under one sovereignty was, in fact, invented by eighteenth- and nineteenth-century European Romantics and revolutionaries who wanted to weave a grand narrative to root their political agitation in a mythical past and secure a large and passionate base of support, building on earlier efforts by absolutist monarchs in the sixteenth and seventeenth centuries eager to create homogenous kingdoms, by force if necessary, to facilitate the ease of their rule. Nationalism took the place of traditional religion as the latter faded as a major political force in Europe. Nationalists successfully claimed the moral high ground by claiming to be a movement for liberation and anti-imperialism. But, as we have seen, nationalism is simply another form of imperialism—internal imperialism—and often substitutes oppression from abroad with oppression closer to home.

Nationalism is an ideology of emotion more than ideas, originally created to prop up and justify authoritarian or revolutionary government but founded on vacuous ideas. The danger of nationalism is not that it encourages us to cultivate loyalty to and affection for our country—which is inescapable—but that it endows the state with almost limitless jurisdiction to reshape culture, imagines the nation as a quasi-religious body, and exacerbates sectarian and ethnic cleavages at home. Christians who uncritically buy into nationalism are giving support to an incoherent secular idea with a troubled historical record and making themselves credulous supporters of a dangerous and thoughtless ideology.

Is there anything good about nations? Anthony Smith suggests we might credit nationalist sentiment for "its rescue of 'lost' histories and literatures; its inspiration for cultural renascences . . . its legitimation of community and social solidarity; its inspiration to resist tyranny; its ideal of popular sovereignty and collective mobilization," and more.[21] These are indeed praiseworthy things, and many social movements aiming at such goals have called themselves "nationalist" and said they were inspired by national feeling. But none of these good things require the myths of nationalism; all of them are possible under patriotism. We don't need to believe that we must define ourselves politically by some shared trait in order to value our cultural traditions, and we certainly do not need to vest government with the responsibility for caretaking our culture. We can have affection for our traditions (patriotism) while rejecting the political agenda (nationalism).

Quite a lot of recent nationalist ferment has been motivated by an angst about the fate of Western civilization. Nationalists, concerned that the left-wing critique of the West has gone too far, want to revive and honor the United States' European heritage because of the positive legacies of the Renaissance, the Enlightenment, and liberal democracy (and some would even add the legacy of Christendom). I agree with quite a lot of this sentiment, though as a Christian my ultimate loyalty is not to the West but to the church, and I find nostalgia for Christendom—with its repressive established churches—baffling. But the place to revive the West, if indeed that is a worthy project, is in the home, the pews, the classroom, the school board, and the city council: localism is far more accountable and carries fewer dangers than nationalism. President Trump's suggestion in 2020 that the United States should adopt more "patriotic" education was half right: children should learn about our past and our heritage and should be encouraged to cultivate gratitude for the best in service of a true and deep patriotism. But the White House is the last place I would look to provide that curriculum. Trump's effort, embodied in "The 1776 Report," nicely proves my point. Education in the United States is and has always been a local affair. Similarly, cultural renewal is a bottom-up project accomplished in the realm of civil society and local reform; efforts to make it top-down by national fiat are likely to fail and cause a backlash. (The one place where national advocacy is necessary is in

---

[21] Anthony Smith, *National Identity* (Reno: University of Nevada Press, 1991), 18.

protecting our fundamental freedoms and constitutional rights, especially religious freedom.) I would be much more impressed with the nationalist project if they spent half as much time serving on the local school board to reform high-school history curricula or lobbying the state legislature to change divorce law as they do trying to elect presidents to troll the libs by tweeting politically incorrect insults. Reviving the West is too important to entrust to Washington, DC.

NATIONALISM AND THE BIBLE

I'VE ARGUED THAT NATIONALISM CONFLICTS with core American ideals of liberty and equality for all, and that, when given a Christian gloss, it amounts to the pursuit of Christian power at the expense of Christian ideals. I've answered a variety of political, theoretical, and historical counter-arguments. But there is another set of arguments I haven't fully considered yet: theological and biblical arguments.

Some have argued that nationality is a biblical idea. They argue that the table of nations in Genesis 10 shows that God has separated humanity into distinct groups, under each of Noah's three sons "by their clans, their languages, their lands, and their nations" (Genesis 10:20, 31). These groups, according to this reading, would be culturally and linguistically distinct and each enjoy their own sovereignty, supporting the main idea of modern nationalism. Later in the Old Testament, when Moses sings praises to God, he sings that, "When the Most High gave to the nations their inheritance, when he divided mankind, he fixed the borders of the peoples according to the number of the sons of God" (Deuteronomy 32:8). Nationalists read an echo of this idea in Paul's sermon in Acts 17:26 in which he says that God made "every nation of mankind to live on all the face of the earth, having determined allotted periods and the boundaries of their dwelling place," again highlighting the divine allotment and prescribed boundaries that keep peoples distinct and sovereign. Above all, the nationalist appropriation of the Bible rests heavily on how they read the story of ancient Israel as a model for nations today. Nationalists view ancient Israel as a model of nationality, a template of how God intended a people to achieve political unity founded on a common culture. That is why nationalists today claim the Bible as a nationalist text.

Similarly, Rich Lowry, whose book *The Case for Nationalism* I reviewed in chapter three, argues that biblical Israel is a template of nationality that we should still look to today. The Torah is a "how-to guide for nationalism,"[1] because "Ancient Israel gave us the template of a nation."[2] Israel shows us how to be a nation; its story in the Bible shows the ingredients of successful nationhood. "Ancient Israel bears all the hallmarks of a nation. The Israelites were a people with a homeland, centered on the holy city of Jerusalem. Their genealogy, history, traditions, law, and language set them out as different. They acted on a deeply felt imperative to govern themselves." Among other things, Israel had its own designated land, a nation-defining law, a covenant with God, a mission in the world, and God-given borders. Israel also "powerfully demonstrates the importance of historical memory and ritual, of texts, language, and reading, to nationalism."[3]

Lowry notes, correctly, that many contemporary nations have taken their cue from ancient Israel. "The Old Testament acted as a conveyor belt carrying biblical notions of nationality directly into the mind of Europe,"[4] the birthplace of modern nationalism. Because of the Bible's general influence and prevalence in Europe, especially during the early modern era as nations were gaining coherence, self-awareness, and harder borders, nation builders looked to the Bible for support and saw what they wanted to see in Israel's story. Lowry finds that "in the story of the ancient Israelites, we see the creation not just of a great religion but of a nation, one that would, through the Torah, spread its example throughout the world."[5] Among other elements, one of the things that contemporary nations have copied from ancient Israel is the notion of being in covenant with God as a special, chosen people. The Bible "depicted a united people, governing themselves in their own land, with their own laws, special relationship with God, and a mission in the world," Lowry notes, adding that "practically any self-respecting nation conceived of itself as the new Israel, a

---

[1] Rich Lowry, *The Case for Nationalism: How It Made Us Rich, Powerful, and Free* (New York: Broadside, 2019), 71.

[2] Lowry, *Case for Nationalism*, 70.

[3] Lowry, *Case for Nationalism*, 70, 76.

[4] Lowry, *Case for Nationalism*, 80.

[5] Lowry, *Case for Nationalism*, 70.

chosen people with its own Promised Land,"[6] a fact that Lowry, amazingly, seems untroubled by.

Yoram Hazony also appeals to the Bible to support nationalism. "The idea that political order should be based on independent nations was an important feature of ancient Israelite thought as reflected in the Hebrew Bible," he argues.[7] Hazony interprets the Bible as condemning ancient empires like Babylon, Persia, and Assyria because of their universal pretensions. "Despite the obvious economic advantages of an Egyptian or Babylonian peace that would unify humanity, the Bible was born out of a deep-seated opposition to this very aim."[8] Again, he argues that "the problem of empire and anarchy is central to the political teaching of Hebrew Scripture," the answer to which is "the distinctive Israelite tradition of the national state."[9] The "Mosaic law offered the Israelites a constitution that would bring them together in what would today be called a *national state*."[10] The priests, prophets, and kings of Israel were drawn from among the people themselves, pictured as a brotherhood; Israel would not be ruled by faraway leaders or teachers. And Israel had specific boundaries to protect itself both from outsiders and from the temptation to imperialism.

One of the most important elements of Israel-as-national-template, for Hazony, is its example of national formation out of tribal elements. Israel was a confederation of tribes, which Hazony sees as a fundamental step in modern political formation: "Heads of clans can unite to form a *tribe* that may have tens of thousands of members. And heads of tribes can come together to form a *nation* whose members number in the millions. Such a process of consolidation is familiar to us, for example, from the biblical history of Israel."[11] That is why, for Hazony, we should understand nations today as simply large families, the extension of familial loyalty to a macro scale. He argues that this tribal consolidation is, historically, how states really form, not through a mythical social contract that brings individuals out of the state of nature.

---

[6]Lowry, *Case for Nationalism*, 81.
[7]Yoram Hazony, *The Virtue of Nationalism* (London: Hachette, 2018), 16.
[8]Hazony, *Virtue of Nationalism*, 17.
[9]Hazony, *Virtue of Nationalism*, 99.
[10]Hazony, *Virtue of Nationalism*, 18.
[11]Hazony, *Virtue of Nationalism*, 68, emphasis original; see also p. 79.

NATIONS IN THE BIBLE

What does the Bible say about nations? Are cultures and peoples supposed to pursue political independence? What does it say about Israel? Is Israel supposed to be a model of nationality? What kind of "nation" was ancient Israel? Lowry and Hazony are correct that the Bible was historically influential in the rise of modern nationalism and that nation builders often looked to biblical Israel as a template for their own projects. But that does not give them the endorsement for nationalism that they think it does. There is good reason to think that early modern nation builders were bad biblical scholars: the Bible does not say what they think it says about Israel, nations, and political order.

The Bible plainly presents humanity as existing in different political, linguistic, and cultural groups, variously defined, according to God's divine ordinance; I do not think the Bible endorses world government. The Bible suggests that at least some of these groupings (not language) are part of the created order, which means we should recognize and, to some extent, embrace our group identities. (I will expand on this idea in chapter ten.) But the Bible says almost nothing about what those group identities should look like. The Bible uses over a dozen different terms to refer to political groups. In Hebrew, we have *'am* (family, people, descendants, inhabitants of a common territory), *goy* (crowd, nation, the Gentiles), *'umma* (nation, group of matrilineal descent), *shebet* and *matteh* (tribe), *mishpachah* (clan), and *melek* (kingdom). In Greek we have *ethnos* (equivalent to *goy*), *genos* (posterity, family), *laos* (equivalent to *'am*, family, people, population), *phyle* (tribe), *basileia* (kingdom), *polis* (city-state), and *glossai* (language group). The Bible does not hold up any single form of group organization as normative; it does not exhort people to organize themselves as one kind of group instead of another. None of these terms carries the exact sense of "cultural unit that enjoys political sovereignty" or "political unit that governs a single, distinct, and complete cultural group." There is no Hebrew or Greek word for "nation-state."

It is especially noteworthy that, to the extent that there is a consistent usage, the Bible tends to use one term for a social, cultural, or religious group (Hebrew *'am* and Greek *laos*), usually translated "family" or "people," and a separate term for a sovereign political entity (Hebrew *goy* and Greek *ethnos*), usually translated "the nations" or "the Gentiles," and it does not assume the two must overlap. The Hebrew 'am, most often used to describe Israel in the Old Testament, is a social, cultural, and religious term which connotes "a people," or "a family," and it gets closest to what we might think of as a tightly knit group of extended kinship ties, while goy, usually used of the Gentile nations, is both more impersonal and political. It is a term applied to a variety of polities, including tribes, city-states, nation-states, and empires. By itself, the separation of these concepts into two terms is telling: the Bible does not assume that a religio-cultural "family" ('am) must also constitute a sovereign polity or "nation" (goy).

The nations in the Bible—Hebrew goy and Greek ethnos—are the peoples who are neither Jews nor Christians. Ethnos is the "most general and therefore weakest of these [Greek] terms, having simply an ethnographical sense and denoting the natural cohesion of a people in general."[12] Ethnos has none of our contemporary political meanings. Its original meaning was simply "a number of people accustomed to live together" or a people under a common rule. An ethnos in biblical times is not the same as the "imagined community" or the thick national units of the modern era in which culture and sovereignty exactly overlap. The nations of modern nationalist aspiration are large, geographically extensive polities governed by impersonal institutions in faraway capitals with pretensions to world-historical status; in that sense, they are closer to the biblical empires of Babylon, Persia, or Rome, the targets of much biblical critique, than to the tribes of Israel or the table of nations in Genesis 10.

But the Bible also does not even use the terms with a high degree of precision or consistency. "The ease with which [the Hebrew terms] could be synonymously paralleled and interchanged indicates a common semantic range," according to one biblical scholar.[13] Another has commented on the "sociological indefiniteness" of the various Greek and Hebrew terms.[14] For example, the Hebrew words for "tribe can designate a population group, a type of social organization, or a geographical area."[15] The Hebrew 'am

---

[12]Gerhard Kittel, ed., *Theological Dictionary of the New Testament*, trans. Geoffrey Bromiley (Grand Rapids, MI: Eerdmans, 1977), 1:369.

[13]Geoffrey Bromiley, *International Standard Bible Encyclopedia* (Grand Rapids, MI: Eerdmans, 1995), 3:492.

[14]Kittel, *Theological Dictionary of the New Testament*, 2:366.

[15]Bromiley, *International Standard Bible Encyclopedia*, 4:904.

referred to a wide variety of nonsovereign units, including small groups, an army, the population of men (excluding women and children), or a labor force: "in fact, it appears that any time two or more individuals were united *in any way*, they could legitimately be identified as an *'am*."[16] Similarly, throughout the Bible "we find that there is no precise definition of what constitutes gôy."[17] *Goy* can carry some meaning of common descent, common rule, and common territory and many even sometimes imply a common worship, language, or army—but just as often not. "It remains unclear to what extent the principle of identification is based on political, territorial, or gentilic consideration."[18]

Whether Israel or the other nations are conceived as *'am* or *goy* does not tell us anything definitive about their form of political organization or even their level of sovereignty and independence. The term *'am* carried no such connotation at all, and while normally a *goy* would also constitute a *melek*, a kingdom with independent political rulership, "the measure of independence enjoyed by such kingdoms naturally varied from case to case"[19] and could include dependent colonies, subordinate fiefdoms, and vassal states. In fact, "The Old Testament never precisely defines what requirements are essential for Israel's existence as a gôy, as it does not in the case of other nations either."[20] Another scholar has suggested that *goy* "does not seem to indicate a natural unit," like a family or tribe the way *'am* does.[21]

Part of this ambiguity simply reflects the fluidity of political rule and the irrelevance of political identity to most people in ancient times. "Ancient perceptions of nationality were diverse and often quite different from modern notions, in which political considerations predominate," according to one scholar.[22] Or, as another argues, "Most Western readers of the Bible will tend to project modern concepts of the nation and state into the Old Testament. However, the ethnic or national consciousness of people in Palestine during

---

[16]Bromiley, *International Standard Bible Encyclopedia*, 3:759, emphasis added.

[17]G. Johannes Botterweck, *Theological Dictionary of the Old Testament* (Grand Rapids, MI: Eerdmans, 2004), 2:428.

[18]Botterweck, *Theological Dictionary of the Old Testament*, 2:426.

[19]Botterweck, *Theological Dictionary of the Old Testament*, 2:428.

[20]Botterweck, *Theological Dictionary of the Old Testament*, 2:429.

[21]A. R. Hulst, "'am/gôy," in *Theological Lexicon of the Old Testament*, ed. Ernst Jenni and Claus Westermann, trans. Mark E. Biddle (Peabody, MA: Hendrickson, 1997), 2:899-919.

[22]Bromiley, *International Standard Bible Encyclopedia*, 3:492.

the formative period of Israel is far from clear."[23] Modern nationalism has taught us to derive a strong sense of personal meaning and self-understanding from our political identities. The average person in the ancient world almost certainly had no such expectation because they were ruled by distant kings with whom they had no contact other than the exchange of taxes for protection, and over whom they had no say or voice. There was no logical overlap between language, ancestry, and rulership, as kingdoms changed hands with the waxing and waning of imperial fortunes. "The boundaries of the territorial states fluctuated, depending on the ability of the king to control his region or incorporate more land."[24] The Bible, having been written in that cultural context, does not reflect a politics in which cultures must aspire to statehood, in which states are expected to overlap precisely with corresponding cultural nations. The crazy-quilt patchwork of peoples, tribes, nations, and languages, which to the nationalist is a heinous crime to be redressed, is simply the accepted shape of the world to the authors of the Bible. As a result, "The Old Testament does not contain any ordered or consistent doctrine of nationhood."[25]

The borders of Old Testament nations were blurry—which, as I argued in chapter four, is true of all nations—and God never commands rulers to make them otherwise. There is simply no biblical command or model for the most important nationalist beliefs: that cultural and political borders must correspond; that cultural distinctiveness merits sovereignty; or that governments should regulate the cultures of their peoples to enforce or safeguard cultural homogeneity. The point of the table of nations in Genesis 10, Moses' song in Deuteronomy 32, and Paul's sermon in Acts 17 is to affirm God's sovereignty over all the world, including its rabble of kingdoms, tribes, families, and peoples, however defined, not to make a point about political organization, group affinity, or the criterion of sovereignty. That the table of nations lists groups "by their clans, their languages, their lands, and their nations" does not mean each clan corresponded with exactly one language, in one land, under one political ruler, or that one ruler ruled over one and only one tribe or language. The peoples of the ancient Near East were a

---

[23]J. Daniel Hays, *From Every People and Nation: A Biblical Theology of Race* (Downers Grove, IL: InterVarsity Press, 2003), 40.
[24]Bromiley, *International Standard Bible Encyclopedia*, 3:493.
[25]Botterweck, *Theological Dictionary of the Old Testament*, 2:428.

jumble of crosscutting and overlapping language groups, religious groups, and political borders; the point of the table of nations is that God is king over them all. (The table, in fact, is probably a description of geopolitical alliances, of vassal-lord relationships, not a family tree of biological or ethnic relationship.)[26]

Nations and empires such as Babylon, Persia, and Rome populate the biblical narrative, but the Bible has little to say about their organization or self-understanding; little, indeed, other than that God rules them (Psalm 22:28), God will judge them (Deuteronomy 9:4; Isaiah 60:12; Joel 3:2), they will eventually recognize God's sovereignty (Psalm 86:9; Isaiah 60:3), and they are not of ultimate importance. Isaiah 40:15 says, "The nations are like a drop from a bucket, / and are accounted as dust on the scales," which hardly gives support to the nationalist fixation on national identity.

ISRAEL: PEOPLE OR NATION?

The much bigger question is Israel. Should Israel be taken as a model for the nations, including nations today? If so, what does that model teach us? What kind of nation was Israel?

First, the extent to which we can or should take Israel as a straightforward model for modern secular states is contentious and not at all clear. In some respects, ancient Israel was far more thickly defined than even modern nationalists would be comfortable with: it was, after all, nearly theocratic, with membership reserved exclusively for those who shared in its beliefs and religious worship, which few modern nationalists advocate and which would obviously be at odds with the American tradition of religious freedom. Setting that aside, we can, perhaps, look for examples of wisdom and prudence in Israel's history (some have seen the separation of powers in the division between priests, prophets, and kings), but viewing Israel that way, as a template of national formation and an early political science experiment, misses the point of what Israel was for. To the extent that the Bible presents Israel as a light for the nations, it is because Israel was meant to be an example of righteousness and obedience (Isaiah 42:6), a unique display of God's mercy, glory, beauty, and power (Isaiah 60), and because Israel was the vehicle for the Messiah who would accomplish salvation for all nations (Isaiah 49:6)—not because of

---

[26] Hays, *From Every People and Nation*, 74-76.

Israel's model of political organization, its tribal confederacy, or its cultural distinctness from other people.

Other nations were not expected to copy Israel in most respects—certainly not in its office as the bearer of the Messiah. There is similarly no suggestion that other nations should seek to be, or understand themselves to be, in a covenant with God akin to Israel's covenant (though they are in the Noahic covenant); God is specific about making his covenant with his particular people. Israel is a model for the nations in how the prophets clearly apply the moral law to other nations, condemning Babylon, Assyria, and Persia for oppression, tyranny, and violence (not, contrary to Hazony, for the expansiveness of their rule; nationalist governments can be just as oppressive and tyrannical as imperial ones). The moral law God specifically revealed to Israel did not apply only to Israel; it applies to all people, everywhere, at all times, and Israel was to be a living embodiment or model of what it looked like to live that moral law out together. Recall from chapter five that I argued governments should not be morally neutral. All peoples—however defined—ought to strive for righteousness and justice, because "righteousness exalts a nation, but sin is a reproach to any people" (Proverbs 14:34). America's "open exceptionalism," in which we strive to be an example of justice and equality for all, is the right way to apply Israel's moral law to ourselves. But that is not the same thing as saying that we should look to Israel as a template of political organization or the process of national formation through tribal confederacy. The Old Testament was not written to make a point about secular political order; it was written to make a point about God's character and his acts of redemption in the world.

But even if we do accept Israel as a model in some limited and qualified ways, the Bible still does not endorse modern nationalism because ancient Israel's self-definition in the Bible is not consistent with the nationalist insistence that culture and sovereignty overlap. Again, Israel was strongly defined and unified by *religion,* by doctrine, belief, and corporate worship, which Lowry and Hazony explicitly deny is their goal. They claim they want to reinforce modern nations' *cultural* identity. But Israel was not culturally homogenous. Israel started out as a pluralistic, multiethnic polity. Abraham was an Amorite; Judah and Simeon married Canaanites; Joseph married an Egyptian; and Moses married a Black African Cushite, all of whose descendants were part of Israel. Many other Gentiles were welcomed into Israel's polity, including

Jethro, Rahab, Ruth, Caleb, and Othniel—again, whose multiethnic descendants were members of Israel. Other Gentiles expressed some measure of belief in the God of Israel, such as Melchizedek, the Queen of Sheba, Naaman, and the people of Nineveh after Jonah's preaching, and were recognized as having fellowship, in some sense, with Israel and its God. Later, Israel mingled with its neighbors through intermarriage, through "foreigners' identification with Israel in its worship," through their incorporation of Canaanite tribes (the Gibeonites), through "dynastic marriages," and more.[27] (The prohibition on intermarriage applied only to the inhabitants of Canaan, not others, and was clearly motivated by concerns that intermarriage would pollute Israel's religion, not its race, ethnicity, or culture.)

Most significantly, when Israel escaped Egypt, it was accompanied by a "mixed multitude" (Exodus 12:38), likely a reference to non-Israelites who joined Israel because of the demonstrated power of its God. This multitude would have been made up of Egyptians and probably Cushites who subsequently became part of Israel. To state it bluntly: Israel started out as a multiethnic and multilingual nomadic people. That may be why Israel had specific provisions in its law to welcome strangers to the Passover table (Exodus 12:48) when the strangers affirmed loyalty to Israel's God. "The presence of other 'peoples' or 'nationalities' at this juncture of the story has strong implications as to the true nature of Israel," according to Hays. "Participation in the celebration of Yahweh's great redemptive act was not based on birth or ethnicity," or culture, "but rather on relationship to Yahweh and his covenant."[28] As a result, "the Israelites of the Old Testament had numerous 'ethnic' affinities with their neighbors in and around Palestine [and] the lines of ethnic demarcation were not hard and fast," and "for much of their history the ethnic boundary between Israel and her neighbors was fuzzy and fluid."[29] Despite its strong identity around religion, ancient Israel was less strongly defined, less politically and culturally distinct, less a nation-state, than modern nationalists claim.

Israel was meant to be marked out by a different defining trait than what separated the other nations of the world from each other. The achievement of either sovereignty or cultural uniqueness was not the main point. God nowhere commands Israel to keep its language separate or even its nonreligious

---

[27]Bromiley, *International Standard Bible Encyclopedia*, 3:493.
[28]Hays, *From Every People and Nation*, 88.
[29]Hays, *From Every People and Nation*, 40, 42.

cultural practices distinct. Hebrew almost certainly mixed freely with Aramaic, Egyptian, Babylonian, and Sumerian throughout the region (part of the Old Testament is written in Aramaic, probably the language that Jesus and the disciples spoke as a first language). Archaeologists and historians have even shown how the Bible itself parallels and echoes some language used in other ancient Near Eastern religious texts—though it differed decisively in how it employed that language and what sort of god it portrayed. The kernel of Israel's special status is not its racial purity, familial bonds, cultural uniqueness, Hebrew language, or political organization, but solely its relationship to its God.

Israel was called to be separate and distinct from the nations of the world and given clear boundaries to enforce—but the boundary was drawn around the common worship of the God of Israel, nothing more and nothing else. That makes Israel a bad model for modern secular states. (Ironically, if we did want to use this more accurate picture of Israel as a model for modern nations, it would lead to a version of creedalism—unity around shared belief, the very idea nationalists oppose—not nationalism.) God promises to make Israel a holy nation if the people "obey my voice and keep my covenant" (Exodus 19:5-6). Their constitution as a people depends on their obedience to God and worship of him: they are a people defined by common trust in God and common worship, not a common cultural inheritance. Similarly, in Deuteronomy 26:5, Moses tells the people to reaffirm the story of their origin: "And you shall make response before the LORD your God, 'A wandering Aramean [Abraham] was my father. And he went down into Egypt and sojourned there, few in number, and there he became a nation, great, mighty, and populous.'" Abraham left Ur in obedience to God's call; it was because of that obedience that he became a great nation. Israel's origin lies in an act of obedience to God. In both cases, we see that the precondition of becoming God's 'am is obeying his voice and keeping his covenant.

Israel's status as the 'am of God referred to its religious unity, not cultural unity or political sovereignty. When God promised to make Israel his *people*, the question of political sovereignty was a non sequitur. Israel was an 'am during its time under slavery in Egypt and continued to be an 'am during its Babylonian captivity and when under Persian and Roman rule, showing that political sovereignty was not essential to Israel's existence as God's people. Naturally, Israel longed to recover its sovereignty and wrongly believed its recovery was the mission of the hoped-for Messiah. Israel's political hopes are why today's nationalists look to it as a template for today's nations. Refuting such political aspirations is one of the main points of the New Testament. By putting their hopes in political deliverance, ancient Israel missed the point of God's redemptive purposes. In 1 Samuel 8, the people of Israel ask for a king, "that we also may be like all the nations." God grants their request but warns that in accepting a king, "they have rejected me from being king over them." Being like other nations was never Israel's purpose. The Messiah's mission was not to make Israel a great nation or a new *goy* but to usher in God's kingdom with a renewed people, a new *'am*.

What kind of new *'am* would this be? In light of the entirety of the Bible's message, it seems clear that the new *'am* is the church. In the Septuagint translation of the Old Testament, *'am* becomes the Greek *laos*—and in the New Testament the term is applied to Christians (e.g., Acts 15:14; Titus 2:14; Hebrews 4:9; Revelation 21:3), not to the Romans or the Gentile nations. *Laos* is the New Testament term for God's people, the gathering of those called by his name who follow him through trust in and allegiance to King Jesus and who count themselves citizens of the kingdom of God, a kingdom that, Jesus reminds us, is not of this world (John 18:36). *Laos* in the New Testament has lost whatever secular or temporal political meaning *'am* might have had in the Old Testament. In this new people, "the biologico-historical or national element is of no significance."[30] Read back into the Old Testament, this layer of meaning suggests that to the extent Israel was true to the best version of itself, its aspiration would focus on being God's people and God's family, not on achieving sovereignty or being known for its greatness among the nations of the earth. Israel was clearly meant to be a model for the church, not for the nations, in which case the question of sovereignty is beside the point.

Israel is not a model for modern nations unless we want to build theocracies. To the extent we look to Israel as a model today, it should be a model for our churches, not our states. For modern nations to emulate Israel, they must either be theocratic, or treat their cultures as the equivalent of Israel's religion, which is a form of idolatry. The point of Israel's boundaries of national identity was not to be an example of homeland security or cultural traditionalism or national liberation, but an example of holiness, of keeping oneself separate and apart from the idolatry of the surrounding peoples.

---

[30]Kittel, *Theological Dictionary of the New Testament*, 4:55.

Israel was called to be separate and distinct from the nations in the world in its righteousness and its worship of God, not its culture. When modern nationalists want to treat national culture with the same reverence and separateness that Israel was supposed to have for its covenant relationship with God, they are treating their national culture as a form of religious worship, the preservation of which is a religious duty, with the nation playing the role of God.

2 CHRONICLES 7:14 AND PSALM 33:12

Some ways in which the Bible inspired modern nationalism are downright dangerous. It is astonishing to me that Lowry can acknowledge and *celebrate* nationalists' role in propagating "chosen nation" mythology throughout Europe and America, a notion that has given direct support to some of the worst episodes of imperialism and oppression in modern history. The Bible nowhere even slightly hints that any other people are ever considered a chosen people or have a divine mission like Israel. When nationalists claim their nation is chosen, a "new Israel," or has a divine commission to accomplish God's purpose in the world, they are reading their secular polities into the biblical narrative, substituting their nation for God's people, a frank admission that nationalism is a religion.

Americans have long thought of themselves as a chosen people. In the eighteenth and nineteenth centuries Americans regularly talked of themselves as a "new Israel." Today, many American Christians routinely cite 2 Chronicles 7:14 ("If my people, which are called by my name, shall humble themselves, and pray, and seek my face, and turn from their wicked ways; then will I hear from heaven, and will forgive their sin, and will heal their land") and Psalm 33:12 ("Blessed is the nation whose God is the LORD") and apply them to the United States, asserting that America is "my people" who are "called by my name" and is "the nation whose God is the LORD." President Dwight Eisenhower took the oath of office in 1953 on a Bible opened to 2 Chronicles 7:14 at Billy Graham's suggestion. In fact, he placed his hand on two Bibles: one opened to 2 Chronicles 7:14 and the other opened to Psalm 33:12. Jerry Falwell cited both verses and directly applied them to America in his 1980 book, *Listen, America!* Ronald Reagan once told someone that his favorite verse was 2 Chronicles 7:14, and, like Eisenhower, took the oath of office on Bibles opened to the verse in 1981 and 1985.[31] Reagan quoted the verse approvingly in public speeches at least a half dozen times, including when observing national days of prayer in 1982 and 1984, at the 1983 National Prayer Breakfast, in a June 1983 dinner honoring Jesse Helms, in an October 1983 talk with women leaders of Christian organizations, and at a 1984 speech to the National Association of Evangelicals.[32]

But the tradition of applying 2 Chronicles 7:14 and Psalm 33:12 to the United States did not start with either Reagan or Eisenhower. It dates at least to the Civil War. In January 1860, the Reverend A. Othman in Danby, New York, delivered a sermon on 2 Chronicles 7:14 noted for being "earnest and forcible, especially in its views on Slavery," so much so that the newspaper reporting on his sermon warned that some readers might find it "severe, if not denunciatory."[33] In August 1861, in Rutland, Ohio, Captain Samuel Titus was mustering troops of the Union Army for service in the Civil War. An onlooker addressed the troops, quoting Psalm 33:12. The *Pomeroy Weekly Telegraph* reported on the benediction and added, "This precept is strikingly verified in the history of our forefathers, who, with few men, and small means, fought the battles of Freedom, and bequeathed to us the rich boon of Constitutional Liberty."[34]

The next month, Reverend B. W. Chidlaw, a Union Army Chaplain, delivered a sermon to troops of the thirty-ninth Ohio Infantry Regiment stationed in St. Louis.[35] He chose for his text 2 Chronicles 7:14, reminding the Union troops that they, the people who are called by God's name, must keep faith with God to secure his blessing, presumably in the form of military

---

[31]Daniel K. Williams, *God's Own Party: The Making of the Christian Right* (New York: Oxford University Press, 2012), 124; "Oath on the Bible Used by Reagan's Mother," *New York Times*, January 21, 1981, www.nytimes.com/1981/01/21/us/oath-on-the-bible-used-by-reagan-s-mother.html; Gajann, Mahita, "These Are the Bible Verses Past Presidents Have Turned to on Inauguration Day," *Time*, January 19, 2017, https://time.com/4639596/inauguration-day-presidents-bible -passages/.

[32]According to a search of the American Presidency Project's materials, www.presidency.ucsb .edu/advanced-search?field-keywords=2+Chronicles.

[33]"New Books," *New York Evangelist (1830-1902)*, vol. 31, no. 2 (January 12, 1860): 8, available via ProQuest, American Periodicals.

[34]"Communicated," *Pomeroy Weekly Telegraph* (Pomeroy, Meigs County, OH), August 9, 1861. Chronicling America: Historic American Newspapers, Library of Congress, https://chroniclingamerica .loc.gov/lccn/sn8402745/1861-08-09/ed-1/seq-2/.

[35]"War News From Missouri," *Cincinnati Daily Press* (Cincinnati, OH), September 30, 1861. Chronicling America: Historic American Newspapers, Library of Congress, https://chroniclingamerica .loc.gov/ lccn/sn84028745/1861-09-30/ed-1/seq-2/.

victory. Reverend Pliny White did the same a few months later in Vermont.[36] In February 1864, Reverend William Patton preached that "the Great National Baptism" was "Certain," by which he meant that "God will so pour out his spirit upon the army, the navy, and the churches," that "the nation [will] stand up redeemed and sanctified," citing 2 Chronicles 7:14, among others, as proof of God's promise to answer prayers to this effect.[37] In February 1864, a group of clergymen spearheading an effort to amend the US Constitution to explicitly acknowledge Jesus Christ and declare the nation's Christian identity issued a press release advertising their efforts. The group invoked Psalm 33:12, calling on all those "who love our country and desire to have it become that 'blessed nation whose God is the Lord,'" to sign their petition and support the constitutional amendment.[38]

A review of biblical references in American literature shows dozens of instances of these verses used in reference to the United States over the following decades. Southerners used them to defend the Confederacy.[39] A pastor invoked them to pray for the nation during the contested 1876 election.[40] The Governor of Vermont issued a call for a day of prayer in 1838, concluding it with Psalm 33:12.[41] The Governor of West Virginia did the same in his call for a day of Thanksgiving in 1866.[42] Reverend Windsor of Red Wing, Minnesota,

---

[36]"Home Duties in Time of War," Orleans Independent Standard (Irasburgh, VT), October 11, 1861. Chronicling America: Historic American Newspapers, Library of Congress, https://chroniclingamerica.loc.gov/lccn/sn84022548/1861-10-11/ed-1/seq-1/.

[37]William Patton, "The Great National Baptist Certain," The Independent . . . Devoted to the Consideration of Politics, Social and Economic Tendencies, History, Literature, and the Arts (1848-1921), vol. 16, no. 794 (February 18, 1864): 2, ProQuest.

[38]"Proposed Amendments to the Constitution," Daily National Republican (Washington, DC), February 16, 1864. Chronicling America: Historic American Newspapers, Library of Congress, https://chroniclingamerica.loc.gov/lccn/sn86053570/1864-02-16/ed-1/seq-1/.

[39]Weekly Standard (Raleigh, NC), February 24, 1864. Chronicling America: Historic American Newspapers, Library of Congress, https://chroniclingamerica.loc.gov/lccn/sn83045706/1864-02-24/ed-1/seq-4/; "A Proposition," The Camden Confederate (Camden, SC), April 6, 1864. Chronicling America: Historic American Newspapers, Library of Congress, https://chroniclingamerica.loc.gov/lccn/sn85042595/1864-04-06/ed-1/seq-2/.

[40]R. P. Johnson, "Sermon," Yorkville Enquirer (Yorkville, SC), November 9, 1876. Chronicling America: Historic American Newspapers, Library of Congress, https://chroniclingamerica.loc.gov/lccn/sn84026925/1876-11-09/ed-1/seq-4/.

[41]Silas H. Jenison, "A Proclamation," Vermont Telegraph (Brandon, VT), November 14, 1838. Chronicling America: Historic American Newspapers, Library of Congress, https://chroniclingamerica.loc.gov/lccn/sn83025661/1838-11-14/ed-1/seq-3/.

[42]Arthur I. Boreman, "Thanksgiving Proclamation," The Wheeling Daily Intelligencer (Wheeling, WV), November 8, 1866. Chronicling America: Historic American Newspapers, Library of Congress, https://chroniclingamerica.loc.gov/lccn/sn84026844/1866-11-08/ed-1/seq-2/.

preached a sermon on Independence Day 1875, and chose Psalm 33:12 for his text, a choice that clearly conveyed the message that the United States is and should remain the "nation whose God is the LORD." "This nation has a controlling Christian power among its people," Windsor preached, calling for "the religious observance" of American national independence and specifically looking to "the church" to partake in "all the enthusiasm of American patriotism."[43] The tradition migrated to other reform movements and popped up during celebrations of civil religion and during moments of national crisis. Reformers invoked the verses to give extra heft to the temperance movement.[44] Others used them to comfort the nation after President William McKinley's assassination.[45] During World War I, both supporters and opponents of the United States' entry into the war invoked the verses, suggesting that Americans, as God's people, were obligated to be either pacifists[46] or crusaders.[47]

These anecdotes occur at different times across decades of history, in different regions of the country, in response to a wide variety of occasions and contemporary events, by different preachers in different denominations. Americans' habit of applying these verses to the United States has not been limited to one tradition, denomination, region, subculture, era, or crisis. It is a pervasive feature of American Christianity. When Billy Graham persuaded Eisenhower to use the verse at his inaugural, he was following a tradition that was already at least a century old. As the Christian Right first started to cohere in the 1940s and 1950s, and then took its modern shape in the 1970s and 1980s, it is unsurprising that it would reinvigorate this American tradition. According to Google's Ngram viewer, citations to both verses in English language material

---

[43]"Patriotic," *The Grange Advance* (Red Wing, MN), July 6, 1875. Chronicling America: Historic American Newspapers, Library of Congress, https://chroniclingamerica.loc.gov/lccn/sn85025567/1875-07-06/ed-1/seq-5/.

[44]H. M. Barker, "Call for a Day of Prayer," *Press and Daily Dakotaian* (Yankton, Dakota Territory, SD), November 1, 1887. Chronicling America: Historic American Newspapers, Library of Congress, https://chroniclingamerica.loc.gov/lccn/sn91099608/1887-11-01/ed-1/seq-3/.

[45]"Emporium Pulpit Remarks on McKinley," *Cameron County Press* (Emporium, Cameron County, PA), September 19, 1901. *Chronicling America: Historic American Newspapers*, Library of Congress, https://chroniclingamerica.loc.gov/lccn/sn83032040/1901-09-19/ed-1/seq-1/.

[46]"Memorial Sunday in Webster City," *Webster City Freeman* (Webster City, Hamilton County, IA), June 1, 1915. Chronicling America: Historic American Newspapers, Library of Congress, https://chroniclingamerica.loc.gov/lccn/sn85050913/1915-06-01/ed-1/seq-5/.

[47]John R. Herndon, "Plea for the Day of Prayer," *The Ocala Evening Star* (Ocala, FL), May 29, 1918. Chronicling America: Historic American Newspapers, Library of Congress, https://chroniclingamerica.loc.gov/lccn/sn84027621/1918-05-29/ed-1/seq-2/.

soared after 1980 to an all-time high in American history, peaking around 2014, suggesting that Reagan's use of 2 Chronicles 7:14, and the Christian Right's heyday more generally, have made the notion of America's chosen status more popular today than at any point in American history. As Christian power has waned, Christian nationalists have become all the more assertive in staking claim to America's status as a chosen people and a Christian nation.

The use of these verses in reference to the United States is part of a broader tendency among some American Christians to view the United States as a divinely chosen nation in a unique relationship with God to carry out his mission on earth. In this most extreme form, Christian nationalism treats loyalty to America as the natural implication of Christian piety. It conflates American identity with Christian identity and treats the good of one as the good of the other. Past generations very clearly argued that our Christian identity gave America a unique moral status, or that the United States was specially privileged by God for a unique mission or destiny. Older generations of Christian nationalists drew inspiration from the Bible's treatment of ancient Israel—especially the idea of Israel as a chosen nation and the narrative of its conquest and possession of the Promised Land—and from the biblical conflict between good and evil culminating in an apocalyptic struggle.[48]

Christian nationalism goes hand-in-hand with a darker understanding of American exceptionalism. In contrast to the "open" view of exceptionalism—America as unique exemplar of justice and liberty—Christian nationalism takes the form of "closed exceptionalism." Closed exceptionalism views America as exceptional because it is Christian, uniquely innocent of the sins that afflict other nations.[49] In closed exceptionalism, Americans' loyalty attaches not to the ideals America strives for, but to the nation doing the striving. In a sense, the nation *is* the ideal; making America the best nation in the world is the purpose and commission of American nationhood. "In nationalism, the nation is placed upon the highest pedestal; its value resides in its capacity as the sole, binding agency of meaning and justification,"[50] according to Peter Alter. At its worst, closed exceptionalism has sometimes applied the notion of divine favor not to the American nation, but to its largest representative group:

---

[48]Philip Gorski, *American Covenant.*

[49]John D. Wilsey, *American Exceptionalism and Civil Religion: Reassessing the History of an Idea* (Downers Grove, IL: InterVarsity Press, 2015), 18.

[50]Peter Alter, *Nationalism*, 2nd ed. (New York: Hodder Education, 1994), 5.

White Protestants. To put it another way, there is only a blurry and indistinct line between American nationalism, Christian nationalism, and the tribal nationalism of White America. In this kind of extreme nationalism, "the cult of the nation becomes an end in itself. . . . The nation that proves itself as the strongest and fittest in a hostile and competing world shall gain the upper hand and ultimately survive."[51]

CHOSEN PEOPLES

Is 2 Chronicles 7:14 or Psalm 33:12 about the United States? Does America have a divine mission to accomplish in the world? Are we God's chosen people? It seems hardly worth the effort to answer these questions because of how obvious the answers should be—yet the overwhelming historical evidence clearly shows that American Christians stand in need of correction, rebuke, and remedial education on a rudimentary point of theology. Christianity teaches that God, in his providence, worked through a specific national community—ancient Israel—to reveal himself and work out his plan for redemption. Christians believe that plan came to fruition in the person of Jesus Christ, the Messiah of Israel. Through Jesus, all people, Jews and Gentiles, Americans and Mexicans, are invited into fellowship with the God of Israel. Israel's sojourning through history prepared the ground for God's global purposes. Through Jesus, we are "grafted on" to the tree of God's favor. Indeed, the true "Israel" is now the collection of all people who trust in the promises of God through Jesus. As Romans 9:8 says: "It is not the children of the flesh who are the children of God, but the children of the promise are counted as offspring" of Abraham, and who constitute a new Israel.

In other words, the "nation whose God is the LORD," and the "people who are called by my name," is the gathering of God's people in Christ across all cultures and in all times. Second Chronicles 7:14 and Psalm 33:12 are about Israel and, in the new covenant, about the church; they are not about the United States or any other secular polity. To apply them to the United States is hermeneutically indefensible, theologically irresponsible, intellectually sloppy, politically dangerous, and borderline heretical. Jesus told Pilate, "My Kingdom is not of this world" (John 18:36) and told his disciples to "render to Caesar the things that are Caesar's" (Matthew 22:21). That is why he spent time

---

[51]Alter, *Nationalism*, 26.

ministering to Samaritans and Romans, why the Spirit gave the gift of languages to the apostles at Pentecost, and why the apostles traveled the world sharing the good news with different peoples and language groups. Jesus saved people for God "from every tribe and language and people and nation" (Revelation 5:9; 7:9). Jesus refused to be king of one national polity because such a title is beneath him.

Seen in this light, the civil religion that equates America with Israel is a prolonged exercise in missing the point. America is not Israel: the church is. Americans are not God's chosen people; those who trust in Jesus from every tribe, tongue, people, and nation are. The divine mission of God's chosen people is not to spread political liberty, national sovereignty, or capitalism; it is to spread the gospel of Jesus Christ. (They are not the same thing.) America is not a "Christian nation," except in the descriptive sense that most Americans have always been professing Christians and Christianity has shaped much of our culture and history. The church is the one and only true Christian nation. In the United States there is and should be no religious test for public office or for citizenship. The 65 percent of Americans who believe that being Christian is essential to being a true American are wrong, and shockingly illiterate about American civics. The First Amendment rightly protects religious freedom for all people, including Muslims, atheists, and even progressives. I love the United States deeply, but America has no eschatological status. It is not a chosen nation. It plays no irreplaceable role in the redemption of the world. Pastors must repeatedly, publicly, and explicitly teach their congregations from the pulpit that 2 Chronicles 7:14 and Psalm 33:12 are not about America and that to read them that way is to abuse the Word of God. The belief that America is somehow chosen by God or has inherited the mantle of ancient Israel is unsupported by biblical evidence, church history, or theological reasoning.

John Winthrop's sermon of 1630 is deeply engrained in Americans' thinking about our country. Winthrop described his band of followers as having "entered into a Covenant" with God in their quest to "seek out a place of cohabitation and consortship under a due form of government both civil and ecclesiastical." Winthrop was not a clergyman and held no office in church governance. He served as governor of the Massachusetts Bay Colony and applied his theological reasoning to the secular government he led, interpreting God's covenant with the church as a covenant with the new colony. The covenant was important because "we shall be as a city upon a hill, the eyes of all people are upon us; so that if we shall deal falsely with our God in this work we have undertaken and so cause him to withdraw his present help from us, we shall shame the faces of many of God's worthy servants." Reagan invoked Winthrop's image repeatedly throughout his presidency, popularizing the notion that America is that shining city on a hill in covenant with God.

The vision of a Christian commonwealth, chosen by God for special favor and a special mission, shining as a city on a hill for all to see, is inspiring. It is right for us to look to that city, to want to build that city, and to yearn to live there. That city is the church and, one day, it will be the renewed creation pictured as a city coming down out of heaven in Revelation 21. If Winthrop had confined his comments only to "ecclesiastical" government—that is, to the church—it would have been perfectly appropriate. The church is, indeed, in covenant with God, a city on a hill, in full sight of the world and charged to keep faith with our God. But Winthrop was wrong when he also claimed that his secular colony was in a covenant with God for the colonization of the New World, commissioned to carry out a special mission of nation building here. Such an assertion gives the state a status it does not merit and an authority God has not granted it. There is nothing in the Bible to suggest that God commissions nations to do anything other than uphold justice and order. God sometimes raises up a nation to chastise and punish other nations—but, notably, he chooses *wicked* nations like Babylon and Persia so as to highlight that *no* nation is righteous and that only he is a perfectly just sovereign.

Nationalism is a form of overrealized eschatology, a utopian attempt to realize the kingdom of God in all its fullness here and now. The Bible speaks quite plainly about the danger of political idolatry. The greatest evil envisioned in the Bible is portrayed as seductive, deceitful political leaders with godlike pretensions. The Prince of Tyre in Ezekiel 28 and the great city of Babylon in Revelation 18 are usually understood to be images of Satan himself and his kingdom, or the kingdoms of the world under his sway. The Prince of Tyre repeatedly claims godhood and grows arrogant in his wealth, wisdom, power, and beauty, for which he is cast down and punished, as Satan was cast out of heaven for sedition against God's kingship. Similarly, the city of Babylon "glorified herself" and gathered the merchants of the earth together because of her vast wealth. It is telling that when the Bible seeks to convey the reality of demonic power, oppression, and deceit, the image or metaphor it uses is a government trying to be a god. When we invest our governments—nationalist, imperialist, fascist, communist, progressive, or any other kind—with sacred meaning or saddle them with the expectations that they act godlike or carry out a divine mission, we are erecting a frighteningly powerful idol.

In the book of Revelation, the nations are God's enemies while the renewed creation of paradise is pictured as a multicultural city—a *polis,* not a nation, and not a homogenizing, idolatrous empire—in which people from every *ethnos, phylos, laos, and glossai,* "from every nation, from all tribes and peoples and languages," worship God together. Revelation points to how we can embrace our group identities—political, cultural, national, ethnic, or linguistic—while guarding against idolatry. This image in Revelation is an answer and complement to another story, much earlier in the Bible, in Genesis 11. There we read the story of the Tower of Babel, in which humanity, unified by a single language, aspires to "build ourselves a city and a tower with its top in the heavens" and "make a name for ourselves." God sees their hubris: "Behold, they are one people"—one *'am,* one family—"and they have all one language, and this is only the beginning of what they will do. And nothing that they propose to do will now be impossible for them." God confuses their language and disperses the people, creating the divisions of language we have today. The story of the Tower of Babel could be spun as a pronationalist text ("when people are united as one family with one language, we can do anything") or an antinational text ("national divisions are a punishment from God for our hubris"). But I think either interpretation is incomplete without looking to how Babel is complemented by the throne room scene in Revelation. When God completes the work of redemption and gathers his people together in the new creation, he does not undo the curse of Babel or remake humanity into one homogenous family of one tribe and one nation with one language. Rather, he calls people "from every nation, from all tribes and peoples and languages" who worship him together, apparently with existing differences intact and not unmade. The existing differences and distinctions among nations, peoples, tribes, and languages remain and are present in the city of God, but now, instead of being a curse and a cause for division, they are a blessing and a reflection of the infinitely deep and broad character of the God in whom all peoples find unity.

This is our ultimate destiny and the truest model of political justice. To the extent we can see a model polity in the Bible, we find the unity of God's universal kingdom embracing the endless and wonderful motley diversity of tribes, peoples, languages, and nations. Local particularism flourishes within the context of a broader, benevolent order. We embrace and celebrate our differences without fetishizing or idolizing them, and we rest in the kingdom of ordered justice without turning it into a domineering imperial center. Unity in diversity, diversity in unity: eschatological federalism, cosmic decentralization. Augustine argued that, "If men were always peaceful and just, human affairs would be happier and all kingdoms would be small, rejoicing in concord with their neighbors. There would be as many kingdoms among the nations of the world as there are now houses of a city."[52] The contrast with the totalizing governments of Babylon and Tyre—and with the homogenizing regimes of nationalist imagination—is stark. We see in the Bible not a homogenizing government that enforces a sameness of culture, language, heritage, or race, but one that, through Christ, redeems and celebrates and ennobles all the glorious differences with which God has blessed humanity. The Bible hardly mandates that we work to make our cultural and political borders correspond, as modern nationalists insist, and it emphatically does not want us to give nations our primary loyalty or affection.

JOHAN GOTTLIEB FICHTE

The religious, idolatrous nature of nationalism is intrinsic to the theory and has been evident for centuries to those aware of its history. Johan Gottlieb Fichte was a German philosopher, tutor, and professor who lived and wrote around the turn of the nineteenth century. Working in the school of transcendental idealism, he wrote widely on various subjects, taking inspiration from Immanuel Kant and working with his contemporaries, Georg Hegel and Friedrich Schelling. As was the case for most thinkers and writers who lived through the French Revolution and Napoleonic wars, he was drawn to reflect on political matters. In 1806, the French Army won a decisive victory at the Battle of Jena and occupied Berlin; Napoleon formally dissolved the Holy Roman Empire, and much of Germany became a French protectorate. German defeat and subservience caused Fichte, like many Germans, to think hard about what it meant to be German, what made a nation, and what defined national identity. Fichte delivered the results of these reflections, his *Addresses to the German Nation,* in 1807 and 1808.

---

[52]Augustine, *City of God*, IV.15, 159.

These lectures transcended their moment and became foundational texts for the era of nationalism just then unfolding. As is often the case when an idea is first explored, this earliest exposition of nationalism was the clearest and most explicit about its true nature because Fichte did not have to dissemble or avoid the bad historical baggage and uncomfortable connotations that nationalism would accrue over the next two centuries. We see in Fichte's writing the overt religiosity inherent in nationalism. Nationalism takes on the form, the structure, and the sentiment of religious attachment. Like R. R. Reno, Fichte believes that it is simply inevitable that human beings will seek to find sacred meaning in this world.

> The natural impulse of man, which should be abandoned only in cases of real necessity, is to find heaven on this earth, and to endow his daily work on earth with permanence and eternity; to plant and to cultivate the eternal in the temporal—not merely in an incomprehensible fashion or in a connection with the eternal that seems to mortal eye an impenetrable gulf, but in a fashion visible to the mortal eye itself.[53]

Fichte embraces this natural desire, rather than try to resist its hubris—shocking in itself—and then asks the logical question: how can we possibly achieve this kind of worldly immortality? For him, the answer is clear: by identifying ourselves with a nation, with what he calls a people:

> What can provide man an opportunity to do this kind of work? Only an "eternal" order. . . . Such an order of things . . . truly exists [in that] from which he himself, with all his thoughts and deeds and with his belief in their eternity, has proceeded—the people. . . . *The life of a people is where the revelation of the divine takes place.* So long as this people exists, every further revelation of the divine will appear and take shape in that people in accordance with the same natural law.[54]

Fichte was quite literal when he claimed that the "life of the divine" takes place in and through the life of a people—that was more or less the argument of his colleague Hegel, who had argued that the "absolute" (his word for God) unfolded and became revealed through history, particularly through the

---

[53]Johann Gottlieb Fichte, "Addresses to the German Nation," in *From Absolutism to Napoleon, 1648—1815*, German History in Documents and Images, vol. 2 (Washington, DC: German Historical Institute), 4, http://germanhistorydocs.ghi-dc.org/pdf/eng/12_EnlightPhilos_Doc.8_English.pdf.

[54]Fichte, "Addresses," 5, emphasis added.

diverse but complementary histories of distinct nations, each of whom contributed some new particular genius or cultural essence to humanity. For Fichte, since a people outlives any individual member, it is essentially immortal. And because its immortality is the vehicle for our own lasting legacy, we owe it our love and devotion. Only through the life of a people or a nation is it possible for individuals to experience and practice the highest form of love at all: "Love that is truly love . . . never clings to what is transient; only in the eternal does it awaken and become kindled."[55] Recall that for Fichte, "the eternal" is not God, but the life of a people, through whom God is revealed. We can only truly love one another insofar as we identify with a people and a nation and make it the object of our devotion.

In Fichte's thought, a people or a nation occupy the same place that God occupies in a religion. Fichte offers a quasi-mystical definition of a people: "This, then, is a people . . . : the totality of men continuing to live in society with each other and continually creating themselves naturally and spiritually out of themselves, a totality that arises together out of the divine under a certain special law of divine development.[56]" In arguing that a people is "creating themselves naturally and spiritually out of themselves" and that it "arises . . . out of the divine," Fichte is offering a pale imitation of the doctrine of divine aseity, or God's independence. In traditional Christian doctrine, God exists in, of, and from himself, without reference to any other thing or person. Fichte is suggesting a doctrine of national aseity—that nations exist in, of, and for themselves and develop from the inner logic of their unique cultures without outside influence. This sort of national aseity arises "out of the divine" under a "law of divine development," again suggesting a strong connection between individual meaning and self-worth, national development, and some kind of divine revelation.

Being a member of such a nation imposes a strong burden of worship and obligation. The people must work to ensure that they continue "without admixture of, or corruption by, any alien element," foreshadowing the nationalists who call for resistance to cultural change or pollution.[57] But more is required: "He to whom a fatherland has been handed down, and in whose soul heaven and earth, visible and invisible, meet and mingle, and thus, and only

---

[55]Fichte, "Addresses," 6.
[56]Fichte, "Addresses," 5.
[57]Fichte, "Addresses," 6.

thus, create a true and enduring heaven—such a man fights to the last drop of his blood to hand on the precious possession unimpaired to his posterity."[58] Fichte calls for citizens to love their nation with a religious love, a worshipful devotion, "to the last drop of his blood." Such a love has a practical function: it inspires men to serve the state, fight for it, and sacrifice for it. Only such a higher purpose can inspire a people to fight for their country because, Fichte believes, they will not fight for a constitution or a creed.

> Not the spirit of the peaceful citizen's love for the constitution and the laws, but the devouring flame of higher patriotism, which embraces the nation as the vesture of the eternal, for which the noble-minded man joyfully sacrifices himself. . . . It is not that love of the citizen for the constitution; that love is quite unable to achieve this. . . . The promise of a life here on earth extending beyond the period of life here on earth—that alone it is which can inspire men even unto death for the fatherland.[59]

Nationalists today are fond of mocking mere creedalism as thin gruel insufficient to bind a great people together; they unconsciously echo Fichte when they do. But the love of nation, people, and fatherland is not merely a pragmatic means by which to inspire martial valor. Inspiring such love is also the very purpose of the state, more important than abstract principles of justice, law, or freedom. The state is subordinate to the nation, a mere tool of the people: "People and fatherland in this sense . . . far transcend the state in the ordinary sense of the word." The state is a set of institutions, but the nation is the eternal being that embodies the meaning and purpose of the lives of its members. That is why love of the nation is more important than law, justice, or freedom. "Love of the fatherland must itself govern the state and be the supreme, final, and absolute authority." Freedom is only needed insofar as it is useful to help achieve "the higher purposes that transcend the state."[60] In other words, government is not primarily an institution commissioned by the people or by God to uphold public order and justice. It is the institutional expression of a people and their culture, designed to reflect and reinforce their love for the nation. This is a very different theory of politics than what we find in either the Bible or any kind of republicanism, democracy, or classical liberalism.

---

[58]Fichte, "Addresses," 6-7.
[59]Fichte, "Addresses," 8-9.
[60]Fichte, "Addresses," 7-8.

Finally, the self is never satisfied to worship itself in isolation. It calls on others to worship it—demands their worship, even at the point of a sword. Fichte writes admiringly of the great man of history who

> takes it firmly into his head once for all that he is one of those exceptional beings who are called to lead the obscure and common folk of the earth. Then, in order to justify this conceit of himself as a divine call, he lets this thought absorb his whole life; he must stake everything on it, and cannot rest until he has trodden underfoot all who refuse to think as highly of him as he does of himself, and until he sees his own belief in his divine mission reflected in the whole contemporary world.[61]

A great people will tread underfoot all who refuse to think as highly of it as it does of itself, until the whole world recognizes and affirms and validates its sense of divine mission. Fichte, among the first to describe and champion nationalism, was also the most honest in disclosing its true heart.

NATIONALISM IS IDOLATROUS

Despite its incoherence and antidemocratic tendencies, nationalism is widely popular around the world and it has been enjoying an upsurge in popularity over the past half decade. Nationalism is an irresistible political tool for leaders looking to win support and whip up enthusiasm. We get enthusiastic about it because we are naturally social creatures and we gravitate toward experiences that help us feel part of something larger than ourselves. The nation is among the largest things of which we ever feel a meaningful part, and the temptation to thicken our national identity, to strengthen our group feeling around some shared commonality, can be irresistible. Simply put, nationalism is fun and feels good. It imitates the thrill of being in a stadium rooting for a sports team alongside tens of thousands of likeminded fans, except with greater gravitas, historical depth, and a sense of religious awe.

Recall from chapter one that Clifford Geertz defined *religion* as "a system of symbols which acts to establish powerful, pervasive, and long-lasting moods and motivations in men by formulating conceptions of a general order of existence and clothing these conceptions with such an aura of factuality that the moods and motivations seem uniquely realistic."[62] A religion is whatever

---

[61]Fichte, "Addresses," 11.
[62]Clifford Geertz, *Interpretation of Cultures*, 90.

framework of values that shapes and defines the most basic contours of our lived experienced. It is our fundamental, gut-level, instinctive, prerational, atavistic certainties as much as our explicit, articulated, rationalized, propositional dogmas—specifically, the certainties that give us a sense of right and wrong, a sense of community, a sense of meaning and worth, and a sense of direction and purpose.

Nationalism fulfills all the criteria of a religion. It is a set of symbols that establishes powerful moods that last for centuries. It describes a general order for life, an orienting framework with a standard of right and wrong, a sense of purpose and direction. And it roots this general order in an "aura of factuality," a story about the nation's ancient roots and primal existence which seems feasible because the nation preexists us and outlives us. I have argued that nationalism is illiberal, prone to oppression, complicit in racism, and more. But those critiques pale in comparison to this final one: nationalism, in its ideal form, is a religion—which means nationalism is idolatry. Loving one's country is a positive virtue, but nationalism, as we have encountered it throughout this book, is the opposite. C. S. Lewis (echoing Augustine) rightly noted that the love of country is good, but all goods must be rightly ordered. The love of country "becomes a demon when it becomes a god."[63]

Although this book has focused on American nationalism, it is worth noting that idolatry tends to characterize nationalism generally, wherever it occurs. In some nations, nationalism sidelines and replaces traditional religion, as in the state-sponsored secularism of Turkey or France, or the state-enforced atheism of North Korea, China, or the former Soviet bloc. This is the typical approach of communist, fascist, and progressive regimes devoted to a secular ideology, and French-style secularism seems to be the goal of the American left. In this arrangement, the state becomes a sort of alternate church and nationalism a new religion. (Some readers might be confused by the idea that progressivism is a type of nationalism because the two are pitted against one another in contemporary American politics. But President Woodrow Wilson, who was both a nationalist and a progressive, would have understood the underlying similarity of the two movements.)

But in most cases, nationalism does not fight religion; it co-opts and merges with traditional religion to create a new object of religious loyalty: Russia with

---

[63]C. S. Lewis, *The Four Loves* (New York: Harcourt and Brace, 1960), 39.

the Orthodox Church, some Latin American countries with the Catholic Church, Pakistan and Saudi Arabia with Islam—and the United States with Protestantism. This seems to be the goal today with Hindu nationalists in India, with Victor Oban's movement in Hungary (his new constitution explicitly proclaims Hungary to be a Christian state), and Jair Bolsonaro's government in Brazil (with Catholicism). As one scholar has noted, nationalism can become "a new *ersatz* and heterodox religion, opposed to conventional, traditional religions, yet inheriting many of their features—symbols, liturgies, rituals, and messianic fervor," and that they "retain many 'religious' features—sacred texts, prophets, priests, liturgies, rites, and ceremonies."[64] Another put it more concisely: "In nationalism, the religious is secularized, and the national sanctified."[65]

This sort of religiously infused nationalism typically comes with a myth of the chosen nation, of having a special historical destiny. "Nationalism is the secular, modern equivalent of the pre-modern, sacred myth of ethnic election."[66] Hans Kohn noted the "inspiration and sometimes revivalist character" of nationalism and noted that, for many nations, "The nationality feels that it has been chosen for some special mission, and that the realization of this mission is essential to the march of history, and even to the salvation of mankind."[67] Americans' habit of comparing ourselves to ancient Israel or imagining ourselves to be in a covenant with God or having a special divine mission is not at all unique. Most cultures with a Christian heritage have imagined the same fantasy for themselves at some point in their histories, including Poland's idea of the "Christ of Europe," Russia's myth of "Holy Rus," the Rastafarian belief that Ethiopians (or all Africans) are God's chosen people, or the Reverend Sun Myung Mood's teaching that Korea is the chosen nation. Even countries without a Christian heritage have imagined a version of national supremacy for themselves, such as China's conception of itself as the Middle Kingdom at the center of the world.

When nations co-opt religious sentiment, they also have to co-opt the churches and other religious institutions. Scholars have a word for this relationship between the church and state: Caesaropapism. In the Byzantine

---

[64]Anthony D. Smith, *Chosen Peoples: Sacred Sources of National Identity* (New York: Oxford University Press, 2003), 13-14.

[65]Alter, *Nationalism*, 5.

[66]Anthony Smith, *National Identity* (Reno: University of Nevada Press, 1991), 84, 36-37.

[67]Hans Kohn, *The Idea of Nationalism: A Study of the Origins and Background* (New York: Macmillan, 1944), 23.

Empire, the emperor had an official status in the hierarchy of the Orthodox Church; he presided over councils, appointed patriarchs, and more. The emperor (Caesar) was dual hatted as a sort of pope or head of the church: thus, Caesaropapism. In the Caesaropapist arrangement, the church is subordinate to the state. The church lacks independence; its role is less to mediate worship, teach spiritual truth, or be a voice of public conscience than to act as a buttress and legitimizing authority to the state, and secular rulers use its moral and religious authority to further their political ends. In other words, the church becomes the propaganda arm of the king, the court chaplain. While the exact institutional configuration of the Byzantine Empire is long gone, the manipulative use of religious sentiment for the state's purposes is probably the most common arrangement of religion and politics in history because politicians recognize they can benefit by harnessing the tremendous power of religious fervor. Nationalism that co-opts traditional religion is an updated version of this old model, and Christian nationalism is a uniquely American form of Caesaropapism.

Regardless of which model we're talking about—either sidelining or co-opting religion—nationalism is almost always idolatrous in the sense of becoming a substitute religion. Though I approach the issue from a different angle than other scholars, my conclusion that nationalism is a religion is more or less conventional wisdom among scholars of the subject. Peter Alter argued, "Nationalism exists whenever individuals feel they belong *primarily* to the nation, and whenever affective attachment and loyalty to that nation override all other attachments and loyalties."[68] Hans Kohn defined nationalism as "a state of mind, in which the supreme loyalty of the individual is felt to be due to the nation-state."[69] He argued that modernity is unique among periods of history in the widespread expectation that "the nation demands the supreme loyalty of man," and that all civilizations are "now dominated more and more by this one supreme group-consciousness, nationalism."[70] Liah Greenfeld observed that in comparison to other identities, "national identity represents what may be called the 'fundamental identity', the one that is believed to define the very essence of the individual, which the other identities may modify but

---

[68] Alter, *Nationalism*, 4, emphasis added.
[69] Quoted in Anthony Smith, *Nationalism: Theory, Ideology, History*, 2nd ed. (Cambridge: Polity, 2010), 9.
[70] Kohn, *Idea of Nationalism*, 12.

slightly, and to which they are consequently considered secondary."[71] Or as Ernest Gellner offered, "Having a nation is not an inherent attribute of humanity, but it has now come to appear as such." In the era of nations and nationalism, a national identity has come to be seen as fundamental to what it means to be human. "A man must have a nationality as he must have a nose and two ears." It is simply who and what we are.[72]

Another word for a person's primary, overriding loyalty, attachment, and affection is their *worship*; the object of such attachment is their god. R. J. B. Bosworth argued that "the nation always boasts a metaphysical side," because it treats its land as sacred and outlives its inhabitants; furthermore, "the acceptance of the national identity carries the religious promise that individuals are not only individuals but rather that they connect with their fellows across time through common membership of the nation."[73] Alter argued that in nationalism, "the nation is consecrated, it is ultimately a holy entity."[74] Benedict Anderson suggested that it has "a strong affinity with religious imaginings," through "a secular transformation of fatality into continuity, contingency into meaning."[75] Michael Billig suggested, "If there is an ideological aura attached to nationhood, then the role of God in this down-to-earth (or, rather, down-to-soil) mysticism is interesting. The order of nations is not designed to serve God, but God is to serve the order."[76] Mearsheimer, in advocating for what he sees as the positive value of nationalism, wrote that "what makes a nation so special is that it provides an existential narrative. It gives members a strong sense that they are part of an exceptional and exclusive community whose history is filled with important traditions as well as remarkable individuals and events. . . . In this sense, nationalism is much like a religion." If so, it is quite obviously a false one.[77]

---

[71]Liah Greenfeld, *Nationalism and the Mind: Essays on Modern Culture* (London: Oneworld, 2006), 7.

[72]Ernst Gellner, *Nations and Nationalism* (Ithaca, NY: Cornell University Press, 2008), 6.

[73]R. J. B. Bosworth, *Nationalism* (New York: Routledge, 2007), 2-3.

[74]Alter, *Nationalism*, 5.

[75]Benedict Anderson, *Imagined Communities: Reflections on the Origin and Spread of Nationalism* (New York: Verso, 2006), 10-11.

[76]Michael Billig, *Banal Nationalism* (London: Sage, 1995), 4.

[77]The religious underpinning of nationalism is clear in the early German philosophers of the movement, such as Herder, Fichte, and Hegel. They talked about national "souls" and argued that nations had unique missions to humanity depending on their particular genius. They argued that "individuals are only free when they are absorbed into the will of the organic state, itself an expression of the national soul" (Smith, *Nationalism*, 15).

Social scientists sometimes talk about the "ideal type" of a concept as a way to isolate its abstract, pure form—a set of ideas taken to their logical conclusion. Most American Christians do not hold to the ideal type of Christian nationalism; they are more likely to hold an inconsistent mix of nationalism, conservatism, Christianity, republicanism, libertarianism, and more. But there is virtue in speaking about the ideal type: it helps us recognize the end point or purest expression of an idea. The ideal type of Christian nationalism cannot go together with Christianity: they are separate, rival, mutually exclusive religions. They make fundamentally incommensurable claims on human loyalty. In its ideal type, you can either be a Christian nationalist, or you can be a Christian: you cannot be both. Christians should be patriots, but true patriotism sometimes means rebuking our country for its sin or even working against it when it is working toward its own self-destruction, as Bonhoeffer worked against the Nazi government of his German homeland. Nationalism is a totalistic political religion that is inconsistent with orthodox Christianity, a false religion that places the nation in the place of the church and the leader in place of God. Thomas Hobbes called the state a "mortal god," and White American Christians have been tempted to dream the idolatrous dream of commanding, or being, that god.

In *The City of God*, Augustine, musing on what constitutes peoplehood, at first considers if a commonwealth could be defined as a people bound together by justice. He rejects that view because he would have to conclude that no true regime ever existed as no true justice had ever been achieved. He concluded: "Let us say that a 'people' is an assembled multitude of rational creatures bound together by a common agreement as to the objects of their love."[78] If nations are defined by the common object of their love, nationalism holds up the nation itself as the object of love. It is thus a form of self-love, in which the nation is invited to love itself: nationalism is little more than political onanism, and about as fruitful.

---

[78]Augustine, *The City of God Against the Pagans*, ed. Robert W. Dyson (Cambridge: Cambridge University Press, 1998), 19.23.

7

THE CHRISTIAN RIGHT'S POLITICAL THEORY

IN 1992, PAT BUCHANAN told the Republican National Convention in Houston, Texas, that voters in that year's presidential election were not merely selecting a president. They were taking sides in a conflict over American identity. The election "is about who we are. It is about what we believe, and what we stand for as Americans." The conflict was, in fact, a war. "There is a religious war going on in this country," he said. "It is a cultural war, as critical to the kind of nation we shall be as was the Cold War itself, for this war is for the soul of America." The other side called for "abortion on demand, . . . homosexual rights, discrimination against religious schools, [and] women in combat units," which Buchanan asserted was "not the kind of change we can abide in a nation that we still call God's country." Winning the religious war and protecting America's identity as "God's country" was the responsibility of the American voter and the Republican Party.

Christian nationalism is not only a set of ideas. It is also a social, cultural, and political movement, a movement that overlaps almost entirely with what came to be called the Christian Right. The history of this movement is an important resource for understanding the full meaning of Christian nationalism. The Christian Right is conventionally defined as "a social movement that attempts to mobilize evangelical Protestants and other orthodox Christians into conservative political action,"[1] according to Clyde Wilcox and Carin

---

[1]Clyde Wilcox and Carin Larson, *Onward Christian Soldiers? The Religious Right in American Politics*, 3rd ed. (New York: Routledge, 2006), 6.

Larson, authors of the standard (and commendably evenhanded) scholarly account of the movement. Understood this way, it emerged in the 1970s by advocating against abortion, pornography, and gay rights, in favor of "family values," Christian education, and a belief in America as a Christian nation. As it matured and played a role in Ronald Reagan's election to the presidency in 1980, it increasingly advocated other right-wing causes, including conservative economic theory and a strong national defense. In its self-understanding, the Christian Right "is a *defensive* movement—one designed to protect their moral values and especially their ability to impart those values to their children. . . . For its supporters, the Christian Right is an attempt to restore Judeo-Christian values to a country that is in deep moral decline." The Christian Right is a response to cultural change—specifically, the change in American society away from (White) Christian cultural dominance. "They believe that secular Americans are waging a culture war on religious conservatives, undermining traditional values and religious practices."[2]

Earlier scholars dismissed religious political activism as a function of disordered psychology, of allegedly "authoritarian personalities" who were intolerant of difference and who prized obedience and conformity. They also ascribed Christian political activism to social misfits who struggled from alienation and isolation. Wilcox and Larson generally dismiss these explanations—few scholars take the "authoritarian personality" seriously, and it turns out that Christian activists are generally *more* socially involved in civic associations than their secular counterparts—though I expect scholars will revisit these arguments in the aftermath of the Trump presidency. Regardless, Wilcox and Larson argue that joining "the Christian Right is rational for Christian conservatives as is joining the Sierra Club or National Organization for Women for environmentalists or feminists . . . because these groups articulate their religious, moral, and political sensibilities."[3] Wilcox and Larson are close to the mark, but defining the Christian Right as a social movement geared toward "conservative" political action takes its stated beliefs too much at face value. Insofar as they recognize that Christian conservatives join the Christian Right to advocate for their particularistic group interest and their definition of American identity, they describe a reality—that the Christian Right is a form

---

[2] Wilcox and Larson, *Onward Christian Soldiers*, 12-13, 24.
[3] Wilcox and Larson, *Onward Christian Soldiers*, 131.

of identity politics or tribal nationalism—but mislabel it as conservatism. Conservatism and republicanism are the Christian Right's stated ideology, but only part of their embodied practice. I would amend Wilcox and Larson's definition to say that the Christian Right is "a social movement that attempts to mobilize evangelical Protestants and other orthodox Christians into *both republican and nationalist* political action."

In this chapter, after reviewing some historical context, I argue that the Christian Right contains an uneasy mix of Christian republicanism and Christian nationalism. I show that, on the surface, the Christian Right's articulated ideology is Christian republicanism (with a small *r*), which is a good and defensible political theory. Republicanism stresses that individual civic virtue is necessary to sustain political liberty. But the Christian Right interprets "virtue" in a unique way: it asserts that Christian values are the necessary precondition of individual virtue. Thus, to sustain the American experiment in liberty, citizens must honor Christian values. This political theory is false— even though its component parts (Christianity and republicanism) are separately true. Worse, this political theory is intolerant because in an increasingly pluralistic nation, citizens will not honor Christian values voluntarily, and so Christians must get and use power to do it for them. The Christian Right's agenda, though in principle expansive and concerned with the common good, in practice tends to prioritize Christian power. This is exacerbated by the fact that, for much of American history, republicanism served as the official propaganda of White Christian power, which makes it hard to disentangle the two today.

THE EARLY CHRISTIAN RIGHT

An early version of the Christian Right started to emerge in the early twentieth century. After the Great War and the 1925 Scopes trial and its fallout, fundamentalists—and, more broadly, politically conservative White Protestants— started to recognize their loss of cultural influence amid sweeping changes. New waves of immigrants and rapid urbanization challenged traditional notions of American identity, a concern that started to push some conservative Christians into the arms of the Republican Party, which was more nativist than the Democratic Party and which spearheaded the restrictive 1924 Immigration Act (although regional differences continued to split White Christians deeply).

A booming economy in the 1920s made new forms of leisure and recreation available to a mass audience. Fundamentalists responded by agitating against promiscuity, dancing, boxing, alcohol, atheism, Catholicism, immigration, and some of what they saw in the newest form of entertainment—cinema. "Fundamentalists invested substantial energy in defending what they understood as traditional, God-given gender and racial roles," a stance which made them similar to, not distinct from, most Americans: "In defending exclusionist racial and gender hierarchies, they did not look like religious radicals at all but more like prototypical White Americans."[4]

But fundamentalists inclined to keep fighting faced a lack of opportunity to engage because conservative Protestants had no organization or institution to bring them together, articulate their agenda, or advocate for their concerns—and the Great Depression and subsequent global war occupied much of the nation's energy in the meantime. The Second World War would prove instrumental. During the war, fundamentalists "baptized Christian fundamentalism in the waters of patriotic Americanism," a change from their earlier message that America was under judgment because of its sins, with the result that "for the rest of the century they positioned themselves as the legitimate guardians of the nation."[5] Conservative Christians came together to found the National Association of Evangelicals in 1942 as an association to represent and advocate for "evangelical" interests on the national stage, choosing a word to distance themselves from the fundamentalist label. The act of founding an organization dedicated to their interests was a tacit admission by conservative Protestants that, because of demographic and cultural changes, they had evolved from being the whole of the nation to being a part, from the embodiment of America itself to being one interest group among many. Yet that recognition was never fully embraced: they continued, then and now, to blur the line between their group interest and the common good, to profess universal values while protecting tribal interests.

Around the same time, a new phrase began circulating with which to describe the United States' cultural and religious heritage: "Judeo-Christian," which served both to broaden the scope of cultural inclusivity to encompass Jews and Christians of all denominations, and to harden the boundaries of

---

[4]Matthew Avery Sutton, *American Apocalypse* (Cambridge, MA: Harvard University Press, 2014), 123.
[5]Sutton, *American Apocalypse*, 266.

exclusion against foreign enemies—fascists and communists—and against domestic cultural and religious dissenters.[6] "Being a Protestant, a Catholic, or a Jew is understood as the specific way, and increasingly perhaps the only way, of being an American," Will Herberg wrote in his famous 1955 book *Protestant-Catholic-Jew*. "To be an American today means to be either a Protestant, a Catholic, or a Jew."[7] Conservative Christian activists initially coalesced around broadcasting rights, anticommunism, and anti-Catholicism. They were supported, in part, by wealthy businessmen who opposed Franklin Roosevelt's New Deal and wanted to fund right-wing thinkers who could link their pro-business agenda to a broader moral movement.[8] Broadly, during the war years, "The faithful came to believe that they not only had a monopoly over the proper interpretation of the scriptures but also truly understood the Christian origins of the United States' sacred documents," according to Sutton.[9]

This early version of the Christian Right found its apogee during the Eisenhower administration. At Billy Graham's suggestion, Eisenhower took the oath of office in 1953 on a Bible opened to 2 Chronicles 7:14, a verse that has become a touchstone and epigraph for the entire conservative Christian political movement.[10] Eisenhower "used religious rhetoric more than most other presidents and repeatedly called for spiritual revival,"[11] according to one historian. In 1954, he helped launch the Foundation for Religious Action in the Social and Civic Order, which he hoped would show citizens how to "take the Bible in one hand and the Flag in the other." Eisenhower said in another speech in 1955, "Recognition of the Supreme Being is the first and most basic expression of Americanism. Without God, there could be no American form of government."

The same year the Republican National Convention announced that the president "in every sense of the word is not only the political leader but the

---

[6]Healan K. Gaston, *Imagining Judeo-Christian America: Religion, Secularism, and the Redefinition of Democracy* (Chicago: University of Chicago Press, 2019).

[7]Will Herberg, *Protestant—Catholic—Jew: An Essay in American Religious Sociology* (Chicago: University of Chicago Press, 1983), 40.

[8]Kevin M. Kruse, *One Nation Under God: How Corporate America Invented Christian America* (New York: Basic Books, 2015).

[9]Sutton, *American Apocalypse*, 283.

[10]"Billy Graham Trivia," Billy Graham Evangelistic Association, https://billygraham.org/story/billy-graham-trivia-which-bible-verse-did-he-suggest-to-president-eisenhower-for-his-inaugural-speech/.

[11]Frances Fitzgerald, *The Evangelicals: The Struggle to Shape America* (New York: Simon and Schuster, 2017), 184.

spiritual leader of our times,"[12] a rather overt admission of American Caesaropapism. Eisenhower's Secretary of State, John Foster Dulles, defended America's Cold War strategy with the same appeal in a 1953 speech on "The Power of Moral Forces": "Our forebears felt keenly that this Nation had a mission to perform," which was to "spread their gospel of freedom, their good news, throughout the world."[13] The US government and White Christian churches—including Catholics—cooperated to reinforce one another during the early Cold War to combat the atheist Soviet Union. Congress added "under God" to the pledge of allegiance in 1954 and declared "In God We Trust" the national motto in 1956. The motto first appeared on paper money the following year. The National Prayer Breakfast, an annual gathering of political and religious leaders in Washington, DC, was inaugurated in 1953.

The new mixture of religion and nationalism in the mid-twentieth century and later differed from the Protestant nationalism of the nineteenth century. In the earlier era White Protestants could plausibly claim to embody the nation because of their size and unchallenged position in the major centers of political, social, and economic power. They didn't have to argue for the importance of their voice because it was obvious who was in charge. By the 1950s, White Protestants had to put out an effort to construct a sense of rediscovered religious national identity. The leaders of the emerging evangelical movement "believed that at its origins, the United States had been governed by biblical principles and that their mission was to lead it back to its righteous foundations," according to Sutton.[14] They had to argue—they could no longer assume—that America was a Christian nation. The nation had grown more diverse and political and economic power was slowly becoming more widely distributed. Eisenhower's famous quip—"Our form of government has no sense unless it is founded in a deeply religious faith, and I don't care what it is"—had some truth to it: the foundation of religious nationalism had broadened slightly by the 1950s, having made room for Catholics and Jews as tolerated guests in the Protestant homeland.[15] In the nineteenth century, Americans did not need "In God We Trust" on their paper money or "under

---

[12]Quoted in FitzGerald, *The Evangelicals*, 185.
[13]John Foster Dulles, "The Power of Moral Forces," October 5, 1953, in Department of State Bulletin, US Government Printing Office, Washington, DC, vol. XXIX, no. 745, p. 510.
[14]Sutton, *American Apocalypse*, 315.
[15]Quoted in FitzGerald, *The Evangelicals*, 185.

God" in the pledge because few would have thought to suggest that America should *not* trust God. It was only when the cultural consensus began to fray that the establishment felt the need to create new symbols to reinforce the old framework. In this—the politicization of religious language to buttress specific conceptions of American identity—we see the beginnings of what blossomed into America's never-ending culture war.[16]

The newly constructed religious nationalism of the 1950s served the interests of both church and state. It was a useful tool of psychological warfare against the atheist Soviet Union. By emphasizing a basic, foundational difference between the Christian West and godless communists, the United States helped deepen the stakes of the conflict and reinforce Americans' loyalty to the cause, turning the Cold War into a veritable religious crusade. At the same time, state sponsorship of religious piety benefited the churches. It gave powerful voice to many Christians' sincere, justified concerns about totalitarianism and oppression around the world. (But just because the United States was on the side of justice in the Cold War does not mean the tactic of religious nationalism was justified, nor that every battle in the Cold War was just.) It also updated and reinforced the old Protestant sense that America had a providential destiny to save the world. According to Sutton, in the 1950s, "Many Americans believed that the United States—like ancient Israel—was a particularly religious nation that had been divinely chosen by God to play a major part in his plan for the ongoing redemption of the world."[17] Throughout the Cold War, statesmen from both parties regularly described the United States as the "leader of the free world," uniquely positioned to save civilization from the menace of Soviet tyranny by upholding the values of democracy and capitalism, a perfect melding of Puritan chosenness with American grand strategy. Finally, the apocalyptic threat of the nuclear standoff between the forces of good and the forces of evil helped drive a surge in church attendance and church membership in the postwar era.

THE CONTEMPORARY CHRISTIAN RIGHT

The conservative Christian political coalition of the 1940s and 1950s collapsed because of two events: the election of John F. Kennedy, a Roman Catholic, in

---

[16]As Gaston says, "What we now call the 'culture wars' were already raging in the 1950s," *Imagining Judeo-Christian America*, 7.

[17]Sutton, *American Apocalypse*, 316.

1960; and the civil rights movement, which split White Protestants between segregationists and moderate civil rights advocates. In 1960 conservative Protestants threw their weight behind Vice President Richard Nixon and waged an anti-Catholic campaign, warning the nation against the dangers of entrusting power to someone who, they believed, owed his ultimate loyalty to the Vatican rather than to the United States (much as they had done in 1928 against Democratic presidential nominee Al Smith). They lost, and Kennedy's presidency, much like the Scopes trial, demonstrated their waning influence and, as the nation moved on from overt anti-Catholicism, deprived them of a common cause to rally around.

More consequentially, the civil rights movement split the nascent Christian Right. Some northerners and elite spokesmen, like Billy Graham, endorsed integration, while southern fundamentalists like Jerry Falwell Sr., Bob Jones Jr., John Rice, and Billy Hargis remained stalwart segregationists during the 1960s, joined at the time by evangelicals like W. A. Criswell. According to Daniel Williams, "While evangelicals such as [Billy] Graham took a moderate position on issues of race, giving cautious support to civil rights legislation, southern fundamentalists lambasted the civil rights movement as a communist plot." Southern fundamentalists "saw the movement as an attack on the nation's well-being and a threat to the right of private institutions, including churches, to exclude anyone they wished."[18] Some of the divide was not regional but between elites in large national institutions and local leaders. The Southern Baptist Convention praised the 1954 Supreme Court decision in *Brown v. Board of Education of Topeka* that struck down segregated public schools and endorsed the 1964 Civil Rights Act, but rank-and-file Southern Baptist churchgoers almost certainly supported the South's campaign of "massive resistance" to integration—an important example of how elites diverged from the population they purported to lead, and how the articulated ideology of republicanism diverged from the social practice of nationalism. White southern churches had, after all, been instrumental in sustaining segregation for decades. As one historian summarized, "Grassroots conservatives' opposition to the liberal state's expansion of individual rights (although not property rights), their concern

---

[18]Daniel K. Williams, *God's Own Party: The Making of the Christian Right* (New York: Oxford University Press, 2012), 4, 70, 76.

with growing federal government power, and their defense of custom and tradition (here understood as the traditions of the White majority) combined to create a strong opposition to federal support for civil rights."[19] Because conservative White Protestants were divided on civil rights, their movement fell into disarray and they had no united voice on public issues through much of the 1960s.

Conservative Christians began to regroup in 1968. Over the next decade, the movement underwent a profound transformation that birthed the contemporary Christian Right and modern conservatism. The movement shed its anti-Catholicism and put disagreements over civil rights behind it, while still maintaining a strong emphasis on anticommunism. "The end of the civil rights movement facilitated the formation of a new Christian political coalition, because it enabled fundamentalists and evangelicals who had disagreed over racial integration to come together," according to Williams.[20] In place of those old causes, conservative Christians—increasingly including Catholics—added several issues, including law and order as a response to the race riots and political violence of the late 1960s; chastity, anti-obscenity, sex education, and "family values"[21] in response to the sexual revolution and the feminist and gay rights movements; the quality of public schooling, opposition to desegregation busing, and the freedom to form private Christian schools; and antiabortion activism. The antiabortion movement was strategically critical because, more than any other issue, it finally bridged the divide between Protestants and Catholics (who had argued against abortion long before Protestants did), turning a traditional target of the old Protestant establishment into a major pillar of the new Christian Right.

On the whole, Christian conservatism took shape as backlash by White, suburban, and middle-class voters against the perceived excesses of 1960s progressivism in the name of the "silent majority" or "Middle America." But attributing the rise of the Christian Right and modern conservatism to a backlash does not mean it was unplanned, inarticulate, or leaderless, nor that it was wholly determined by underlying structural forces. The movement

---

[19]Lisa McGirr, *Suburban Warriors: The Origins of the New American Right-Updated Edition* (Princeton, NJ: Princeton University Press, 2015), 182.

[20]Williams, *God's Own Party*, 6.

[21]Seth Dowland, *Family Values and the Rise of the Christian Right* (Philadelphia: University of Pennsylvania Press, 2015).

required leaders to identify, exacerbate, and exploit grievances animating the voter base. That is why race is not absent from the story: race was too potent and too salient an issue not to use in forging a new political coalition, even if racial appeals were more subtly articulated than previously. Some of the private schooling movement was designed, in part, to evade integration,[22] and a high-profile case in which the IRS stripped Bob Jones University of its tax-exempt status because of its discriminatory racial policies was an early mobilizing cause. Richard Nixon's "southern strategy" in the 1968 presidential campaign reflected and capitalized on the mix of cultural concerns, including race, circulating on the right as the Christian Right was being born.[23] Other issues, such as Nixon's calls for "law and order" and Reagan's criticism of "welfare queens"—calls which the Christian Right echoed—had implied racial overtones. As importantly, the alliance between economic conservatism, libertarianism, national security hawkishness, and Christian "family values" changed the political identities of each member in the coalition. Christian activists became, through association, heirs to a range of political positions that were only tangentially related to Christianity.[24]

The difference between the Christian Right of the 1970s and Christian activists of the nineteenth century and the first half of the twentieth century was not that White Christians were asserting a felt duty to define the American nation on their terms; such an effort is a perennial theme in American history. Rather, the difference was that the nation had changed and become less receptive to their efforts. Earlier Christian political movements had been more proactive, forward looking, and optimistic, seeking to harness the active energies of the nation toward an Anglo-Protestant vision of social order; they faced far less meaningful opposition from within and had the wind at their backs. Earlier Christian nation builders were often postmillennialists; they had an optimistic (and naive) belief in their ability to build the kingdom of God on earth. But the erosion of the Anglo-Protestant establishment by the 1960s raised an obvious question: What will fill the void? The fight to craft a new American identity kicked off what we today call the culture war in which the

---

[22]Randall Balmer, "The Real Origins of the Religious Right," *Politico*, May 27, 2014, www.politico .com/magazine/story/2014/05/religious-right-real-origins-107133.

[23]Dan T. Carter, *From George Wallace to Newt Gingrich: Race in the Conservative Counterrevolution, 1963-1994* (Baton Rouge, LA: LSU Press, 1996), chap. 2.

[24]Joseph E. Lowndes, *From the New Deal to the New Right: Race and the Southern Origins of Modern Conservatism* (New Haven, CT: Yale University Press, 2008).

Christian Right arose as the standard bearer for older, more traditional understandings of American identity.

In this light, the Christian Right is best understood as a response to the long-term decline in Anglo-Protestant power that had roots in the nineteenth century, but was dramatized by the radical transformations of the 1960s. The twentieth-century Christian Right was more reactionary than its predecessors, facing a changing and increasingly oppositional culture, and were often premillennialists who believed the world would gradually deteriorate into anarchy and oppression until Jesus' return. By the mid-twentieth century, the nation was more diverse, less Christian, and less biddable to the White Christian agenda. That, in turn, forced conservative White Christians to approach their Christian nation building project differently than in the past: they became more partisan, and their agenda came to include, even prioritize, preserving Christian power and securing symbolic recognition of the nation's Christian heritage. Such an agenda would have been superfluous in previous ages because few could have denied the overwhelming fact of White Christian dominance in American history, culture, and politics. Nineteenth-century White Christians did not need symbols to represent the power no one denied they had. By contrast, many late twentieth-century White Christians felt a gnawing anxiety about their loss of power, as reflected in the nostalgia, defensiveness, and attention to historical symbolism in their movement.

JERRY FALWELL SR.

With this background in mind, we can turn attention now to the Christian Right's articulated agenda, its avowed agenda and theory of political engagement, for which we can use the work of Jerry Falwell Sr. as representative. Falwell has a good claim to being one of the chief founders, spokesmen, and architects of the Christian Right, alongside Pat Robertson, Oral Roberts, James Dobson, and (later) Ralph Reed. Falwell, born in 1933, was the pastor of Thomas Road Baptist Church in Lynchburg, Virginia; founder of Liberty University in 1971; and founder of the Moral Majority in 1979, the most prominent political institution of the Christian Right in the 1980s. Falwell was the author of over twenty books; for our purposes, his 1980 book *Listen, America!* was his political manifesto and his agenda for the new movement.

Falwell articulated a version of civic republicanism, reinterpreted with a Christian or Christianized gloss on some of its core concepts. Civic republicanism is a mix of ideas that emphasize freedom from foreign rule and internal tyranny; the right of citizens to participate in their own government; a mixed constitution and checks and balances to prevent concentrations of power; the priority of the common good over private interests; the rule of law; and the importance of civic virtue to stave off corruption. Early modern republican theorists, and the American founding fathers, drew heavily on classical Greece and Rome, renaissance Italy, and early modern Britain to argue for the superiority of republicanism and the importance of citizens' virtue in sustaining republican freedom.

Falwell similarly argued that Americans' virtue was essential to sustaining American freedom, though he was more explicit and insistent about the religious foundation of virtue. He warned against the "moral decay . . . that is destroying our freedoms" and cautioned that "America can only be turned around as her people make godly, moral choices." He suggested that "how we stand as a free people at the end of this decade [the 1980s] will depend upon the moral decisions we as a people make in the very near future." Americans' moral decisions depend on their religious identity: "It is only as we abide by those laws established by our Creator that He will continue to bless us with these rights," as established in the Constitution. "We are still a free nation because we have the blessing of God upon us."[25]

At this point Falwell's argument is not substantially different, on its face, from older generations of civic republicans who argued that citizens' virtue is essential to sustaining republican freedom. He, like they, argued that a religious culture was the vital pillar of political freedom and, consequently, the government should promote a religious culture. Niccolò Machiavelli had counseled in the sixteenth century, "Princes and republics who wish to maintain themselves free from corruption must above all things preserve the purity of all religious observances, and treat them with proper reverence; for there is no greater indication of the ruin of a country than to see religion condemned."[26] Machiavelli, of course, was more concerned about the show of religion and its role creating social cohesion and an obedient population than

---

[25]Jerry Falwell, *Listen, America!* (New York: Doubleday, 1980), 6-8, 18.
[26]Niccolò Machiavelli, *The Prince and the Discourses*, trans. Luigi Ricci (New York: Random House, 1950), 149.

he was with true heart piety or avoiding the judgment of God. But most of the American founding fathers had similarly declared their beliefs about the importance of religion for public morality and political liberty, probably with more sincerity.

The key difference is that Falwell understands "virtue" differently than had Machiavelli, the founding fathers, or other civic republicans. Virtue, for older republican theorists, meant public spiritedness, informed involvement in the affairs of the city, patriotic loyalty and fellow feeling with other citizens, vigilance against self-dealing by public officials, and a willingness to place the good of the commonwealth ahead of one's individual good. They thought of virtue in an Aristotelian sense as striving for excellence; public or civic virtue as striving for the common good. John F. Kennedy's inaugural exhortation to "ask not what your country can do for you; ask what you can do for your country," perfectly captures a classically republican sentiment. Civic virtue was understood to be formed from many sources. Good republics constantly exposed their citizens to formative, shaping experiences and institutions that taught and reinforced the value of civic duty, patriotism, and public service, including through education, the family, military service, the public traditions and rituals of civil religion, and opportunities to participate in governance.

By contrast, Falwell thinks of virtue in a sectarian, theological way. Virtue, for him, is holiness, or obedience to the Bible. Because Falwell (rightly) believes that the God of the Bible is the exclusive source of morality, he also believes this God has blessed and will bless America as a reward for her obedience. A lack of virtue will bring God's judgment in the form of national decay or calamity. This is the crucial step that opens a pathway between Christian republicanism and Christian nationalism. "I believe that God promoted America to a greatness no other nation has ever enjoyed because her heritage is one of a republic governed by laws predicated on the Bible," he wrote. "Any diligent student of American history finds that our great nation was founded by godly men upon godly principles to be a Christian nation."[27] Falwell describes a cause-and-effect relationship between spirituality and politics: "When a nation's ways please the Lord, that nation is blessed with supernatural help." This is specifically true with regard to political liberty. "God is the author of our liberty, and we will remain free only as long as we

---

[27]Falwell, *Listen, America!*, 15, 25.

remember this and seek to live by God's laws. . . . [The founders] made it clear that they were guided in their thinking, their decisions, and their writings by scriptural teachings."

For Falwell, civic virtue and Christian obedience are synonymous; Christianity is the essential foundation for republican liberty. The founders designed a constitutional system premised on the idea that "these rights were given to us with the condition and the responsibility of acknowledging and obeying Him. Freedom *is* conditional upon precisely that—the acknowledgment of and obedience to the laws of our Creator." In sum, we "are a nation that was founded upon Christian principles, and we have enjoyed a unique relationship toward God because of that foundation." Among the features of American society that Falwell attributes to biblical teaching are the free-enterprise system, the work ethic, private property, competition in business, and "ambitious and successful business management," a striking overlap with the principles of economic conservatism and the Republican Party. Additionally, and most importantly, the principles of the Constitution "are based directly on the Ten Commandments."[28]

Falwell's theory—that biblical obedience causes political liberty—is nonfalsifiable because we can never prove or disprove that any given historical event, like the American founding, was directly caused by divine reward for human religious observance or divine punishment for disobedience. That explains why providential history is so important to the Christian Right: retelling American history as a story of obedience and blessing, and disobedience and fall—telling American history the same way Israel's history is told in 1 and 2 Kings and 1 and 2 Chronicles—is the closest the movement can get to proving its political theory. History is inextricably entwined with political theory because it is the testing ground, the case study, to illustrate the principles of politics at work. If American history is really a complex story with interweaving political, economic, and cultural causes and effects, it challenges the Christian Right's most fundamental political belief that political liberty is the straightforward reward for biblical obedience.

For Falwell, American liberty is in danger because of the loss of Christian virtue. The fundamental problem is sin, understood as individual moral wrongdoing: "Until man realizes that his greatest problem is sin and that this

---

[28]Falwell, *Listen, America!*, 12, 21, 26, 41, 45, 221.

is what has alienated him from God, his Creator, there can be little hope of curing the chaotic conditions in our nation and world." With sin comes national decay: "With our erosion from the historic faith of our fathers, we are seeing an erosion in our stability as a nation." As the nation decays, Falwell worries, so too will our liberties. "If America continues down the path she is traveling, she will one day find that she is no longer a free nation. Our nation's internal problems are direct results of her spiritual condition."[29] America's loss of freedom is seen as God's judgment on America, a straightforward application of the Old Testament's treatment of Israel: obedience leads to blessing and national prosperity, disobedience to punishment and national disgrace.

When civic republicans worried about the loss of virtue, they tended to focus on corruption, by which they meant self-dealing and the subversion of public interests for private gain. Falwell's lists of sins that he worries are eroding American virtue and American democracy have a different emphasis, focusing on the loss of individual self-control, especially sexual self-control. He lists drugs, pornography, abortion, family breakdown, the absence of school prayer, too much television, rock-and-roll, the Equal Rights Amendment, feminism, and the "homosexual revolution." The consequences he frets about include the budget deficit, the size of government, bureaucratic regulations, inflation, welfare, high taxes, foreign aid, communism, and a weak national defense. He concludes the book with a call for national repentance, focusing on five specific sins: abortion, homosexuality, pornography, humanism, and the fractured family, calling for a "moral crusade for righteousness." Among America's sins that might undermine American virtue and American freedom, Falwell—who had supported segregation in the 1950s and 1960s—nowhere mentions racism or inequality.[30]

The connection between Falwell's understanding of virtue and political liberty is—compared to the classical republican understanding of virtue—far from clear. Classical republican virtue was directly concerned with the virtues required for public life, paramount among them being the subordination of self-interest to the common good. Most of Falwell's virtues have only an indirect influence on public life, if that. Pornography is sinful, but Falwell's specific claim is not that it is wrong but that it undermines American democracy.

---

[29]Falwell, *Listen, America!*, 55, 103, 213.
[30]Falwell, *Listen, America!*, 17, 233.

This seems doubtful. Pornography, rock-and-roll, television, and promiscuity have never been more widely prevalent, yet they are hardly the driving cause of inflation, big government, international communism, domestic extremism, or other dangers to American democracy. Such individual vices are, at most, proxy variables that could suggest deeper underlying problems, such as a lack of self-control, faithlessness, and hedonism, which in turn perhaps undermine the habits necessary for democratic citizenship. But Falwell does not make that argument or spell out this causal logic, which seems unnecessarily convoluted in any case. If our concern is with republican virtue, it seems easier to argue for the importance of the rule of law, combating self-dealing, prioritizing the common good, and participating in the public square, none of which are paramount among Falwell's concerns, which seem more focused on promoting Christian sexual ethics than on classical republican concerns. Falwell's concern for family breakdown is more relevant to public life, but overall Falwell's equation of republican virtue with biblical obedience hurts his case and weakens the persuasiveness of the republican argument. (It also amounts to a political prosperity gospel that trivializes holiness, as if the main point of sanctification is to safeguard democracy, not to honor God by emulating his character.)

Regardless, Falwell's solution to these crises is national repentance, religious revival, individual moral virtue, and a return to America's Christian roots. "America must not turn away from the God who established her and who blessed her. It is time for Americans to come back to the faith of our fathers, to the Bible of our fathers, and to the biblical principles that our fathers used as a premise for this nation's establishment." That for Falwell American identity and Christian identity are synonymous is clear in how he addresses his audience: it is time for "Americans" to come back "to the biblical principles" of the American founding. His free mixture of American and Christian terms here is indicative; he might have rightly called Christians to return to biblical principles of the church's founding, or Americans to return to the constitutional principles of the country's founding. But to call *Americans* to return to the *biblical* principles of the *American* founding is a rudimentary category error. On the basis of that error, Falwell believes that to save American freedom the consequences of American sin, citizens must reaffirm America's Christian identity and revive personal morality in their lives. Falwell's policy prescriptions thus focus on two levels: the nation and the individual. Citizens must rediscover God, and the nation must publicly avow its identity as a Christian nation. Falwell has little to say about *institutional* injustices or institutional reform (except for the public school system, the solution to which is a return to school prayer).[31]

Falwell's two main concepts—America's Christian identity and its legacy of political liberties—are inextricably entwined, as they are for all advocates of Christian nationalism. In language strikingly similar to that used by Samuel Huntington, Rich Lowry, and Yoram Hazony, Falwell argues that American religion and American liberty are of a piece: "Our religious heritage and our liberty can never be separated," Falwell wrote. "America is in trouble today because her people are forgetting the origin of their liberty."[32] Because the origin of our liberty is our Christian heritage, Falwell argues that we must sustain that heritage. He laments that schools no longer teach "respect for our nation's heritage," and quotes approvingly Senator Jesse Helms, who argued that the devil tempted "nations [to] disavow their Christian heritage," and that those nations who gave in found themselves "deceived, betrayed, and then destroyed."[33] Falwell's political program bears a superficial resemblance to civic republicanism because of the linkage he draws between virtue and freedom. But, because he defines virtue as Christian obedience, his operative agenda is to protect and revive the nation's Christian heritage, which can only be accomplished by advancing Christian power. The more power Christians have in government, the more they will be able to protect the nation's Christian heritage and inculcate Christian values, thus securing God's blessings and protecting American liberties. Falwell illustrates how the Christian Right's political theory makes use of the language and rhetoric of civic republicanism but is functionally indistinguishable from Christian nationalism.

FIVE OBSERVATIONS ABOUT THE CHRISTIAN RIGHT

The effort to harmonize biblical principles with a republican form of government goes back at least to the eighteenth century, and many of its arguments are persuasive. For example, because Christianity teaches that all humans are equally made in God's image, they should also have equality under law. The Old Testament prophets condemned tyranny and oppression, so Christian republicans advocate for the rule of law, typically under a mixed

[31]Falwell, *Listen, America!*, 43, 213.
[32]Falwell, *Listen, America!*, 25.
[33]Falwell, *Listen, America!*, 24, 179.

constitution that recognizes some form of popular sovereignty. Because Christianity also teaches the sinfulness of humankind, republicans also counsel caution against concentrations of power and for the diffusion of power through branches and levels of government and checks and balances between them. Most of the founders could probably be described as Christian republicans, though the Christian component varied considerably among them. (It is striking, however, that Falwell employs almost none of these arguments in his book.)

Christian republicanism has strong merits as a political theory. It is clear that Christianity has political implications and—notwithstanding John Rawls—Christians should unashamedly and unapologetically advance their religiously grounded political convictions in the public square (which is different from advocating for tribal power or prerogative). As the ethicist David Barr describes it, American evangelicals believe that "virtue . . . makes political freedom sustainable; it allows for self-regulation without government intervention." As such, "many evangelicals see limited government and the political and economic freedom that comes with it as an organic, obvious aspect of their moral and religious values."[34] As political theories go, this is a pretty good starting point, and Christians should continue making this argument in their public lives. To that end, Christian political thinkers could do worse than to reacquaint themselves with the writings of classical republican theory—from Cicero and Machiavelli to the early modern British republicans and the American founding fathers—and reappraise them in light of contemporary political conditions.

But, following Falwell, Christians routinely overestimate the unique importance of Christianity to their republicanism and underappreciate God's common grace. They rightly prioritize the former over the latter in their political thinking, which elides into protecting Christian power at the expense of republican principles: their ideology functionally becomes Christian nationalism more than Christian republicanism.

What accounts for this obvious (to us) contradiction? In this context it is important to recall that the American founders, and generations of Americans before and after, had advocated for Christian republicanism while

---

[34]David Barr, "Evangelical Support for Donald Trump as a Moral Project: Description and Critique," *Religion and Culture Forum*, January 16, 2018, https://voices.uchicago.edu/religionculture/2018/01/16/evangelical-support-for-trump-as-a-moral-project-description-and-critique/.

simultaneously sustaining slavery and segregation and giving voice to centuries of anti-Catholic bigotry. Christian republicanism existed side by side with racial and religious tyranny for most of American history. So, we may well wonder why they bothered professing republicanism at all. What *function* did republicanism play in American political life if its ideals were not taken seriously or implemented consistently? Benjamin Lynerd has insightfully noted that republicanism "furnishes a conceptual framework beyond factional self-interest to defend Christianity as the lodestar of American culture."[35] Christian republicanism gave slave owners, segregationists, and Protestant sectarians a language that sounded fair, disinterested, and morally legitimate. They used the moral legitimacy of republicanism to cloak their racism and sectarianism. Christian republicanism gave unprecedented freedom to White men while also serving as the official propaganda of the White Protestant nation; a cipher for White Christian power. Republican ideals are sound, which is why generations of racists found it useful to exploit it as a prop for their power.

The history of Christian republicanism as the propaganda of White Christian power still lingers in our national understanding. It is extremely difficult to separate the articulated ideology of Christian republicanism—which is admirable on its face—from the embodied social reality of White Christian power and the nationalist movement to preserve it. For most of American history, the ideology of Christian republicanism was little more than the moral fig leaf that White supremacy wore. Until very recently in American history, White Christians were insincere in their republicanism—or, at least, transparently hypocritical—because they talked about liberty while sustaining slavery and segregation. That history means that, when many Americans hear the ideas of Christian republicanism, they still hear those historical echoes, which makes it extremely hard for them to believe that White Christians use republican principles today in good faith.

In light of the history and political theology of the Christian Right, a few things come into clearer focus. First, the Christian Right's effort to define America as a Christian nation and to assert ownership over American identity is not a novel movement. White Protestants have been doing much the same for most of American history. White Protestants have always treated the

---

[35]Benjamin Lynerd, "On Political Theology and Religious Nationalism," *Religion and Culture Forum*, January 26, 2018, https://voices.uchicago.edu/religionculture/2018/01/26/on-political-theology-and-religious-nationalism-a-response/.

political projects of North America as a religious mission, including the Puritans in the colonial settlements, the evangelicals and abolitionists of the Second Great Awakening, and the activists, prohibitionists, and social gospelers of the early progressive era. American nation building has been, from its start, a religious project by Anglo-Protestants who have felt a sense of ownership over America, cultivated a close identification with it and believed its success to be their success and its failures a punishment for their sin. Much (not all) of the just and the unjust, the right and the wrong, the sin and the grace of American life through the mid-twentieth century can be attributed to White Protestants simply because of their sheer numerical dominance.

Second, what we today call the culture war is also not new: it is only the most recent contest to define American nationhood. The meaning of American nationhood has been contested from its beginning. For most of American history the contest took place among White Protestants, pitting John Cotton against Roger Williams and other dissenters; New England Congregationalists against southern Anglicans (later Episcopalians) and both against Baptists; orthodox Protestants against Deists, Quakers, Unitarians, Mormons, and above all Catholics; abolitionists against slavers; northerners against southerners; urban against rural; and fundamentalists against modernists. Americans also disagreed over the nation's racial identity, but even then some White Protestants were typically at the forefront of advocating for non-Whites—along with a few prominent non-Whites, like Frederick Douglass—because their number and prominence in American life meant that they were at the forefront of any influential social movement. America's increasing diversity has continued to elevate non-White and non-Christian voices to new levels of prominence.

Third, the post-1960s culture war redrew battle lines and took on new sharpness as it seemed to pit secular progressives against Christianity (though many Christians continued to identify with the left), a conflict that led to the reconciliation between American Catholics and Protestants and the end of one of the longest running bigotries in American life. The Christian Right is the old wine of White Christian political advocacy in the new cultural wineskin of twentieth- and twenty-first-century America. It is a traditional approach to politics among America's White evangelical ethnoreligious group ("evangelical" in the tribal rather than theological sense) transplanted into a novel environment in which that group no longer has the unquestioned dominance it once had. The different circumstances account for why the Christian Right is more defensive and reactionary than its predecessors, why it has increasingly focused on the preservation of its own power, and why it seems blind to the concerns and critiques of other Americans.

Fourth, changing circumstances also explain a key difference between the Christian Right and its predecessors. American nationalism until the mid-twentieth century was overtly racist and sectarian, advocating for White supremacy and Protestant dominance. The Christian Right's articulated ideology does neither. The change is due in part to a sincere change in heart among some Christian activists who recognize the sins of past generations. It is also because racist and sectarian language no longer reliably wins elections. Instead of race and sect, the Christian Right has adopted the language of culture, heritage, and values. The Christian Right is an effort to reformulate traditional American nationalism without relying on an explicitly racist or sectarian understanding of American identity. Members of the Christian Right disclaim discrimination against non-Whites and non-Christians; define American identity by reference to culture, not race or religion; claim anyone can assimilate to Anglo-Protestant culture; but still insist that that culture should rightfully define America.

That means, fifth, the Christian Right is, partly, a nationalist movement—containing elements of nationalism alongside republicanism—and therefore at least partly illiberal. Like nationalist movements before it, the Christian Right seeks to privilege Anglo-Protestant or Judeo-Christian values, norms, or habits in the public square, and its agenda still has illiberal effects—effects that are not consistent with the classically liberal ideas of democracy and individual rights. Every effort to enforce a specific cultural identity to the nation is illiberal—American history has repeatedly born that out—and we should expect to see the same from the contemporary Christian Right. Importantly, these illiberal effects exist side by side with its republican beliefs and with many beneficial things the Christian Right has accomplished and the just causes it advocates, such as its activism against abortion and in favor of religious liberty. The Christian Right's political activism comes with the same mixture of some noble inspiration and just causes with some unjust, illiberal ones as had characterized past generations' efforts.

The Christian Right, as the current manifestation of Christian nationalism, has illiberal strains within it. Its illiberalism takes a different, subtler form.

Even if we grant that culture can be fully separated from religion or ethnicity (which I grant for the sake of argument, though I doubt such a move is actually as straightforward as nationalists suggest), shifting the principle of exclusion from religion or race before the 1960s to culture afterwards softens but does not eliminate its illiberalism. Cultural nationalism involves the state asserting jurisdiction over the cultural identity of the nation, which necessarily means it will police the culture of the nation, pick sides in cultural disputes, privilege cultural insiders, and disadvantage cultural outsiders. While I acknowledge the theoretical difference between the *cultural* claims of the contemporary nationalism of the Christian Right and the racist and sectarian nature of earlier American nationalism in their respective articulated ideologies, in the next chapter I argue that the two overlap with troubling regularity in their embodied social practice.

CONCLUSION

The Christian Right contains a contradictory mix of Christian republicanism and Christian nationalism. Republicanism and nationalism differ strongly. Nationalism does not use Christianity as the source of principles to support certain political institutions. Nationalism pays less attention overall to the institutional machinery of government and to specific regime type. Rather, Christian nationalism ascribes a Christian identity to the nation and advocates for the defense and promotion of that Christian culture. Christian republicans assume that republicanism is good and worthy of defense; and they arrive at that conclusion because of their Christian principles. But they do not claim their principles are the only ones possible that could ground republicanism. They would point to Greece and Rome as clear examples of non-Christian republics, and Venice and Florence as non-Protestant ones. Christian nationalists, by contrast, routinely claim that Christianity (usually Protestantism) is *the essential precondition* for liberty, and that liberty cannot be sustained without a Christian heritage, which means preserving the Christian heritage is the paramount goal of public policy. The cohabitation of Christian nationalism with Christian republicanism is a kind of ideological fragmentation in which the movement occupies contradictory self-conceptions simultaneously. To the extent that Christian nationalism predominates, the Christian Right is identity politics for tribal evangelicals, a response to the decline of

Anglo-Protestant power, more than a movement of ordered liberty and equal justice for all.

Once we have taken the argument this far—recognizing that the Christian Right includes nationalism in its political agenda—we have to take one step further. Nationalism has a particular history in the United States, a history inextricably entwined with racism and sectarianism. Barr notes that "it is an empirical fact that republican theology, Christian nationalism, and racism often overlap in our society."[36] Past American nationalists believed that their race, their religion, and their politics went together, that they were religiously obligated to define their polity in religious and racial terms and to seek affirmation of and support for their religious goals; and it was precisely these beliefs that led to their worst, most oppressive behavior. If the Christian Right is at least partly the inheritor of the nationalist mantle in the United States, we should expect to see antidemocratic strains show up somewhere in its social and political practice. That is, we should look for echoes of racism and sectarianism in contemporary White Christian practice.

This is where some readers who are sympathetic to the Christian Right may feel defensive because they rightly insist that they do not espouse White supremacy or sectarianism. But because ideology takes some of its meaning from attendant social practice, we have to examine both. In the next chapter, I argue that the embodied cultural movement beneath the ideology—the vast and sprawling collection of churches, advocacy organizations, lobbyists, publishing houses, radio talk shows, musicians, folk art, and the voting base of the Republican Party—shows more nationalism and less republicanism, more concern for restoring Christian power than for shoring up the institutions and norms of republican governance. Christian republicanism is cast in universal terms and could, in principle, be an ideology by and for all people. But White Christianity is culturally particularistic, and White Christians tend to argue for principled, universal values while acting to defend the interests of their tribe. It tends to be blind to its own particularity, and blind as well to the enduring realities of racial inequality in America.

---

[36]Barr, "Evangelical Support."

8

THE CHRISTIAN RIGHT'S ILLIBERALISM

I ARGUED IN CHAPTER FOUR that nationalism is inherently illiberal. Nationalist movements have to construct the nation they imagine and can only do so through compulsion or force in the face of resistance from minorities who do not want to conform to the cultural template put forward by nationalist advocates. Past iterations of American nationalism, including White nationalism and Protestant nationalism, were clearly and explicitly racist and sectarian, and the conflict between them and the tradition of American liberty and equality defined much of American history. If the Christian Right is at least partly a nationalist movement, it is at least partly illiberal, conflicting with the Christian Right's own professed dedication to Christian republicanism. How and where do we see its illiberality?

We are likely to see it most clearly in the movement's embodied practice, its revealed preferences, its priorities and blind spots—and in the unarticulated, implicit presuppositions behind them. In this chapter I want to examine these aspects of the Christian Right. What does the social practice of politically engaged White American Christians suggest about the beliefs that actually animate their social and political choices? I want to describe the embodied movement to highlight the differences between the Christian Right's republican theory and the Christian nationalism evident in the social practice of tribal evangelicalism. I also want to highlight that Christian nationalism is not just an elite project by a small handful of scholars. I want to describe how tribal evangelicals really think, vote, and behave, regardless of what elite and churchgoing evangelicals profess. Christian nationalism is a social, cultural, and political movement embodied in millions of Americans' attitudes, activism, and voting behavior.

JACKSONIAN AMERICA

The first way I want to get at this is by exploring what Walter Russell Mead has called "Jacksonian America," America's predominant subculture, the folk community of the South and Midwest, the heartland of tribal evangelicalism. Mead's characterization of Jacksonian Americans is essentially an ethnography of Anglo-Protestants, or at least a subset of them that live in the American South and West, and his ethnography enables us to see their lived social and cultural practice and their occasionally illiberal habits and leanings. Jacksonians are key to understanding Trump and his relationship to White evangelicals. Trump's rise was not sui generis; he did not invent nationalism or the yearning for Christian power. He exploited a preexisting but neglected reality, one long simmering in a part of America long overlooked by many of its elite institutions.

As Mead wrote when he originally described Jacksonians twenty years ago, "The Jacksonian school represents a deeply embedded, widely spread populist and popular culture of honor, independence, courage, and military pride among the American people."[1] Jacksonians are a little hard to define because they are a people, a culture, and a history more than an ideology or a statement of beliefs. Jacksonianism is "less an intellectual or political movement than it is an expression of the social, cultural, and religious values of a large portion of the American public,"[2] or, put another way, they are a "community of political feeling."[3] The Jacksonian tradition is America's "folk community," rooted in the heritage of the Anglo-Saxon settlers of New England and, more so, the Scotch-Irish settlers of the South and, later, the frontier West. Jacksonian America was shaped by its experience on the frontier: the battle with the wilderness and with Native Americans shaped a people who prized self-reliance, hard work, tribal loyalty, patriotism, a farmer's bond with the land, the warrior's code of honor, and the citizen's skill with weaponry.

---

[1] Walter Russell Mead, *Special Providence: American Foreign Policy and How It Changed the World* (New York: Routledge, 2013), 88.
[2] Mead, *Special Providence*, 226.
[3] Mead, *Special Providence*, 224.

The Jacksonian agenda, as Mead described it, is the platform of Trump's Republican Party. They are "suspicious of untrammeled federal power, skeptical about the prospects for domestic and foreign do-gooding (welfare at home, foreign aid abroad), opposed to federal taxes but obstinately fond of federal programs seen as primarily helping the middle class."[4] At the same time, they are not orthodox conservatives or civic republicans. "Jacksonians believe that the government should do everything in its power to promote the well-being—political, moral, and economic—of the folk community"—that is, they freely practice identity politics for themselves—"*any means* are permissible in the service of this end,"[5] which points toward a tension between Jacksonian nationalism and republicanism, to which "any means" sounds like an invitation to tyranny. And while Jacksonians are fiercely patriotic, they are sometimes loose with the details of the American creed. They are, for example, impatient with some of the complicated and inefficient features of the US Constitution: "They don't need administrative or constitutional safeguards on the will of the majority."[6] And Jacksonians have a rather uncomfortable tendency to "look to a popular hero to restore government to its proper function," according to Mead. "The Jacksonian hero dares to say what the people feel and defies the entrenched elites," Mead wrote, remarkably fifteen years before Trump was elected president.[7]

Jacksonians are also Christians, though Mead does not emphasize it, and "Christian" in this sense needs qualification. Calling Jacksonians Christians does not mean they are churchgoers. Their attitude toward their Christianity is closer to the Old World's attitude: religion is an inherited trait that naturally goes with one's tribal and national loyalties. They are Christians in the sense that they identify with a White Christian ethnoreligious group by default; they are tribal evangelicals, whether or not they also happen to be churchgoing or religious evangelicals. One's theological education or fidelity to a statement of beliefs is incidental; Jacksonian Christianity can be a cultural Christianity of outward conformity as much as a heartfelt faith or belief in the historic doctrines of the church. (Roger Williams quipped in the seventeenth century that the "Christian world" would "swallow up Christianity," a warning that

---

[4]Mead, *Special Providence*, 224.
[5]Mead, *Special Providence*, 238, emphasis added.
[6]Mead, *Special Providence*, 238.
[7]Mead, *Special Providence*, 239.

Christian culture could grow to become opposed to actual Christianity.) To be an American in the Jacksonian heartland simply means to be a Christian.

And Jacksonian Christianity comes with a sense of entitlement to own and define the American brand; they are nationalists who believe that their culture should define the nation. Historian Darren Dochuk, in documenting the migration of White southerners to the rest of the Sunbelt in the early and mid-twentieth century, describes how their politics "came wrapped in a package of Christian, plain-folk Americanism, an all-encompassing worldview that gave White southerners especially a sense of guardianship over their society."[8] Dochuk argues that the southern migration caused a "southernization" of American conservatism and, I would add, American Christianity. When the Christian Right emerged in the 1970s promising a return of Christian power, Jacksonians were its voting base. Today, Jacksonian America is what we call Middle America, or red-state America, the prevailing culture of the South and most of the inland West, and they are the political base of American nationalism.

Jacksonianism was, historically, racist. Calling this a movement of "Whites" is not entirely accurate, as Jacksonians in the nineteenth century worked hard to exclude other Whites, including Germans, Irish, Italians, Catholics, and European Jews. It was originally a movement of Protestant Britons who directed their ire at other Europeans as much as any other group. Indeed, Jacksonians' exclusionary tribalism was one of America's besetting sins. "Through most of American history the Jacksonian community was one from which many Americans were automatically and absolutely excluded: Indians, Mexicans, Asians, African Americans, obvious sexual deviants, and recent immigrants of non-Protestant heritage have all felt the sting."[9] Rogers Smith gets at something similar when he argues that a provincial or exclusionary understanding of American identity is not an aberration but a major contributing strand to American history.[10]

In other words, there is nothing new about a populist movement of working-class Whites reasserting native-born American identity and

[8]Darren Dochuk, *From Bible Belt to Sunbelt: Plain-Folk Religion, Grassroots Politics, and the Rise of Evangelical Conservatism* (New York: Norton, 2010), xx.

[9]Mead, *Special Providence*, 236.

[10]Rogers M. Smith, *Civic Ideals: Conflicting Visions of Citizenship in US History* (New Haven, CT: Yale University Press, 1997).

advocating a return to traditional Christian values over against immigrants, non-Whites, and non-Protestants. Such a movement constitutes one of the major strands in American political culture. The American Party of the 1850s (the "Know-Nothing" Party) was an anti-immigrant nativist movement founded on fears that hordes of Irish and German Catholic immigrants imperiled America's Protestant heritage. The Ku Klux Klan was founded to combat the enfranchisement of African Americans and, in its twentieth-century incarnation, Catholics. Congress passed the Chinese Exclusion Act in 1882, and the Immigration Act of 1924 severely restricted immigration into the United States globally, especially from Africa and Asia. Waves of anti-German and anti-Japanese sentiment swept the United States during the World Wars. Senator Strom Thurmond ran for president in 1948 on a segregationist platform, and George Wallace did the same in 1968. Wallace's party, the American Independent Party, is still around and nominated Donald Trump as their party's nominee in 2016. We like to say that racism is un-American. While it is clearly inconsistent with American ideals, racism is all too consonant with American history.

That does not mean Jacksonian nationalism is still racist today in the same way as it was in the nineteenth century. American history has also shown that Jacksonians can adapt and expand the boundaries of their clan. This is the crucial distinction that has enabled Jacksonians to moderate their tribal instincts, shed much of their racism, and harmonize with the American creed of universal equality. While Jacksonianism is historically rooted in British Protestantism, over the course of the twentieth century it made peace with German, Italian, and Irish Catholics; Jews; and Mormons. Since the civil rights movement, it has expanded even further to include ethnic and religious minorities it deems to be hard working and honorable. Jacksonian tribalism is *culturalist*: they discriminate, fundamentally, on the basis of culture. Jacksonian exclusivism is neither more nor less than tribal loyalty, the universal human instinct to stick with insiders and treat outsiders with suspicion until they prove themselves.

If you are wondering whether I am defending or accusing Jacksonian America, I am doing both. Jacksonians have often been guilty of tribalism and racism, but consider the historical alternatives. Jacksonian tribalism is not the "scientific" racism of eighteenth-century slaveholders, nineteenth-century social Darwinists, or early twentieth-century progressive eugenicists, for whom non-Whites were predestined by God or their DNA to inferiority. Racism in America has come in many forms, most of them much harder edged and worse than Jacksonian tribalism. Jacksonians have often been willing to give outsiders a chance to prove themselves; they admit, in principle, that outsiders can be let in. There isn't anything, biologically or theologically, that makes it impossible for someone to adopt the Jacksonian code and become part of the tribe, or at least a respected ally. The boundaries are permeable. "As folk cultures go, Jacksonian America is actually open and liberal," in Mead's estimation.[11]

But one enduring problem with Jacksonian nationalism is its amnesia about its own past; its insensitivity to how it sounds to outsiders; its tendency to identify the nation with its largest demographic group; its tendency to blame inequality entirely on personal failings to the exclusion of systemic or structural factors; and the potential for it to lapse back into old habits of equating culture with color. Jacksonians still have a knee-jerk habit of defining American nationality as the folk community of White Protestants. Jacksonians like to affect the mien of being "real Americans," implying that others—coastal professionals, non-Whites, naturalized immigrants, and non-Christians—are fake, second-class, or temporary Americans. That very posture is ironically *un-American* in its refusal to recognize true equality among all Americans. And Jacksonians often show little awareness of, or contrition for, America's historical sins. They seem to believe that love of country means overlooking past wrongdoings, that focusing on the sins of the past is somehow unpatriotic. Jacksonians are right that values and culture matter, but they sometimes seem to believe that the values that matter are the Jacksonian code of honor rather than the tenets of the American creed. The two overlap, but not perfectly. At its worst, Jacksonian America still occasionally uses color as a proxy for culture and looks on ethnic minorities with suspicion, as if they are presumptively suspect until proven truly American. Those who feel no discomfort with an almost homogeneously White political movement centered around American nationalism are, on the best possible reading, historically ignorant and willfully insensitive about the racist legacy of such movements in the United States.

The clearest manifestation of the problems with Jacksonian culture is its fondness for Confederate symbols. Today, there are over seventeen hundred

---

[11]Mead, *Special Providence*, 260.

Confederate statues, and memorials, and place names in the United States, almost entirely in the South and Midwest, according to the Southern Poverty Law Center, most built or named either in the 1890s, at the height of Jim Crow, or the 1960s, in defiance of the civil rights movement and government-mandated integration. These symbols are clear evidence of Jacksonians' insensitivity to historical sins and insistent pride in "heritage," regardless of its effects on others and regardless of the *content* of that heritage. To the rest of America, nostalgia for Confederate symbolism is baffling and offensive, amounting to little more than romantic depictions of traitors and slavers who nearly destroyed America, killed more Americans than the Nazis, Soviets, and al-Qaeda combined, and did it all in the service of a repugnant ideology of human servitude. Jemar Tisby is right that such monuments have "inscribed White supremacy into the landscape of public spaces."[12] There is a reason why the national outcry following the Charleston massacre of 2015, the Charlottesville rally of 2017, and the murder of George Floyd in 2020 all resulted in attacks on Confederate symbols. Americans instinctively understood that one way to respond to the injustice of anti-Black terrorism and police brutality was to reassert control over the nation's symbolism, to strip it of symbols that represented its racist past, and to demand symbols that can represent, inspire, and unify all Americans. The Southern Baptist Convention rightly passed a resolution in 2016 calling on Christians to discontinue the display of the Confederate flag. I would go further: the only place a statue of Robert E. Lee or Jefferson Davis should be found is a museum, a battlefield, a cemetery—or a junkyard.

CHRISTIAN NATIONALISM IN 2020

Another way to describe the social practice of American evangelicals is through the work of two American sociologists, Andrew Whitehead and Samuel Perry, who drew on years of polling data to draw a picture of Americans' attitudes and feelings toward our country with specific attention to how Americans' religious and civic identities mix. Their work is helpful because it illustrates Christian nationalism as a popular phenomenon, a collection of interlocking attitudes, and a lived experience, one with clear antidemocratic tendencies.

---

[12]Jemar Tisby, *The Color of Compromise: The Truth About the American Church's Complicity in Racism* (Grand Rapids, MI: Zondervan, 2019), 116.

They argue that Christian nationalism is an identifiable and distinct set of beliefs that offers more predictive clarity about Americans' political and cultural attitudes than other categories, such as "conservative" or "liberal." In their words, "Christian nationalism is a cultural framework—a collection of myths, traditions, symbols, narratives, and value systems—that idealizes and advocates a fusion of Christianity with American civic life."[13] As they describe it:

> Data from the 2017 Baylor Religion Survey (BRS) shows that 29 percent of Americans agree that "the federal government should declare the United States a Christian nation." . . . In addition, in the same survey 42 percent of Americans agreed that "the success of the United States is a part of God's plan." Using slightly older data from 2013, almost two-thirds of Americans either mostly or completely agreed with the statement, "God has granted America a special role in human history."[14]

These beliefs track closely with the articulated ideology of Christian nationalism I presented in chapter three, not with the ideas of Christian republicanism. The Christian nationalist worldview "blurs distinctions between Christian identity and American identity, viewing the two as closely related and seeking to enhance and preserve their union."[15] Put another way, "the American Christian nation narrative is potent because it enlists traditions and symbolism from Christianity and intertwines them with the United States' national story. Narratives and origin stories are vital aspects of cultural frameworks—telling us about where we come from, where we should be going, and how we should get there."[16] Christian nationalists "wish to institutionalize conservative 'Christian' cultural preferences in America's policies and self-identity"[17] and "want Christianity to be privileged in the public sphere and reflected in the national identity, sacred symbols, and public policies of the United States."[18]

Whitehead and Perry categorize Americans into four groups based on their attitude toward Christian nationalism: ambassadors, accommodators, resisters, and rejectors, highlighting that nationalism exists along a sliding scale

---

[13] Andrew L. Whitehead and Samuel L. Perry, *Taking America Back for God: Christian Nationalism in the United States* (New York: Oxford University Press, 2020), 10.

[14] Whitehead and Perry, *Taking America Back*, 6.

[15] Whitehead and Perry, *Taking America Back*, 15.

[16] Whitehead and Perry, *Taking America Back*, 17.

[17] Whitehead and Perry, *Taking America Back*, 153.

[18] Whitehead and Perry, *Taking America Back*, 114.

of intensity. They estimate about 52 percent of Americans qualify as ambassadors or accommodators, falling somewhere along a spectrum from cautiously accepting to enthusiastically supporting the Christian nationalist worldview, including 77 percent of self-identified evangelical Protestants, 52 percent of mainline Protestants, and 55 percent of Catholics. These numbers are almost certainly an overestimate, but they are suggestive of the wide reach that nationalism has within Christian circles.[19] The most ardent supporters believe "that America has been and should always be distinctively 'Christian' . . . in its self-identity, interpretations of its own history, sacred symbols, cherished values, and public policies—and it aims to keep it that way."[20] Ambassadors "tie our prosperity as a nation to our heritage of obedience to God's commandments as laid out in the Christian Scriptures," believe that "the United States has a special relationship with God," and that "the federal government should formally declare the United States a Christian nation and advocate for Christian values." Ambassadors tend to be older, Whiter, more southern, more rural, and less educated than the national average. As I argued earlier, sometimes Christian nationalism is most evident not in its political agenda, but in the sort of attitude: an unstated presumption that Christians are entitled to primacy of place in the public square because they see themselves as the true heirs of the American past, that Christians have a presumptive right to define the meaning of the American experiment, or that Christians deserve recognition as America's architects, first citizens, and guardians.

In one of their most important findings, Whitehead and Perry argue that Christian nationalism is different from Christianity. Christianity is a set of beliefs about ultimate things—most importantly, about the life, death, and resurrection of Jesus Christ. Christian nationalism is a political ideology about American identity. The two things overlap insofar as Christian nationalists invoke Christian rhetoric to justify their political views. But, according to

---

[19]Whitehead and Perry's numbers overestimate the prevalence of Christian nationalism. One of the questions they use to measure it is whether someone agrees that "The federal government should advocate Christian values." That question is ambiguous and could be interpreted in non-nationalist ways. I've argued that the government should not be morally neutral and that Christians should seek justice and the common good, which are Christian values—but that is not a nationalist argument. Nonetheless, we can view their numbers as indicative of a broad trend, even if their numbers are high.

[20]Whitehead and Perry, *Taking America Back*, 15.

Whitehead and Perry, "Christian nationalism often influences Americans' opinions and behaviors in the exact opposite direction than traditional religious commitment does." For example,

> Being an evangelical [religiously understood] does not lead one to enthusiastically support border walls with Mexico; favoring Christian nationalism does. Being an evangelical does not seem to sour Americans' attitudes toward stronger gun control legislation; endorsing Christian nationalism does. Being an evangelical was not an important predictor of which Americans voted for Donald Trump in 2016; supporting Christian nationalism was.[21]

Similarly, Whitehead and Perry describe Christian nationalists as keen to define and defend group boundaries. But the two sociologists found that "personal religiosity, unlike Christian nationalism, seems to have a softening effect when it comes to the policing of group boundaries."[22] Traditional religious believers who reject nationalist views of America are more comfortable with permeable group boundaries, with the mixing and blurring of different groups. Similarly, "Americans who are more religious," but who do not identify as nationalists, "are actually less likely to vote for Trump [in 2016], less likely to ostracize immigrants, less likely to espouse anti-black prejudice or fear Muslims."[23]

Whitehead and Perry found evidence of illiberal views associated with Christian nationalism in the polling data. They found that Christian nationalists are more likely to believe immigrants increase crime (they don't) and undermine American culture. They tend to believe that it is important to have been born in the United States and to have American ancestry to be accounted fully American, rejecting naturalized citizens and recent immigrants as coequal citizens. They are the most likely to admit they would feel uncomfortable if their daughter married an African American, to believe that the police treat Blacks and Whites equally, and to blame police shootings of African Americans on the victim rather than the police. They are most likely to perceive Muslims and atheists as a threat. The strongest supporters of Christian nationalism support prayer in schools and the display of religious symbols in public life and believe that being a Christian is important

---

[21]Whitehead and Perry, *Taking America Back*, 20.
[22]Whitehead and Perry, *Taking America Back*, 115.
[23]Whitehead and Perry, *Taking America Back*, 143.

to being truly American. None of these beliefs have any logical connection to Christianity or to Christian republicanism, and many of them are directly opposed to it.

Whitehead and Perry are careful to acknowledge that "Christian nationalism is not just repackaged ethnocentrism, racial resentment, or authoritarianism."[24] Nonetheless, the movement has some troubling attitudes toward race and identity. The two sociologists concluded that "Christian nationalism intensifies in-group bias to see white Americans as good, decent, and law-abiding, and black Americans as probably deserving whatever force the police felt compelled to use."[25] One of the reasons this is so is that "the flipside of thinking Christian beliefs, values, and institutions should be privileged is perceiving that other religious systems or groups pose a potential threat to those things."[26] If "we" are the good guys, then "they" are not, however defined, which is why Christian nationalists support immigration restrictions to protect American national identity. Most immigrants to the United States in recent years are non-White Christians, suggesting they pose no threat to American Christianity—which raises the question about which identity Christian nationalists are trying to protect. Whitehead and Perry conclude the worst:

> Christian nationalism gives divine sanction to ethnocentrism and nativism. Recall that prominent Ambassadors rationalized stronger borders on the grounds that God himself uses walls to protect and preserve his people . . . it is likely that biblical justifications are simply masking ethno-racial understandings of "us" and "them." In effect, Christian nationalism lets them neutralize disputed assumptions about American identity and who belongs by cloaking their views in religious symbolism.[27]

Whitehead and Perry overstate their conclusions. They seem intent on ascribing bad motives to Christian nationalists, which may be true for some, but others are likely prey to motivated reasoning, groupthink, and confirmation bias. Christian nationalists intuitively "know" what kind of society is right and what is wrong, and it is easy to cherry-pick evidence, selectively remember the past, and explain away aberrations to avoid cognitive dissonance. There is

---

[24]Whitehead and Perry, *Taking America Back*, 20.
[25]Whitehead and Perry, *Taking America Back*, 33.
[26]Whitehead and Perry, *Taking America Back*, 109.
[27]Whitehead and Perry, *Taking America Back*, 98.

nothing unique about Christian nationalists doing so; indeed, it would be surprising if they somehow avoided such common errors. Regardless, Whitehead and Perry are nonetheless correct that Christian nationalism "allows those who embrace it to express a racialized identity without resorting to racialized terms,"[28] and Christian nationalism is illiberal toward ethnic and religious minorities.

Christian nationalism unconsciously or subconsciously replicates many of the same racial outcomes that White nationalism had intentionally established (such as generational inequality and unequal access to education and employment), without invoking racist reasoning or racist rhetoric. "Christian nationalism has provided the unifying myths, traditions, narratives, and value systems that have historically been deployed to preserve the interests of those who wish to halt or turn back changes occurring within American society," Whitehead and Perry argue.[29] Christian nationalism is reactionary, an instinctive or habitual opposition to social and cultural change. At its worst,

> Christian nationalism idealizes a mythic society in which real Americans— White, native- born, mostly Protestants—maintain control over access to society's social, cultural, and political institutions, and "others" remain in their proper place. It therefore seeks strong boundaries to separate "us" from "them," preserving privilege for its rightful recipients while equating racial and religious outsiders with criminality, violence, and inferiority.[30]

This is a typical response seen across the world by declining demographic groups facing the reality of their loss of power and influence. They seek to use the vestiges of their power to entrench their position and prevent further decline, typically at the expense of other groups. But saying that some White Christians are acting in a way typical of other social groups is not an excuse or justification; it is an accusation. Some White American Christians are acting like a typical ethnoreligious sect that fears its decline and seeks its own perks and privileges, not the common good. "This is Christian nationalism— Christianity co-opted in the service of ethno-national power and separation,"[31] they write. "Christian nationalism is, therefore, ultimately about privilege. It

---

[28]Whitehead and Perry, *Taking America Back*, 16.
[29]Whitehead and Perry, *Taking America Back*, 151.
[30]Whitehead and Perry, *Taking America Back*, 118-19.
[31]Whitehead and Perry, *Taking America Back*, 145.

co-opts Christian language and iconography in order to cloak particular political or social ends in moral and religious symbolism."[32]

FOUR MANIFESTATIONS OF ILLIBERALISM

In recent decades the Christian Right has an admirable record of opposition to abortion, support for school choice and private education, and support for religious liberty, drawn from its republican ideology. But alongside or underneath its avowed republicanism, the Christian Right has also embraced nationalism as part of its functional political theory. The Christian Right insists that America is, was, and should continue to be a "Christian nation." Whether one agrees with that statement is probably the best single determinant of Americans' tribal affiliation. Christian nationalists' understanding of America's Christian identity may seem like so many performative or symbolic gestures that are ultimately of little consequence. But they are not. There are at least four ways in which the Christian Right's nationalism and its demand to recognize America as a "Christian nation" is illiberal and contradicts its avowed Christian republican beliefs—and we should recognize these downsides even despite the many good things the Christian Right has advocated.

First, symbols, rhetoric, and words matter. Words are both the primary tool and substance we work with in constructing our social reality. Recall again Clifford Geertz's definition of culture as "a system of inherited conceptions expressed in symbolic forms by means of which men communicate, perpetuate, and develop their knowledge about and attitudes toward life." If so, words are the substrate, the fundament, the marrow of culture. "Man is an animal suspended in webs of significance he himself has spun," Geertz said. We spin those webs with words. In the first chapter of the Bible, we read that God *spoke* the universe into being. In a very real sense, we follow suit. Words create the social and cultural world we inhabit. The whole idea of an "American experiment" depends on there being words about liberty and equality that we collectively strive to bring to life. This is a nation that was founded by a declaration before it was brought into being by a war. Words incept ideas and interpret behavior.

When we say that America is a Christian nation, we are employing words to construct a national identity that erases the non-Christian (and often,

---

[32]Whitehead and Perry, *Taking America Back*, 153.

implicitly, the non-White) component of our history and our identity—which is a profoundly uncharitable, unloving, even unchristian thing to do, besides being inconsistent with a republican commitment to the equality of all citizens. When nationalists argue that America is a Christian nation, they are implicitly asserting that there is a hierarchy of Americans and that Christians are on top. They are saying that being a Christian is a privileged worldly status, which is theologically false, and they are arguing that Muslims, Buddhists, Hindus, and Sikhs (most of whom are non-White), as well as Jews, atheists, and agnostics are not true or real Americans, or at least are not as truly American as their Christian counterparts. At some points in American history, Christian nationalists have been quite explicit on this point, as when a group of ministers proposed a "Christian amendment" to the US Constitution during the Civil War. The amendment did not propose to turn the United States into a theocracy, but its proponents "did want to give Christianity a privileged place in America,"[33] by proclaiming America to be a Christian nation. Their effort failed because other Americans rightly felt that such an amendment would have contradicted other provisions of the Constitution that explicitly forbade the establishment of a state religion, guaranteed the right of religious worship to all, and banned religious tests for public office.

America has been shaped by many atheists, agnostics, and Deists, including Thomas Jefferson, Benjamin Franklin, Mark Twain, Ernest Hemingway, Robert Frost, Frank Lloyd Wright, William Howard Taft, Thomas Edison, Walt Whitman, Joyce Carol Oates, Camille Paglia, Edgar Allen Poe, Thomas Paine, and James Watson. It would be strange to argue that Mark Twain, author of some of the quintessential American novels, was somehow less than fully American because of his heterodox religious beliefs. The same could be said of the contributions of Jewish Americans, including Albert Einstein, Supreme Court Justice Louis Brandeis, literary critic Harold Bloom, political scientist Seymour Martin Lipset, cartoonist Bob Kane (inventor of Batman), US senators Joe Lieberman and Barry Goldwater, historian Barbara Tuchman, nuclear physicist Robert Oppenheimer, biochemist Gertrude Elion, philosopher Hannah Arendt, and a host of others too numerous to list.

[33]John Fea, *Was America Founded as a Christian Nation? Revised Edition: A Historical Introduction* (Louisville, KY: Westminster John Knox, 2016), 24.

The second way we see the illiberality of the Christian Right is how it sometimes calls for the reestablishment of some features of the old Protestant dominance. Some conservative Christians still lobby for the reintroduction of prayer in schools as part of their broader agenda, though the pro-life movement has overtaken those concerns in urgency. A school prayer amendment gained serious momentum in the 1960s, and again in the early 1980s when Reagan gave it his support. In January 2020, President Trump promised to "safeguard students' and teachers' First Amendment rights to pray in our schools"[34] while campaigning at an evangelical megachurch. Few take these policy proposals seriously in part because Christians concerned about public education have turned in droves to private schooling and home schooling. But Trump's use of school prayer as an election-year, culture-wedge issue in 2020 worked because the issue, even if it is widely recognized to be unrealistic, plays powerfully on evangelical nostalgia for the old Protestant establishment. Christians probably complain about school prayer as a culture war battle cry, using it to dramatize otherwise legitimate concerns about religious freedom in the twenty-first century.

Christian republicanism would celebrate the achievement of true religious freedom for all, including for non-Christians, and true disestablishment, even of Christian churches. Christians are right to worry about some of the legal developments of recent decades and about the deterioration of public schooling. But the solution is not to resurrect the old Protestant establishment. When Christians make our focus the restoration of Christian cultural power, when we evince nostalgia for the old establishment, we send a clear signal that our true priority is preserving tribal privileges or getting a legal carve-out for our preferences, not achieving equal justice for all. Rather, Christians should join with Americans across the political spectrum of any faith in fighting to preserve religious liberty, disestablishment, and the rights of conscience— following the example of Roger Williams, not the Puritans; of the First Amendment, not the Protestant schools; of the Catholics and other dissidents who fought for American liberties, not the Protestants who tried to deny them.

Third, the Christian Right is illiberal in how it teaches history. There is a thriving and continuous cottage industry among Christian nationalists and

---

[34]Seung Min Kim and Sarah Pulliam Bailey, "Trump Courts Latinos," *The Washington Post,* January 3, 2020.

Christian historians to prove, theologically or historically, that America is a Christian nation, that the founders were Christians, that they were motivated predominantly by Christian principles, that America's providential destiny is proven by how God has uniquely blessed the United States, or that the United States is somehow commissioned to carry out a special purpose on earth.[35] The Christian nationalist narrative tends to portray an inspired founding moment followed by a decline and fall as America turned away from its Christian heritage. The best that can be said of this literature is that it tends to tell a highly selective, overdetermined, providential just-so story, and it has rightly prompted a range of responses from more intellectually rigorous Christian historians.[36] While most of the founders were professing Christians, and while Christian principles certainly played a role in the American founding, that is different from asserting that America is therefore a "Christian nation," bound to respect and replicate its Christian heritage as a matter of public policy. A Christian republican understanding of American history would at least recognize the undemocratic elements of the founding and see subsequent history not as a straightforward decline and fall, but partly as a gradual story of progress as republican ideals were more fully realized over time.

RACIAL INEQUALITY

The fourth way in which the Christian Right shows illiberal tendencies is how it thinks about and relates to race, racial identity, and the history of racism in America. White evangelicals tend to have a blind spot for the realities of inherited, intergenerational racial inequality; they do not see the problem or prioritize its solution; or they blame the problem, and therefore assign the solution, exclusively to individuals. White evangelicals' passivity toward racial inequality means that they accept its continuation and replication into the future as an accepted feature of American life. There is no tension, apparently, between their vision of America as a Christian nation, which most White evangelicals share, and the ongoing realities of racial inequality, which they

---

[35]See, for example, the works of David Barton: *America's Godly Heritage, Setting the Record Straight, Separation of Church and State*, and others. See also Peter Marshall, *Sounding Forth the Trumpet, The Light and the Glory, and From Sea to Shining Sea.*

[36]John Fea, *Was America Founded as a Christian Nation? A Historical Introduction*, rev. ed. (Louisville, KY: Westminster John Knox Press, 2016); Mark David Hall, *Did America Have a Christian Founding?* (Nashville, TN: Nelson, 2019); John D. Wilsey, *One Nation Under God? An Evangelical Critique of Christian America* (Eugene, OR: Wipf and Stock, 2011).

tend not to see. By contrast, Christian republicanism would recognize racial inequality as a major injustice deserving time, attention, and effort.

This is a fraught subject; one distinction that will help is between different uses of the word *racism*. Sociologist Michael Emerson has helped to clarify various meanings of the word. Most White people define racism as individual personal animus and the legal enforcement of racial hierarchy or official persecution of people on the basis of their skin color. Because this kind of racism has dramatically decreased since the 1960s, most Whites believe that racism is no longer a serious problem, and they might dismiss the talk about how the history of racial inequality matters today. But Emerson points out that despite these changes, the United States is still a highly racialized society: that is, a society in which a person's race or ethnicity plays a large role in determining that person's life experiences, opportunities, and outcomes. That is indisputably true: on average Hispanics and African Americans have narrower opportunities and worse life outcomes than Whites (and Asian Americans), including worse living conditions, family structures, schools, educational outcomes, access to nutrition, health, access to higher education, job opportunities, lifetime earnings, life expectancy, and more.

Whites overwhelmingly believe that persistent racial disparities are due primarily, even exclusively, to individual choices, merit, and hard work, and to cultural qualities, such as habits of lawfulness, long-term planning, and personal investment in education. Emerson argues that racial disparity also results from other phenomena, which he calls other kinds of racism, specifically, ones that "(1) are increasingly covert, (2) are embedded in normal operations of institutions, (3) avoid direct racial terminology, and (4) are invisible to most Whites."[37] Glenn Loury, an economist, has sensibly argued that individual choice, cultural mores, and structural features all play a role in creating and perpetuating racial inequalities. Yet Loury argues that the fact that individuals and cultural emphases play a role in inequality does not undermine the case for structural problems and therefore structural solutions. "It seems morally superficial in the extreme to argue, as many conservatives do, that 'those people should just get their acts together,'" he argues. "Their culture may be implicated in their difficulties, but so is our culture complicit in their

---

[37]Michael O. Emerson and Christian Smith, *Divided by Faith: Evangelical Religion and the Problem of Race in America* (New York: Oxford University Press, 2001), 9.

troubles; we bear collective responsibility for the form and texture of our social relations."[38]

For example, the American system of funding public schools from local property taxes ensures that most White neighborhoods fund excellent schools for their White children, while Black neighborhoods, which are disproportionately poorer, have predictably inferior public schools. Black children thus grow up with inferior education and fewer subsequent life opportunities in ways attributable neither to individual merit nor individual bigotry. Black children cannot close the gap with White children simply by working hard to get ahead or pulling themselves up by their bootstraps: their individual merit is not the determining factor, nor is African American culture. If White and Black children strive equally hard, White children are likely to achieve more because they have more support, smaller classroom sizes, better technology, more enriching extracurricular activities, more dedicated programs for the talented and gifted, and so forth. Black children get less reward for the same amount of effort: in economic terms, White children have a larger marginal benefit for each hour of time invested in their education. Black children would have to work harder than White children *just to keep up*, let alone close the gap.

And this unequal system has come about not because of today's White parents' personal animus or secret Machiavellian design to keep Black children down (though that may have been the case in some localities when the public-school funding system was originally designed). It results simply from inherited inequality perpetuated across the generations by institutions following their procedures. The reality that African Americans (and others) have to expend more effort for less reward and still face unequal life outcomes is what scholars mean when they speak of "systemic" or "structural" racism. No individual White parent has to be personally bigoted for the system to continue producing unequal outcomes along racial lines. All they have to do is want the best for their children and think that other parents' problems and broader social ills are not theirs to solve. The social system itself, the structure of American society, reinforces and replicates racial inequality on bureaucratic autopilot—an autopilot that Whites have no incentive to change and often do

---

[38]Glenn C. Loury, "Why Does Racial Inequality Persist? Culture, Causation, and Responsibility," *The Manhattan Institute* (May 2019): 15, https://media4.manhattan-institute.org/sites/default /files/R-0519-GL.pdf.

not even notice. In fact, Whites have no incentive to notice because if they noticed, they would likely recognize that their children's relative privilege is not due solely to merit. White Americans may dislike calling this "systemic racism" and may prefer a different term, such as *institutional inequity*, or *inherited inequality*, or *racially unequal outcomes*. Regardless of the label, the underlying reality is true.[39]

Many White Christians are unwittingly complicit in this kind of inherited, transgenerational racial inequality because of some features intrinsic to how we think about the world. Emerson lists three features of what he calls the "White evangelical toolkit" that he argues contribute to our blindness to racial inequality: "accountable freewill individualism," "relationalism," and "anti-structuralism." (Emerson is best understood as analyzing "White evangelicalism" as a cultural practice and way of viewing the world, not as a theological category.) White evangelicals tend to believe that we are all individual moral actors fully accountable for our freely chosen decisions, instead of recognizing the way our social and cultural environment shapes and limits those choices. Because of their overriding emphasis on the importance of one's relationship with God, White evangelicals tend to believe that right relationships are at the root of right conduct and a rightly ordered society, once again without recognizing how "poor relationships might be shaped by social structures, such as laws, the ways institutions operate, or forms of segregation." And White evangelicals have a blind spot for the reality of social structures and institutions and the impact they have on individual lives. "White conservative Protestants believe that sinful humans typically deny their own personal sin by shifting blame somewhere else, such as on 'the system.'"[40] These are broad-brush generalizations and some Christian leaders are pushing back on these beliefs and trying to teach a fuller view of social life, but Emerson's description rings true as reflective of broad trends.

James Davison Hunter suggested something similar when he described American evangelicals' operative political theory as believing that "the essence of culture is found in the *hearts and minds of individuals*—in what we

---

[39]In 2020 and 2021, conservative evangelicals raised a cry of warning against critical race theory. Technically, the argument I am making here benefits from insights generated from CRT scholarship, though I find the term unhelpful. What evangelicals and conservatives railed against was generally not CRT scholarship itself, but a caricatured version of it, and against the racial essentialism implicit in some forms of "antiracist" advocacy.

[40]Emerson and Smith, *Divided by Faith*, 76, 78-79.

typically call 'values.'" Therefore, such Christians believe, "change the values of the common person for the better and a good society will follow in turn." Like Falwell, they tend to believe that "the problems society faces can be traced back to a loss of spiritual vitality and moral propriety." Hunter traces this to an even more fundamental idea: that ideas are the main driving forces in history. Change people's ideas, and you change the world. This kind of idealism ignores "the institutional nature of culture and disregard[s] the way culture is embedded in structures of power." Hunter rightly argues that this theory of political and cultural change is simply false—or, at least, radically incomplete. Culture and cultural change are products of history, institutions, elites, and networks as much as, if not more than, the heart and mind of the common person. Ideas matter, but not often in ways that can be orchestrated in advance. As Hunter says, "Culture takes form as the slow accretions of meaning in society over long periods of time" which means it is "much less an invention of the will than it is a slow product of history."[41]

Some of the overlap between White Christians' political convictions and attitudes about race can be empirically demonstrated through public opinion polling. Robert Jones, the founder and CEO of Public Religion Research Institute, a polling firm, demonstrated as much in his book *White Too Long*. Jones relates his experience growing up in the Christian South and his observations of southern White Christians' casual racism. To that, he adds historical arguments about how Christian theology and Christian institutions supported racism. Most damningly, he adds statistical data—his specialty—illustrating the persistent and widespread presence of what he calls racialized attitudes among White Christians today. Jones constructed a racism index aggregating respondents' replies to fifteen questions about Confederate monuments, racial inequality, African Americans' economic mobility, African Americans' treatment by the criminal justice system, and perceptions of race and racial discrimination, comparing White Christians' views against other racial and religious groups. Jones's data shows that "White Christians explicitly profess warm attitudes toward African Americans," which is unsurprising given the public stigma surrounding overt bigotry.

---

[41]James Davison Hunter, *To Change the World: The Irony, Tragedy, and Possibility of Christianity in the Late Modern World* (New York: Oxford University Press, 2010), 6, 9, 27, 33.

But the data also shows that, compared to other racial and religious groups, White Christians "strongly support the continued existence of Confederate monuments to White supremacy and consistently deny the existence not only of historical structural barriers to black achievement but also of existing structural injustices in the way African Americans are treated by police, the courts, workplaces, and other institutions in the country."[42] Similarly to Whitehead and Perry, Jones found that majorities of White American Christians of all backgrounds and denominations—but especially self-identified evangelicals—held views that were more shaped by race than religion. Another scholar compared White evangelicals to non-White evangelicals and concluded that, "To a large extent, evangelical political attitudes depend on whether one is White or non-White."[43] Jones calls this evidence of racism or racialized attitudes, but even if we call it something more benign—like racial insensitivity, cognitive blindness, or motivated reasoning—it is true that Whites overwhelmingly blame Blacks for their worse life outcomes when the evidence for a more complex view is overwhelming.

Strikingly, Jones found that White non-Christians were far less likely to hold these attitudes than White Christians: it seems that something about White American Christianity itself makes Whites' racial attitudes *worse*, not better. He concludes that "White Christians think of themselves as people who hold warm feelings toward African Americans while simultaneously embracing a host of racist and racially resentful attitudes that are inconsistent with that assertion."[44] Wilcox and Larson get at something similar when they note that "although African Americans and Whites read from the same Bible, the meaning of the text is socially constructed in different ways in the two traditions. Most black churches interpret the Bible as a book of liberation, equality, and social compassion."[45] Similarly, Seth Dowland noted that, even though many African Americans shared the same "family values" as White Christian activists, they rarely organized their political agenda in those terms.[46]

---

[42]Robert P. Jones, *White Too Long: The Legacy of White Supremacy in American Christianity* (New York: Simon & Schuster, 2020), 162.

[43]Janelle Wong, "The Evangelical Vote and Race in the 2016 Presidential Election," *Journal of Race, Ethnicity, and Politics* 3, no. 1 (2018): 81-106.

[44]Jones, *White Too Long*, 171.

[45]Clyde Wilcox and Carin Robinson, *Onward Christian Soldiers? The Religious Right in American Politics* (New York: Routledge, 2018), 63.

[46]Seth Dowland, *Family Values and the Rise of the Christian Right* (Philadelphia: University of Pennsylvania Press, 2015), 5, 18.

In other words, neither Black Christians nor White non-Christians see things the way White Christians do. White Christians' distinctive worldview is not a simple function of their Christianity (or else Black Christians would agree with them), nor of their whiteness (or else White non-Christians would agree with them), but of the interaction between them: there is a distinctive ethno-religious historical community of White Christianity, or Anglo-Protestantism, that interprets the world in a unique way, one that is uniquely blind to the realities of racial inequality and a racialized society. And a nation defined by that brand of Anglo-Protestantism will not only be blind to those racial realities but will allow those realities to be built into its very self-definition.

THE PARTICULARITY OF ANGLO-PROTESTANTISM

The claim that Anglo-Protestantism, or White Christianity, is a particular ethnoreligious historical community is itself one of the major arguments of this book and one of the major interpretive lenses I have used throughout, though I have avoided foregrounding it too much until this point. It is the premise of the claim that Christian nationalism is the identity politics of Anglo-Protestants. The claim is likely to be uncontroversial, even obvious, to historians or political scientists, for whom the cultural and historical particularity of White Protestant Anglo-American culture is a given. But I have found some resistance to this claim among evangelical pastors and theologians—and their flock in the pews—who prefer to think that their theology and their approach to the world is founded on the Bible alone and thus represents unmediated universal truth rather than cultural particularity—especially when I suggest the way in which our cultural particularity influences our thought is to make us insensitive to, or passive in the face of, racial inequality. This is an important point because White American Christians' prioritization of group self-interest above republican principles manifested in their lack of attention to racial equality is the clearest proof that their operative political theology is nationalist, not republican, and that nationalism is illiberal and results in racial injustice.

To skeptics of this view I respond, first, that it is impossible, epistemologically, to achieve a universal vantage point. The Bible is universal truth, but our interpretations of it are always historically and culturally conditioned. Second, the statistics by Whitehead, Perry, Jones, and others are hard to interpret any other way: most White American Christians have a unique way of interpreting the world and the Bible that is not shared by any other group or sect, including by other Christians. Third, I do not mean that White Christianity is uniquely evil, or that the fact of its particularity is evidence of its wickedness. Every culture, tradition, and community is particular and none has a universal standpoint. Fourth, I am, in one sense, simply taking nationalists at their word when they argue there is a distinct culture of Anglo-Protestantism, but I am highlighting that this culture is a part, not the whole, of American identity; and it is only one expression, not the unmediated ideal, of Christianity. We often speak of Black churches and Black Protestantism without discomfort— we understand that Christianity embodied in the Black experience often comes with particular theological emphases and worship practices because of African Americans' unique history and traditions. Why would it be different for White Christianity?

But fifth, I want to highlight the ways in which many White American Christians are acting from their cultural particularity rather than their avowed universal principles in politics, how they prioritize their cultural or tribal interests above the ideals they profess. Cultural particularity is inevitable, but making its defense a central political conviction is not, nor is the effort to pass off one's culture as a universal template or the embodiment of justice. Majorities around the world often adopt an implicit cosmology in which they see themselves as a microcosm of the whole, the whole as a macrocosmic reflection of themselves, and thus hold their culture out as a standard by which others should be compared. Minorities never have that illusion. Many White Christians profess an ideology that presents itself in universal terms—Christian republicanism—while acting in ways specific to their cultural or tribal interests and seeing no tension between the two. Mark Noll has shown that in the nineteenth century some White American Protestants supported slavery from the Bible based on their "commonsense" interpretation—which was an interpretation no other Christians in the world supported then or later. They used the claim of "commonsense" to give their particular—and particularly wrongheaded—interpretation a universalistic gloss. Dowland notes in his survey of conservative Christian political activism in the twentieth century that "conservative Protestants used the term evangelical (or, often, simply 'Christian') to portray a narrow theological vision as a widely held belief."[47] Or

---

[47]Dowland, *Family Values*, 15.

as Kristen du Mez recently argued, "Despite evangelicals' frequent claims that the Bible is the source of their social and political commitments, evangelicalism must be seen as a cultural and political movement rather than as a community defined chiefly by its theology."[48] Today, self-identified White evangelicals are more likely to report going to church "seldom" or "never" (27 percent in 2020 compared to 16 percent in 2008), suggesting that many White Americans are increasingly open about using "evangelical" as a cultural rather than theological identity.[49]

Recall again that for most of American history, Christian republicanism was the official propaganda of White Christian power, the legitimizing narrative we told to give our cultural and political dominance a moral veneer. The problem is not the story of Christian republicanism, which is good; nor is it the fact of cultural particularity, which is inescapable. The problem is believing the story wholly sanctifies the culture, that the culture is the full and final culmination of the story, that there is no tension between story and culture that needs examination or resolution. Acting as if our culture is the full embodiment of true justice leads naturally to the view that preserving and defending our culture is a moral and political imperative—the flip side of treating other groups' disadvantages as unimportant. Republicanism and the doctrine of "free culture" allows for the possibility that our culture is imperfect, other cultures have contributions to make, and thus group disparities are injustices that hurt the common good. Christian republicans would judge their culture by their ideals; nationalists judge their ideals by their culture, which leaves little room to seek justice for those outside their culture.

Some may wonder why White Christians shouldn't embrace their particularity and frankly adopt a posture of identity politics for themselves and others. What is wrong with advocating for our tribal interests, as other tribes do? I respond, first, that White Christians have in fact been doing just that for much of American history, and the results do little credit to the Christian public witness. Second, as I argued in chapter five, identity politics are corrosive of national identity and undermine equality under law. Third, White Christian identity politics either embraces White identity—which obviously would be

---

[48] Kristin Kobes Du Mez, *Jesus and John Wayne: How White Evangelicals Corrupted a Faith and Fractured a Nation* (New York: Liveright, 2020), 297-98.

[49] Ryan Burge, Twitter post, April 8, 2021, https://twitter.com/ryanburge/status/138018460406 6332673.

troubling—or sidelines race and emphasizes Christian identity. But advocating for "Christian" tribal interests alone has its own problems.

In 1941, C. S. Lewis warned against forming a "Christian Party," because such a party would inevitably represent only a part, not a whole, of Christianity, and would necessarily ally itself with non-Christian allies. "The principle which divides it from its brethren and unites it to its political allies will not be theological," but social, cultural, and political. This party would not represent "Christianity," but one particular gathering of Christians and non-Christians bound together by a common political agenda. "It will be not simply a part of Christendom, but a part claiming to be the whole," which is both bearing false witness and using the name of the Lord in vain. "By the mere act of calling itself the Christian Party it implicitly accuses all Christians who do not join it of apostasy and betrayal." Forming such a party and calling it "Christian," succumbs to "the temptation of claiming for our favourite opinions that kind and degree of certainty and authority which really belongs only to our Faith." In time, Christians in the Christian Party would see their political goals as holy crusades and become willing to justify any means in their pursuit.[50] Lewis' warning is apt for today's White American Christians tempted to view themselves as the "Christian Party," or America as a "Christian nation."

The evidence of American history suggests that White American Christians rarely learned to differentiate between our particular culture and the universal values we professed. Contemporary polling data suggests that the social practice of the Christian Right often continues to prioritize the former over the latter. White American Christians have a history of believing themselves to have access to a universal vantage point and an unmediated interpretation of the Bible, and using that moral high ground to ride roughshod over the perspectives of those who disagree with them. There is demonstrably something within the White evangelical way of thinking—what Emerson called their intellectual "toolkit"—that does not come straightforwardly from the Bible—because many others reading the same Bible do not read it that way—but for which they claim biblical authority. (This is not unique to White American Christians; probably most Europeans in the modern era had similar

---

[50]C. S. Lewis, "Meditation on the Third Commandment," 1941, https://web.mit.edu/bcf/www/BSJ97/cslewis.html

pretensions about their access to universal truth until the mid-twentieth century, thanks to the Enlightenment heritage.)

To Emerson's description of the White evangelical toolkit, I would add a few more features of White evangelical thought that distort our ability to see racial inequality or make its solution a political priority. White Christians sometimes stress a gospel of individual, inward, spiritual salvation from sin, death, and hell with no implications for salvation here and now from worldly suffering or injustice. They present this as a straightforward implication of the Bible, but it is theology that other Christians do not find there. Such a gospel functions as a prop for whatever injustices exist in the world because it tells those who are suffering that their suffering does not matter very much—in fact, is not actually *real*—compared to the overwhelming reality of future salvation in heaven, and it tells would-be activists that their efforts are effectively meaningless and even futile in the face of endemic sin and corruption. "Major human intervention is futile, since the world is beyond anything but divine redemption," as Jones characterizes this view. This outlook is closer to Buddhism, with its emphasis on detached acceptance of this world's suffering because of its ultimate unreality, than to the God of the Bible who freed his people from slavery or the Savior who cured leprosy, blindness, and death, a part of the gospel often stressed by other Christian traditions. It is also a departure from Christian republicanism, which is very much concerned with achieving equal justice for all citizens.[51]

Some White Christians match this gospel of spiritual salvation with a selective quietism and self-interested fatalism about what can actually be achieved in this world, and with an eschatology that envisions a disembodied, spiritualized future state. They cite Jesus' admonition that "you always have the poor with you" (Matthew 26:11) as suggesting that poverty is ineradicable and, by extension, other social reform efforts, such as environmentalism and racial equality, are similarly pointless. If the highest good in life is salvation from sin, death, and hell and an escape from this fallen world into a disembodied heaven after death, then this world does not matter very much since it

---

[51]The opposite error is the prosperity gospel, which preaches that God *guarantees* this-worldly health, wealth, and prosperity in exchange for faith; and the Social Gospel, which emphasizes social reform to the exclusion of preaching and evangelism. The Bible presents a more complex picture: that salvation in some sense begins in this life with a gradual and always-incomplete dawning of new life, often including greater flourishing and liberation from this world's ills, but that we will always have to contend against the world's sin and corruption.

is all going to burn anyway, as evangelicals say when they interpret passages like 2 Peter 3:10-13 about the end of the world. They again present this view as a straightforward application of the Bible when it is an interpretation other Christians, including many other White Christians, do not share.

There is a long legacy of White Christians pursuing social reform, from abolitionism, Prohibition, anticommunism, and antiabortionism, and their own avowed commitment to Christian republicanism, with its emphasis on the rule of law, fairness, and justice for all, should motivate them to reject apathy in the face of injustice. White Christians appear hypocritical when they selectively apply quietism and fatalism only to social ills whose solutions are inconvenient to themselves, like racial inequality and institutional reform, while simultaneously mobilizing a massive, generational effort against abortion or in favor of religious liberty. The simplest explanation is that they are prioritizing group interest above republican principle; they are nationalists, not republicans. Falwell, famously, had declared in 1965 in response to the civil rights movement that preachers should stay out of politics before doing an about face the next decade to advocate for a host of other causes. This is *motivated fatalism*: fatalism when it best serves their interests.

When White Christians today exhibit the antistructuralism, preach a spiritualized gospel message, practice selective quietism, and succumb to motivated fatalism—all of which serve to prop up and perpetuate the existing status quo in society, including its racial inequalities—their intellectual toolkit and social apathy contradicts Christian republican principles and functionally allows continuing racial disparities throughout American life. The antistructuralism and other features of historic Anglo-Protestant thought are the parts of the castle that were not abolished when the wing of White supremacy was torn down. There are the support beams and structural foundations around and underneath the wing of White supremacy. Contemporary White evangelicalism took down the wing, but not the support structure. White evangelicalism underwent surgery to take out the largest cancerous mass but left a host of smaller tumors spread throughout the body.

It is telling that Falwell, who opposed civil-rights legislation and supported segregation during the 1960s, does not mention race in his 1980 book. Though he repudiated his past support for segregation, he clearly did not think racism was an enduring problem and did not make racial justice a priority. In his book Falwell did not list racism as one of the sins from which America must repent, he did not spend time discussing racial injustice as a public policy problem to be solved, and he did not mention racial inequalities among the damaging national consequences that prove America has lost its virtue. Falwell simply passes over the entire subject in silence, the result of which is to give tacit support and approval to the racially unequal status quo of his day. In this, Falwell typifies many White evangelicals who cannot or will not see racial inequality as a present and enduring problem in America.

Christian nationalism is the political corollary of the White evangelical toolkit. The toolkit tends not to see racial inequality as a public problem requiring policy solutions and argues that solutions must be individual and private, rather than collective and public—a stance which has the effect of leaving racial inequality unaddressed and ensuring its continuation into the future. Public policy, meanwhile, is addressed to a different priority: making America a Christian nation, ensuring Anglo-Protestant cultural preeminence, which is presumed to be coterminous with the common good. The two stances are mutually reinforcing: nationalism reinforces one group's traditional privilege while the toolkit denies the reality of another group's traditional disadvantage. Whether nationalism motivated the toolkit, or the toolkit motivated the nationalism, or whether both come from a prior underlying commonality is a complex question—but it is also beside the point for our purposes. We can simply note that, in practice, they go together, and observe that this choice of political priorities is where Christian nationalism departs most troublingly from Christian republicanism.

With the exception of a few institutions, the Christian Right never made fighting racism or advocating for racial justice an important item on its agenda, again despite that authentic Christian republicanism would prioritize equality of citizenship for all. White American Christians overwhelmingly reject the notion that they, today, have an obligation to take positive steps to close the gaps in American life. White Christians tend to think of *justice* as procedural justice, following agreed-upon rules, and accepting whatever outcomes those rules generate. Substantive justice, the conditions of flourishing and shalom for all, including the widow, the orphan, and the stranger, is largely absent from contemporary White evangelical political theology and praxis, despite its presence throughout Scripture.[52] These features of the White evangelical toolkit foster intellectual blindness, historical insensitivity, and complicity with the perpetuation of racial inequalities throughout American life, a complicity that comes from its selective, misleading version of American history that reflects a distorted, shrunken, shallow vision of who "we" are. If "we" are only the inheritors of Anglo-Protestant cultural dominance, as nationalists believe, we face no significant problems with racial inequality, because racial inequality benefits "us." "Achieving a well-ordered society, where all members are embraced as being among us, should be the goal. Our failure to do so is an American tragedy. It is a national, not merely a communal, disgrace," Loury argues. "Changing the definition of the American 'we' is a first step toward rectifying the relational discrimination that afflicts our society, and it is the best path forward in reducing racial inequality."[53]

CONCLUSION

Nationalism is the logical conclusion of tribal evangelicalism's blind spots; it is a political agenda constructed on the framework of a White evangelical intellectual toolkit that does not recognize the realities of racial inequality. Is this connection intrinsic to White evangelical tribalism, or is it an especially unfortunate accident? In other words, is the problem with White evangelical tribalism itself, separate from politics, or does the problem arise only when White evangelicals adopt nationalism as their political theory? In a sense, it does not matter because both things are real and their damaging influence on American public life is real regardless of their historical relationship. And the question pushes beyond the boundaries of this book, which is concerned mostly with political theory. Nonetheless, I'd like to offer a few speculative thoughts.

There are clear examples of White Christians who do not succumb to these temptations, like Roger Williams, the seventeenth-century Puritan who fought against the religious authoritarianism of his contemporaries, and George Bourne, a nineteenth-century evangelical abolitionist who was persecuted for his ministry against slavery. It is important to embrace these precedents as a usable past for today's Christian activists who need to take

---

[52] See Timothy Keller, *Generous Justice: How God's Grace Makes Us Just* (New York: Penguin, 2012) for a discussion of justice in the Bible.
[53] Loury, "Why Does Racial Inequality Persist?," 15.

inspiration from a legacy of principled Christian political witness. White evangelicalism, when it acts from universal principles rather than tribal interest, has not always had these blind spots, does not have to align with nationalism as its political theory, and has often been true to its avowed ideology of Christian republicanism. Even today the Christian Right still has within it a strain of Christian republicanism, evident in its campaign against abortion and in favor of religious liberty, which are just and right and have nothing to do with Christian nationalism.

But I suspect that Christian nationalism is becoming more and more central to White evangelical culture, though I admit that this is impossible to prove. I am sharing an educated impression based on a life lived mostly within White evangelicalism coupled with my occasional forays outside of it, based on my reading of history, and, perhaps uniquely, based on my international experience. Anglo-Protestantism arose and has existed entirely within a historical time period in which either Britain or the United States has been the preeminent geopolitical power in the world. Protestants and Puritans had been persecuted earlier, during the Wars of Religion, but shortly afterwards, and for roughly the last three centuries—since Protestantism won its battle in the Glorious Revolution (1689) and Britain emerged as a preeminent power in Europe over the next century—the distinctive tradition of Anglo-Protestantism grew and developed under unique historical and political conditions. White American and British Protestants were represented on the world stage by the greatest powers of their day during a historical period in which their countries drove a staggering, unprecedented amount of historical change around the world. They played starring roles in the invention of liberal democracy, the scientific and industrial revolutions, and the construction of world order. White American and British Protestants had reason to feel that they were the strongest, richest, safest, most educated, most innovative, most successful human beings in history.

There is much to admire about their legacy—but such an environment is not spiritually healthy. Jesus warned that the rich have little chance of entering the kingdom of heaven and exhorted us to be as little children to come to him. The Bible is replete with exhortations that suffering, not riches, is the sure path to sanctification and to spiritual maturity. The rich young ruler left Jesus dejected because he found himself unable to separate himself from his worldly power and follow Jesus with his whole being. I suspect this is true corporately as well as individually. If I can speak in broad generalizations for a moment, comparatively speaking, Anglo-Protestants have not suffered very much. I do not mean to minimize the sacrifice and suffering of missionaries, activists, and ministers who have given their lives in service to the gospel around the world, nor the activists who suffered in the cause of abolitionism or the pro-life movement. But neither can we minimize the truthful historical context: as a whole, considered corporately, Anglo-Protestantism has lacked the accountability and the humility that comes from suffering, persecution, or simply from being relatively small and powerless. "As iron sharpens iron, so one man sharpens another" (Proverbs 27:17). But that only works between two pieces of iron; Anglo-Protestantism, in its power, is tempered steel. I do not mean that as a compliment: I mean that Anglo-Protestantism has been so powerful that it has sometimes been hardhearted and ignorant, historically insensitive to what it is like not to be Anglo-Protestant, which means it was not shaped by the iron-sharpening feedback of other historical communities, other Christian traditions, that could have helped sand off its rough edges or hold up its reflection to itself. Anglo-Protestantism has been, in historical terms, rich, powerful, and secure. Why would we expect it to be spiritually healthy?

The historical wealth, power, and influence of our Anglo-Protestant heritage has given us, I fear, a growing spirit of insularity, self-satisfaction, completeness, and entitlement. Such attitudes stem, I think, partly from our avowed independence from (or ignorance of) church history and our confidence that we, at last, have figured out the Bible's complete meaning without reference to past generations, church tradition, other denominations, other Christians around the world, or external authority. We are, of course, heavily indebted to the past, which only means that our dependence on historical conditioning is matched by our refusal to acknowledge it. To be blunt, tribal evangelicalism is cocky and entitled in the way powerful men are when they have been in charge too long without accountability. I suggested earlier that American Christians often operate with an unstated presumption that Christians are entitled to primacy of place in the American public square because we think of ourselves as the heirs of the true or essential heritage of American culture, that we have a presumptive right to define the meaning of the American experiment because we see ourselves as America's architects, first citizens, and guardians. It sounds noble, but it amounts to Christian tribal chauvinism.

White evangelicalism's cocky power is a double-edged sword: it can be dangerous and destructive, but it is also a major reason why it has been so successful in shaping the world and driving change. Most people in history would not have dreamed that they could reorder the foundational principles of political order or understand and manipulate the forces of nature as Anglo-Protestants did in the early modern era. It takes a degree of self-confidence and self-aware power verging on narcissism to mount generational efforts to remold society around one's moral values, yet Anglo-Protestants have often come close to doing just that. Anglo-Protestants have an awe-inspiring historical record of moral and political crusading. The settlement and development of the United States itself was essentially an Anglo-Protestant nation building crusade for much of the nineteenth century.

Contemporary Christian activists often take confidence from this record of social reform and might invoke it to push back on the narrative of their blindness, individualism, quietism, fatalism, or racial insensitivity. It is true that Anglo-Protestantism was different in the past, and evangelicals today can take pride in some of its legacies. But three things counsel caution. First, not all of its crusades were admirable. British imperialism, American slavery, and anti-Catholicism were also justified in their day as Anglo-Protestants crusades. While some northern White Protestants made opposition to slavery a religious crusade, virtually all southern White Protestants made its *defense* a moral crusade. The American Civil War was a religious civil war between rival crusaders. Indeed, in one of history's great ironies, progressivism itself—the target of White evangelicals' newest crusade in the twenty-first century—is essentially an Anglo-Protestant heresy, a movement that slipped its chain and got loose from its founding theological tradition and turned into an endless revolution with no orienting moral horizon. White Christian activists today have a selective historical memory when we only take credit for the moral crusades which are still admired today. Our uneven record of moral crusading actually *strengthens* the case that we have a faulty moral and political vision.

Second, over the past century conservative White Protestants (later including Catholics) have been increasingly on the defensive, which has gradually but fundamentally changed the orientation of the movement. As other communities and other nations have gained power and made demands, many conservative White Christians have implicitly leaned more and more heavily on the tradition of selective quietism and motivated fatalism to ignore other causes. As a result, they have a far less expansive vision of social reform than their Anglo-Protestant forebears, which is why their vision of reform today seems shrunken and shallow, as if every moral issue could be reduced to opposing abortion and protecting religious liberty. Those are good causes, but they are not the only good causes. It is very difficult to imagine today's conservative Christian activists mounting generational reform efforts against child labor or unsafe working conditions, as they did a century ago. There are some Christian organizations devoted to fighting sex trafficking and advocating for racial justice, yet the fact that they have not captured the energy and imagination of the broader movement or come to define the agenda of the Christian Right proves the point. Insofar as younger evangelicals have sought to broaden the movement's political vision, they have often had to gravitate to other religious traditions for guidance.

Finally, and most consequentially, as conservative White Christians have felt their power ebbing, they have made the preservation of their power itself into their last great moral crusade. America's White Christian ethnoreligious sect has convinced itself that its own power is essential to the nation's future, and, consequently, that preserving its power is a selfless, moral act. To be clear, pursuing power is not immoral, and any Christian who wants to influence policy for the better must pursue political power as part of that goal. But there is a subtle and crucial difference between seeing power as a means to an end, a necessary precondition for pursuing justice, on the one hand, and seeing power as intrinsically good, as if power in the right hands is inherently righteous, on the other. Many White American Christians seem to be gravitating to the latter view of power, the view that the identity of the person who wields power sanctifies its use: Power in the hands of Christians is by definition good and thus the pursuit and preservation of Christian power must be our preeminent goal. A political agenda defined that way is best understood as a form of identity politics or ethnoreligious nationalism. A shorter way of saying that is that the Christian Right is a nationalist movement, despite residual traces of republicanism. Whatever label we put on it, it is the effort to revive and entrench Anglo-Protestant power, to privilege Christian culture, a nostalgic movement to recover the quasi-establishment of Protestant Christianity in American culture. In that sense, Christian nationalism is truly a natural fit with politically active right-wing White Christianity as it exists today—with tribal evangelicalism—because nationalism is the political expression of group cockiness.

Nationalism is an invitation to take one's group identity and make it an official state creed, an irresistible temptation for a movement marked by confidence in its own righteousness and a history of having its claims and its creeds alter the councils of state. Nationalism is a graduation of sorts: it is the next step for a social movement that has found worldly success and power, a necessary step for them to entrench and preserve that power. Nationalism is the effort by social movements to gain the heft, prestige, and resources of a government, to use that government to solidify its privileges and pursue its goals. Conservative White Christians continue to believe they are entitled to "own and operate the American brand," as Lynerd says. He rightly notes the difference "between searching out the implications of the Christian gospel for politics and leveraging this gospel to advance the social position of American Christians. When evangelicals disguise the latter in the robes of the former, not only do they engage in dishonesty, but they also give fuel to the cynical view that there really is no difference—that the theological is nothing more than a cloak for the political."[54]

Which one is more important: Is it republican institutions or Christian culture? Having a free and open society or having public symbols of respect for Christianity? Christian principles or Christian power? Political liberty or political victory? Christian nationalists would reject the framing of these questions as a false choice because they claim the two sides must go together, while Christian republicans would be far more comfortable advocating for republicanism with or without a Christianized culture. The ideal test of republican sincerity would come if the two were ever to conflict—if republican principles led to a political result disadvantageous to White Christian influence, if Christians had to choose between preserving their power or remaining faithful to republican principles. We would want to see White Christians accept republican principles that distributed power and influence fairly and equitably, even if it meant their own loss of influence. The test came in 2016.

---

[54]Lynerd, "On Political Theology and Religious Nationalism."

EVANGELICALS AND DONALD J. TRUMP

9

IT SHOULD BE EASIER TO UNDERSTAND NOW why Donald Trump's direct appeal to Christians during his campaigns and throughout his presidency resonated so deeply and was so successful. Most White American evangelicals voted as nationalists, prioritizing group power over republican principles. Recall, again, some of Trump's campaign appeals. In June 2016: "We will respect and defend Christian Americans."[1] In August 2016: "Your power has been totally taken away," but under a Trump administration, "you'll have great power to do good things."[2] In September 2016: "[In] a Trump administration, our Christian heritage will be cherished, protected, defended, like you've never seen before. Believe me."[3]

One event was especially noteworthy. On the eve of the Iowa caucuses, in January 2016, Trump addressed a crowd at Dordt College in Sioux Center, Iowa. "We're Christians. I'm Protestant, I'm Presbyterian," Trump told a crowd at a Christian college, creating a sense of unity with his audience before channeling that unity into a shared experience of persecution. "Christianity is under tremendous siege," he said. "We are getting less and less powerful." He noted that Christians make up a majority of Americans, "yet we don't exert the

---

[1]Donald Trump, "Remarks at Faith and Freedom Coalition Conference," June 10, 2016, www.c-span
.org/video/?410912-4/donald-trump-addresses-faith-freedom-coalition-conference.
[2]Donald Trump, "Remarks in Orlando, Florida," August 11, 2016, www.c-span.org/video/?413877-1
/donald-trump-addresses-evangelical-leaders-orlando-florida.
[3]Donald Trump, "Values Voter Summit Remarks," September 9, 2016, www.politico.com/story
/2016/09/full-text-trump-values-voter-summit-remarks-227977.

power that we should have." Then he turned their shared fear into shared anger at the establishment: "There's nothing the politicians can do to you if you band together; you have too much power, but the Christians don't use their power." The solution was to vote for Trump. "Christianity will have power," he said. "If I'm there, you're going to have plenty of power. If I'm there, you're going to have somebody representing you very, very well." In less than four minutes, Trump used the words *Christian*, *Christmas*, or *true believer* seventeen times, and the words *power* or *strength* eleven times.[4] Trump campaigned on a promise to restore Christian power, which had been one of the chief aims of the Christian Right for four decades.

During the election, Eric Metaxas, an author and radio host, argued that whatever his flaws, Trump was a superior choice to Hillary Clinton because his presidency would be a necessary and drastic push against the Democratic Party. "Sometimes you have to hold your nose and vote for the person who is going to do the least damage or who is maybe going to pull you back from the brink," Metaxas was quoted as saying. "You can even hate Trump, but I'm saying you better be sure that you understand what a Hillary Clinton presidency brings." Metaxas analogized the 2016 election to wartime: "When you are in a war mentality, you say 'who is going to stand up where we need to stand up?'" He also feared that the 2016 election might be Americans' last chance to preserve their form of government. "The DNC, the Democrats, have been trying hard to make open borders," Metaxas said. "That means we are demographically never going to be able to elect somebody who is a Constitutionalist again. We are just not going to have the numbers. It is that desperate."[5] Metaxas's argument sounds, on the face, concerned with republican principles. But he was arguing that immigrants were unlikely to assimilate and thus would dilute loyalty to the ideals of the American experiment, echoing Huntington's misguided fear that Hispanic immigration would somehow erode the foundations of political liberty. Metaxas was using republican language to express a racialized understanding of American ideals.

Similarly, during the election, Wayne Grudem, professor of theology and biblical studies at Phoenix Seminary and author of a widely used *Systematic*

---

[4]Trump, "FULL Donald Trump Campaign Event in Sioux City," www.youtube.com/watch?v =ATuWvlYwdEY. See especially segment from about 50:15 to 54:00.

[5]Casey Harper, "Leading Evangelical Makes the Case for Christian Support of Trump," *The Daily Caller*, July 18, 2016.

Theology textbook, argued that "if this election is close (which seems likely), then if someone votes for a write-in candidate instead of voting for Trump, this action will directly help Hillary Clinton, because she will need one less vote to win." Grudem explained, "This year we have an unusual opportunity to defeat Hillary Clinton and the pro-abortion, pro-gender-confusion, anti-religious liberty, tax-and-spend, big government liberalism that she champions. I believe that defeating that kind of liberalism would be a morally right action." Grudem, like Metaxas, saw the election in almost existential terms: "This election is not just about Hillary Clinton. It is about defeating the far-left liberal agenda that any Democratic nominee would champion," which was close to fruition because with a Clinton presidency the left would be "gaining permanent control of the nation with a five-vote majority on the Supreme Court, and then relentlessly imposing every liberal policy on the nation not through winning elections but through a relentless parade of one Supreme Court decision after another." Grudem specified the court's influence over abortion, religious liberty, religious association, free speech, and others as issues at stake in the election. Grudem's and Metaxas's views are illustrative of the thought process many Christians (particularly conservative White evangelicals) went through in 2016: Trump has flaws but would be superior to Clinton, especially on Supreme Court nominations. Many self-identified White evangelicals were so fearful that progressive governance represented an existential threat to their beliefs and their way of life that they believed Donald Trump was the safer option.

However, that is not the full story. In January 2016, before Trump won the primary election and when Ted Cruz, Marco Rubio, and a dozen other candidates were still in the race, 52 percent of White evangelicals believed Trump would make a "good" or "great" president—the highest number for any candidate in the race—suggesting a majority of evangelicals felt enthusiastic about Trump independent of how he compared to Hillary Clinton.[6] Evangelical support for Trump was uneven across income, racial, ethnic, and age groups: it was not solely motivated by religion or concern for the Supreme Court. Long after Trump benefited by comparison to Clinton, he still sustained a high level of approval from White evangelicals: in October

---

[6]"Faith and the 2016 Campaign," Pew Research Center, January 27, 2016, www.pewforum.org/2016/01/27/faith-and-the-2016-campaign/.

2019, 82 percent of White evangelicals said they preferred Trump to be the Republican nominee in 2020, according to a PRRI poll. According to PRRI analysts, "White evangelical Protestants are the only major religious group to view Trump favorably."[7] In June 2020, amid the coronavirus pandemic and shortly after nationwide protests against police brutality, 72 percent of White evangelicals approved of Trump's job performance, by far the highest among any group, even though that represented a *decline* among Trump's usual level of support among White evangelicals.[8] Between 76 and 81 percent of White evangelicals voted for Trump again in 2020,[9] and self-identified White evangelicals who attended church weekly voted for him at higher rates (85 percent) than those who did not regularly attend (70 percent).[10]

Even if we grant that many self-identified White evangelicals voted for Trump in 2016 simply because they thought he was better than Clinton—which some polling data belies—their continued approval of him since then and in the 2020 election needs more explanation. Historian John Fea, himself an evangelical Christian, argued that White evangelicals supported, and continue to support, Trump because of a mixture of fear, nostalgia, and a desire for power. White evangelicals fear cultural and social change that threatens their status in a country that was run by White Protestants for most of its history. Some are nostalgic for an era that was more hospitable to their values, status, and prestige. That is why Trump's support is stronger among older Americans who remember that history (or a romanticized version of it) and indulge in such longing, despite that previous eras were typically uncomfortable or

---

[7]"Fractured Nation: Widening Partisan Polarization and Key Issues in 2020 Presidential Elections," PRRI, October 20, 2019, www.prri.org/research/fractured-nation-widening-partisan -polarization-and-key-issues-in-2020-presidential-elections/ and "White Evangelical Support for Donald Trump at All-Time High," www.prri.org/spotlight/white-evangelical-support-for -donald-trump-at-all-time-high/. See also "Partisanship Trumps Gender," www.prri.org /research/abortion-reproductive-health-midterms-trump-kavanaugh/.

[8]Michael Lipka and Gregory A. Smith, "White Evangelical Approval of Trump Slips, but Eight-in-Ten Say They Would Vote for Him," Pew Research Center, July 1, 2020, www.pewresearch .org/fact-tank/2020/07/01/white-evangelical-approval-of-trump-slips-but-eight-in-ten -say-they-would-vote-for-him/.

[9]"Exit Poll Results and Analysis for the 2020 Presidential Election," *Washington Post*, December 14, 2020, www.washingtonpost.com/elections/interactive/2020/exit-polls/presidential-election -exit-polls/; "Understanding the 2020 Electorate," NPR, November 3, 2020, www.npr.org /2020/11/03/929478378/understanding-the-2020-electorate-ap-votecast-survey.

[10]Ryan Burge, Twitter post, February 11, 2021, https://twitter.com/ryanburge/status/13600629 33238243328.

hostile to everyone else. And we all feel the temptation to seek power to protect and advance our own tribe's interests.[11]

John G. Stackhouse agrees. Evangelicals' support for Trump has "only a little to do with evangelicalism as a particular form of Christianity and much more to do with *White American evangelicals*' up-and-down relationship with American cultural power," he writes. "When we speak of 'evangelical' support for Trump, we are talking about a specific segment of American evangelicals, namely, those who feel their cultural, racial, and political power is under attack and must be preserved." Trump recognized White evangelicals' status anxiety and directly appealed to it. "The evangelicals who enthusiastically voted for, and still support, Donald Trump largely do so because they (correctly) recognize the waning of their influence, and Trump has promised to fight on their behalf."[12] Black evangelicals did not feel their cultural power was declining, did not share White evangelicals' status anxiety, and thus were not attracted to Trump's promise to restore Christian power. It is not a leap of faith to suggest that Black Christians are perhaps not eager to revive the cultural and political dominance of White Christians.

Fea's and Stackhouse's explanation is persuasive because the demographic decline of White Christians in America is real and helps explain the rise of evangelical tribalism. "In 1976, roughly eight in ten (81%) Americans identified as White and identified with a Christian denomination," according to PRRI. "By 2006, that number dropped to 54%. . . . Today, only 43% of Americans identify as White and Christian—and only 30% as White and Protestant."[13] As numbers shrink, so does political and cultural clout. This demographic decline helps explain why many White evangelicals feel they are victims of discrimination or persecution and feel the need to fight back, culturally and politically: White evangelicals are far more likely than non-White evangelicals to believe that White Americans face discrimination and the least likely to agree that non-White Americans face discrimination. They are far more likely than

---

[11]John Fea, *Believe Me: The Evangelical Road to Donald Trump* (Grand Rapids, MI: Eerdmans, 2018).

[12]John Stackhouse, "American Evangelical Support for Donald Trump: Mostly American, and Only Sort-of 'Evangelical,'" *Religion and Culture Forum*, February 2, 2018, https://voices.uchicago.edu/religionculture/2018/02/02/american-evangelical-support-for-donald-trump-mostly-american-and-only-sort-of-evangelical-a-response/.

[13]Robert P. Jones and Daniel Cox, "America's Changing Religious Identity," Public Religion Research Institute, September 6, 2017, www.prri.org/research/american-religious-landscape-christian-religiously-unaffiliated/, 18.

White non-evangelicals to believe that Whites face more discrimination than Muslims—and 89 percent of those who believed that voted for Trump.[14] These numbers suggest that most White evangelicals are consumed with worry for their tribe's political and cultural fate. In the midst of this decline, Trump campaigned on promises to protect and advance Christian interests, and White evangelicals took him at his word.[15] Trump's movement was and is fueled in part by status anxiety among nonelite White Christians, among whom evangelicals are predominant.[16]

Andrew Whitehead and Samuel Perry's measure of Christian nationalism presents another angle on evangelical support for Trump, one that gets to the heart of the difference—and overlap—between tribal evangelicalism and religious evangelicalism. They show that among self-identified White evangelicals, those who scored highest on measures of Christian nationalism were overwhelmingly more likely to vote for Donald Trump in 2016. By their measure, nearly 86 percent of White evangelical "ambassadors" (those most enthusiastic for Christian nationalism) voted for Trump, compared to 60 percent of White evangelical "accommodators," 33 percent of White evangelical "resisters," and 27 percent of White evangelical "rejectors." In other words, support for Trump varied considerably *within* White evangelicalism, and the variation was driven by nationalism. Other political and religious groups showed identical trend lines: ambassadors most likely to support Trump and declining levels of support down to rejectors (though White evangelicals showed the highest overall level of support in all categories of Christian nationalism).[17] Similarly, another team of scholars found that voters' attitudes toward Christian nationalism was a stronger predictor of Trump support than frequency of church attendance. Nearly 90 percent of strong Christian nationalists who did not attend church regularly voted for Trump; only around 15 percent of regular

---

[14]Janelle Wong, "The Evangelical Vote and Race in the 2016 Presidential Election," *Journal of Race, Ethnicity, and Politics* 3, no. 1 (2018): 81-106.

[15]For a parallel view, see Philip Gorski, "Why Evangelicals Voted for Trump: A Critical Cultural Sociology," in *Politics of Meaning/Meaning of Politics*, ed. Jason Mast and Jeffrey C. Alexander (New York: Palgrave Macmillan, 2019), who argues that Trump support is a secularized version of White Christian nationalism.

[16]Khazan, "People Voted for Trump Because They Were Anxious, Not Poor," *The Atlantic*, April 23, 2018, www.theatlantic.com/science/archive/2018/04/existential-anxiety-not-poverty-motivates-trump-support/558674/.

[17]Andrew L. Whitehead and Samuel L. Perry, *Taking America Back for God: Christian Nationalism in the United States* (New York: Oxford University Press, 2020), 63.

attenders who rejected Christian nationalism did; and more regular church attendance decreased support for Trump at all levels of Christian nationalism (a trend that seemed to reverse in 2020).[18]

One important implication is that simply being White and evangelical does not fully explain Trump support; rather, one's attitude toward Christian nationalism, toward American identity and Christianity's social position in American life, and toward other ethnoreligious groups was a stronger predictor of one's level of support for Trump. Some evangelicals—those who rejected Christian nationalism—also rejected Trump. Religion affects how people vote, but indirectly; it is how people interpret the political fortunes of their religious group that matters. As the team of scholars wrote, the effect of religion on politics has to do with "the ways people use religious narratives in everyday life to construct and defend symbolic boundaries. At a time when fewer Americans attend religious services, religious narratives about Christian nationhood may have their strongest political effects when, and perhaps because, they are detached from religious institutions."[19]

Those who interpreted their ethnoreligious identity in nationalist terms saw in Donald Trump the best reflection of their political aspirations for a revival of Christianity's social and cultural predominance in the United States. By definition, this describes tribal rather than religious evangelicalism because it describes social, cultural, and political behavior rather than theological beliefs or religious practice. The two kinds of evangelicalism cannot be neatly disentangled—we cannot estimate that, say, 50 percent of self-identified evangelicals are of the tribal variety and the other half are of the religious variety because the two surely overlap in many evangelical hearts and minds. The question is not "how many tribal evangelicals are there?" but "which kind of evangelicalism predominates when evangelicals vote and speak in the public square?" The polling and voting data suggest that the more evangelicals are defined by theology and practice, the less likely they are to embrace nationalism or support Trump. Unfortunately, the polling and voting data also suggest they are a minority among self-identified White evangelicals in America.

Near the end of Trump's term in office, in June 2020, the White House released a video of Trump's visit to St. John's Church across Lafayette Square

---

[18]Samuel Stroope et al., "Unchurched Christian Nationalism and the 2016 US Presidential Election," *Sociological Forum* 36, no. 2 (2021): 405-25.
[19]Stroope et al., "Unchurched Christian Nationalism."

amid nationwide protests and riots against police brutality and racial injustice. Trump had just given a press conference in the Rose Garden in which he floated the idea of deploying US military forces to American cities to restore law and order before visiting the church. The thirty-second video—wordless, set to soaring, inspirational music—shows Trump, flanked by the attorney general, the White House chief of staff, and the secretary of defense, walking to St. John's Church, holding up a Bible in front of its iconic steps and spire, and walking back to the White House past a line of armored riot police. Without words, only the symbolism speaks: symbols of the presidency and American nationhood; symbols of power, authority, and strength; and symbols of Christianity—mingled together in a jumble of free association, overlapping meaning, and provocative, unstated connotation: power, Christianity, and America, a trinity of national identity and a perfect icon of Christian nationalism. Despite his many personal failings, Trump did not betray the values of the Christian Right: he fulfilled them.

ELITE EVANGELICALISM

The division between tribal and religious evangelicalism needs more explanation. Evangelical support for Trump was strong, but not unanimous. Support for Trump appears to be strong in the pews, but views about Trump appear more mixed among evangelical leaders. In 2018 I led a research project for the Ethics and Religious Liberty Commission (ERLC) about the relationship between faith and American democracy. My team and I interviewed scores of evangelical leaders across the country in late 2018 and early 2019. Our study mostly focused on broader trends driving the polarization and fragmentation undermining American democracy.[20] But in the course of our research, we also asked evangelical leaders—on the record—for their views about President Trump. What I heard painted a more complex picture than has usually been portrayed about the relationship between Trump and the evangelical community. These institutional and intellectual leaders articulated a different view, far more circumspect about Trump and what he stands for. They gave voice to a minority of self-identified evangelicals who, in their public lives, prioritized Christian republicanism and saw Trump as a threat to those ideas, compared

---

[20]Paul D. Miller, *Faith and Healthy Democracy*, Ethics and Religious Liberty Commission, September 26, 2019, https://erlc.com/resource-library/white-papers/faith-and-healthy-democracy/.

to what I've called "tribal" evangelicals who believed in Christian nationalism and saw Trump as their defender and champion.

Several evangelical leaders appeared hesitant to express their full or unvarnished views because the interviews were on the record. A few declined to answer questions about Trump or any partisan politics because they believed answering those questions could compromise their ability to pastor congregants who disagreed with them politically, or could appear to wrongly conflate the gospel with a political agenda. Evangelical leaders are aware of the extraordinary loyalty Trump has inspired from his political base, many of whom sit in the pews they preach to or read the publications that they write for. Some of my interlocutors appeared to go out of their way to find things to praise about the president—including overwhelming and virtually unanimous praise for his judicial appointments—perhaps to guard against the perception that their critiques were unfair, dogmatic, or fueled by resentment. Many volunteered that they did not vote for Trump (often coupled with an affirmation that they did not vote for Hillary Clinton either). The most common response when I asked, "What are your views on President Donald J. Trump?" was nervous laughter. There was a palpable climate of anxiety, even fear, around conversations about Trump within elite evangelical circles because they know how large the gulf is that separates their views from the evangelical layperson.

Most of the evangelical leaders I spoke to had serious criticisms of the president. Some focused their criticisms on him personally: they thought he was unqualified to serve as president because of his dishonesty, character, or temperament. They stressed that evangelicals had long argued, rightly, that character matters in public officials, and that we would be hypocritical to ignore Trump's well-publicized failings. Alan Noble, an author and assistant professor at Oklahoma Baptist University, offered that, "He is unfit for office" because "he is immoral" and "deeply incompetent." Noble believed that "his pandering to the church is insulting and demeaning and . . . is very superficially, obviously insincere." Peter Wehner, a senior fellow with the Ethics and Public Policy Center and former official in the George W. Bush administration, believed that Trump is carrying out a "full-scale all-out assault on truth" because he is "a pathological liar" and that evangelicals' support for him was "discrediting the gospel and the Christian witness" because we had (rightly) criticized Bill Clinton for many of the same failings. (Wehner also praised Trump's judicial nominees and deregulatory policies.) Andy Crouch, author and partner for theology and culture with Praxis, offered that Trump is the "very embodiment of what the Bible calls a fool." Ray Ortlund, pastor of Emmanuel Church in Nashville, said, "I think he is a tragic human being, a bad example to a nation, volatile, unpredictable, unprincipled, and Hillary Clinton would have been even worse" (he clarified that he voted for neither).

Others worried about the deeper cultural impact of the Trump presidency and of evangelicals' close association with him. Matthew Lee Anderson, a research fellow at Baylor University and cofounder of the *Mere Orthodoxy* online journal, judged that whatever political or legal progress might happen under the Trump presidency would be more than offset by how Trump would "set back the cultural gains that we had been making." Keri Folmar—an author, former Capitol Hill staffer, and longtime pro-life advocate—worried that Trump has accelerated the loss of moral consensus in the United States and worried, "I'm not sure that we can ever recover from that." Former Obama administration official Michael Wear believed Trump has "helped to normalize a nakedly manipulative form of politics." Tim Keller, an author and pastor of Redeemer Presbyterian Church in New York, worried that "the plausibility of our cause has been greatly undermined amongst younger people, amongst non-White people," because Trump is "staining [our beliefs] and making them implausible to a lot of people." Cherie Harder, president of the Trinity Forum, believed that "we've had political leaders in the past who did try to encourage people towards the better angels of their nature. And I think what's happening now is instead a deliberate stoking of division and tribalism and alienation. And I think that is the mark of a dangerous leader."

African American and other non-White interviewees were among Trump's harshest critics. Bishop A. B. Vines, senior pastor of New Seasons Church in San Diego, California, said that Trump is "a narcissist." Vines believed that Trump is "doing good stuff for the city, for the nation," although he also characterized him as "vicious" and believed that "our testimony has been ruined for the next decade" because of evangelicals' support for him. Adron Robinson, senior pastor of Hillcrest Baptist Church in Country Club Hills, Illinois, offered that Trump is "a very egotistical person. . . . He's feeding into the hate speech, the demonizing anyone that doesn't agree with you, not listening to the other side. He's pulling politics down to a lower level." Jemar Tisby, an author and cofounder of The Witness: A Black Christian Collective, said that

Trump "is at heart a reality TV star." He added, "He mastered that genre of entertainment by capitalizing on boorish self-centered behavior. And now that's enshrined in the Oval Office." He also lamented that Trump's election had "done enormous damage to the cause of racial reconciliation in the church." Byron Day, pastor of Emmanuel Baptist Church in Laurel, Maryland, said simply, "I think he is a racist."

Jason Cook, associate pastor of Fellowship Memphis in Tennessee, gave a considered answer worth quoting at length because it exemplifies so well the balance so many strove for in their assessment of the president.

> President Trump is a human being created in the image of God who because of that reason has dignity and value and worth and I want that to be the first thing that I say about him. . . . I believe that his rhetoric has resonated with much of middle America in a way that they finally see someone speaking for them, and I think that since he has been president, he has made some good decisions.
>
> I find him to be a rancid human being. I find him to morally lack any allegiance. I find him to be one who pounces on political convenience, a man who is not led by many scruples or morals other than the bottom line. I find him to be reprehensible in many ways and yet, the Bible calls me to respect the authority that is over me. . . .
>
> I don't think President Trump cares about minorities until it is convenient for him politically. I believe he cares about his base and what people think. . . . But I will fully and readily admit and recognize where I think he is doing a good job. I do think the appointment of Justice Gorsuch to the Supreme Court was a great decision. I think the unemployment numbers are great. . . . When I think about President Trump being our president it brings great shame to me for a host of reasons. That's what I think about President Trump.

Many evangelicals reportedly voted for Trump in the hopes that his election would lead to the appointment of conservative justices to the US Supreme Court who would overturn *Roe v. Wade*. I asked evangelical leaders if such an outcome would make Trump's election worth it. Most refused to answer the question. Among those willing to answer, almost everyone said no. They said that even if his presidency led to a major change in constitutional law regarding abortion, Trump was doing so much harm in other areas as to make his presidency a net loss for the country. Matthew Lee Anderson worried that "we'll get our justices and we might change the legal framework but we might lose a generation," echoing widespread sentiment that positive changes in the law have been offset by negative changes in the culture. Thabiti Anyabwile, pastor of Anacostia River Church, believed that the victory of the pro-life movement "has to be bigger than overturning *Roe.*" It should include cultural victories that support fatherhood and families, and "has to also include winning in a procedurally just way." Considering that evangelicals have, for forty years, considered abortion a form of murder, it is extraordinary that some believed Trump's presidency was nonetheless causing more harm than good.

Among the few willing to argue that the Trump presidency was a net positive, one issue dominated: not abortion, but the federal judiciary. Bethany Jenkins, a vice president of The Veritas Forum, emphasized in 2018 that Trump's nominations affected more than just the Supreme Court. By the end of his term, Trump had nominated over 230 federal judges to the Supreme Court, the US Courts of Appeals, and US District Courts. Such appointments matter because most federal cases are decided at the district and appellate levels; relatively few actually make it to the Supreme Court. She said that Trump's appointments to federal courts were a "generation shaping" event that affected not only abortion but a wide array of issues including religious liberty, marriage, and bioethics. Cathi Herrod, president of the Center for Arizona Policy, similarly judged that with Trump's election, "Maybe God gave us a little bit of a reprieve where we had a chance to not lose the Supreme Court for the next forty or fifty years. . . . I'm relieved that Trump is president because of what I see on the judicial front and the pro-life front, and the religious freedom front." Wayne Grudem, echoing his arguments from 2016, similarly argued, "the number one greatest problem facing the United States is the excessive role of judges in creating new laws that aren't justified by the written text of the Constitution or legislation that has been passed . . . and President Trump is moving with incredible speed and effectiveness in straightening out the number one problem in the country."[21] (Grudem also identified other positive elements he saw in the Trump administration, including "in his moving the embassy to Jerusalem, in his

---

[21]Wayne Grudem, "Why Voting for Donald Trump Is a Morally Good Choice," *Townhall*, July 28, 2016, https://townhall.com/columnists/waynegrudem/2016/07/28/why-voting-for-donald -trump-is-a-morally-good-choice-n2199564; and "If You Don't Like Either Candidate, Then Vote for Trump's Policies," *Townhall*, October 19, 2016, https://townhall.com/columnists/waynegrudem /2016/10/19/if-you-dont-like-either-candidate-then-vote-for-trumps-policies-n2234187.

strengthening the military, in protecting and securing the border, favoring school choice," and more.)

Why did the rest of the evangelical leaders we spoke to so strongly criticize the president and believe his presidency was not worth whatever benefit might be gained from it? What exactly is the harm Trump was doing? They expressed a wide array of concerns, including about Trump's chronic lying, for what they characterized as his cruel rhetoric, for his effect on American political culture, and especially for his effect on racial relations. Some expressed opposition to Trump's identity politics because they believe identity politics, regardless of whose identity is being advanced, are bad for American democracy. Many expressed these concerns even while expressing agreement with specific policy issues, such as national security, judicial appointments, or immigration policy.

The best summation I heard was that Trump was a threat to the basic norms of a free and open society—and this was two years before Trump's effort to overturn the results of the 2020 election and before the January 6, 2021, attack on the US Capitol by Trump supporters. Michael Wear listed the "culture of our politics" and "basic functioning of our democratic institutions" as among the top issues Christians should be concerned about. Anyabwile concurred, listing the integrity of "government institutions and constitutional authority," and the "rule of law" among top-tier issues. Some of our interviewees warned that the culture of democracy in America is ailing or imperiled. Trevin Wax compared the moment to performing surgery to remove cancer with infected instruments (Trump being the infected instrument). Some of Trump's critics warned that the downside of his administration was its effect on American political culture. Matthew Lee Anderson shared that "a lot of the concerns [about Trump] are broader, cultural . . . about the way in which the atmosphere and the ethos of the presidency through this person has changed." These interviewees represented evangelicals who are genuinely committed to Christian republicanism and who believed Trump was a threat to those values. Many supported Trump's judicial nominees because of the nominees' reputation for conservatism, limited government, and the Constitution, but they criticized Trump for all the ways in which he broke democratic norms and damaged American political culture.

My interviewees were approaching a truth that became clearer toward the end of Trump's presidency: that Trump's movement was a threat to republican principles, to democracy, the rule of law, and even the US Constitution. In 2018, my interviewees tended to focus on Trump's character, his public bullying, lying, and cruelty. Those things are bad, but it became clear that Trump was not simply deceitful and unkind: he was a nationalist and a demagogue, which are inconsistent with republicanism and the norms of a free and open society. Nationalism is an illiberal ideology of exclusion, not a temperamental or character flaw. As such, it will not go away despite that Trump has left office and it cannot be cured by reminding people to be civil to one another. The failure of Trump's words stem from a prior, more fundamental failing: a failure to understand the meaning of the American experiment, a failure to appreciate and defend the republican and democratic norms that undergird it, a failure to value the *ideas*—rather than the culture—that comprise our national identity, to include all Americans in the story he tells about who we are. If I can interpret and build on my interlocutors' concerns, the biggest problem with Trump's political movement is the ideas it embodies, ideas that a supermajority of White evangelicals have uncritically embraced.

These views come from evangelical leaders, or what we might call the professional evangelical establishment: theologically conservative, college-educated evangelicals who not only attend church weekly but lead churches or parachurch organizations or do the intellectual work of articulating evangelicalism and its public agenda, including pastors, seminary professors, cultural commentators, authors, and institutional leaders. In mid-December 2019, during Trump's first impeachment, Mark Galli argued in the pages of *Christianity Today* that Trump should be removed from office because of his abuse of power and immorality. Three days later I published an op-ed in the *Christian Post* arguing the Senate should convict Trump because "the Constitution is more important than abortion,"[22] because without the Constitution and the rule of law, "pro-life advocacy would be meaningless." Only within a constitutional system that allows popular participation is any kind of political activism meaningful, which means that protecting the system has to take precedence over any particular issue. These views were overwhelmingly unrepresentative of the broader evangelical political movement. A few

---

[22]Paul D. Miller, "Convict Trump: The Constitution Is More Important Than Abortion," *The Christian Post*, December 22, 2019.

months earlier, a public opinion poll found that an astonishing 99 percent of White evangelical Republicans opposed Trump's impeachment or conviction.[23] Clearly, the views expressed by the professional evangelical establishment are far more critical of Trump than those expressed by most self-identified White evangelicals.

EXPLAINING THE TRUMP COALITION

Evangelical elites who cared enough about republican principles to criticize and publicly oppose Trump were a minority of the broader evangelical movement. Who are the evangelicals who supported Trump, and why? What led them to value Trump? Democrats look at Trump's movement, see a homogeneously White and Christian political movement reasserting traditional American values, and interpret it as nothing more than eighteenth-century racial hatred imported into the twenty-first century. It is more accurate to say that Trump's movement is the latest manifestation of Christian nationalism in Jacksonian America. It is a backlash by Middle America, a reassertion of what they believe to be American nationality, which they feel is under threat from immigration, globalization, and progressives' century-long onslaught on American ideals. Trump's nationalist movement is overwhelmingly made up of White Christians living in red counties. Like any populist or nationalist movement, it invokes boogeymen as a mobilizing tactic, including Muslim terrorists, Mexican rapists, Chinese factory workers, Antifa and BLM rioters, campus radicals, and social justice warriors.

In 2016, sociologist Arlie Hochschild described what she termed the "deep story" of the political right: a feeling among White Christian men that they have patiently waited in line and worked hard to achieve the American dream, but they are stuck and even moving backward because immigrants, minorities, and women are cutting in line, cheating their way to the front through affirmative action, identity politics, welfare, and outright discrimination against Whites and men.[24] These White American men strongly identify with the United States—Hochschild does not use the word *nationalist*, but that is the reality she is describing—and feel that attacks on their country are attacks on

---

[23]PRRI, "Fractured Nation."
[24]Arlie Russell Hochschild, *Strangers in Their Own Land: Anger and Mourning on the American Right* (New York: The New Press, 2018), 104.

themselves, attacks that have grown so widespread and overt in recent years that they feel like "strangers in their own land." Their response is to reassert "traditional" American identity, which is also how they reassert their proper place in line up front. Hochschild later added to her analysis, arguing that Trump has become part of the "deep story," including his defiance of elites, his suffering on behalf of his movement throughout his embattled presidency, and a mythology of a new lost cause in his 2020 defeat in what he and some of his followers believe was a rigged election.[25] Loyalty to Trump has become a fundamental part of the political and national identity of a large swath of American voters, which is why even after leaving office he still inspires an unusual depth of passion and loyalty.

Historian Lisa McGirr, in her study of the emerging conservative movement in Orange County, California, similarly concluded that the movement was explicable as a response to the rapid pace of change in the mid-twentieth century's modernizing economy. "The people of Orange County were often steeped in nationalism, moralism, and piety that were part of the warp and woof of the communities from which they hailed." In the 1960s, their nationalism and moralism encountered the sexual revolution, the civil rights movement, the movement against school prayer, and the battle with international communism. "In a region where change seemed constant, the Right offered a reassuring message of solidity, of moral certainties and strong moorings. . . . A belief in staunch conservative values provided some stability, firm grounding, and a sense of cohesive community." Religion was a major part of that anchoring. "Social conservatives articulated a vision of the United States as a fundamentally Christian nation," and they argued that "the American nation was the political embodiment of Christian principles." Their view of religion was refracted through their understanding of American history; their vision of American identity as shaped by the American past was central to their project. "Their mythic vision of the nation's past gave conservatives a sense of coherence and represented an effort to legitimize themselves as the true upholders of national good." American history became almost a substitute form of religion and community. "The creation of a mythical American community provided a sense of rootedness. . . . The

---

[25]Derek Thompson, "The Deep Story of Trumpism," *The Atlantic*, December 29, 2020, www .theatlantic.com/ideas/archive/2020/12/deep-story-trumpism/617498/.

national past was such a community."[26] There is a portion of the American electorate that believes American national identity—which they closely associate with themselves—is imperiled, the solution to which is to reassert a past (mythical) version of nationhood which also serves to restore that group's particular fortunes.

Robert Bellah argued over fifty years ago:

> A return to primordial loyalties in the face of cultural and social breakdown can be defensive, based more on fear than joyous reaffirmation. Where the motive is the protection of one's own property and privilege against the threat of other competing groups, the political implications can be quite serious. One man's "cultural pluralism" can then become another man's "nativism," with all the classic elements of violence and repression that that entails.[27]

One way of thinking about the division among evangelicals is by heeding how Americans are divided by social location, or their place in society as defined by race, religion, education, income, and more. For example, in 2016 Trump won rural voters 62–24, reflecting a perennial divide between traditionalist citizens in rural areas and more cosmopolitan city dwellers. Interestingly, Trump did *not* win the voters in the lowest income categories, but he overwhelmingly won (78–19) those who believed their family's financial situation had worsened: Trump's support did not come from the poor but from those most afraid of being left behind, those who might feel they have the most to lose from the turmoil and change of a global economy and a pluralistic culture.[28]

Another way to highlight the social division is by looking at education. Americans are sharply divided between the highly educated and the rest. Hillary Clinton won college-educated voters by nine points in 2016; Trump won those with some college or less by eight points, according to the Pew Research Center: "This is by far the widest gap in support among college graduates and non-college graduates in exit polls dating back to 1980." When race and education are added together—probably the two most important

---

[26]Lisa McGirr, *Suburban Warriors: The Origins of the New American Right-Updated Edition* (Princeton, NJ: Princeton University Press, 2015), 9, 156-57, 162, 166-67.

[27]Robert N. Bellah, *The Broken Covenant: American Civil Religion in Time of Trial* (Chicago: University of Chicago Press, 1992), 109-10.

[28]Jon Huang et al. "Election 2016: Exit Polls," *New York Times*, November 8, 2016, www.nytimes.com/interactive/2016/11/08/us/politics/election-exit-polls.html

determinants of Americans' social location—the picture is stark: Donald Trump won the votes of Whites with no college degree by a staggering 39 points in 2016,[29] reflecting a trend that had been growing in recent election cycles but which peaked in 2016 (Trump's share of this vote declined slightly in 2020).[30] Trump's core voter was a blue-collar, red-state, White Christian Boomer with a high-school education.

Evangelicals—and Baptists specifically—are one of the least formally educated religious groups in America. Only 25 percent of White evangelicals have a college degree, falling to just 19 percent of Baptists, compared to 39 percent of White Catholics and 61 percent of Jews.[31] This is hardly news: Mark Noll published his attention-getting book, *The Scandal of the Evangelical Mind*, a quarter-century ago.[32] Those who go to college and graduate generally see the world differently than those who do not. College graduates are more likely to trust the findings of experts and to believe in the results of scientific inquiry (like the reality of climate change or the importance of wearing masks and getting vaccinated during a pandemic). They are more likely to believe that elite education should confer a privileged status on their opinions. They are also more likely to feel the confidence and responsibility to critique their own leadership. They are more likely to believe that the United States is a meritocracy—that achievement and success are a direct result of hard work and merit. They tend to believe, on balance, that the system works—because it did, for them. Those without a college education tend to believe the opposite.

This dynamic appears to be reflected in evangelicals' attitude toward authority. Nearly half (47 percent) of evangelicals agreed that they should "support my favored leader even when they say or do things I disagree with," according to a poll by the Billy Graham Center Institute, compared to just 27 percent of Americans who are not evangelical.[33] I suspect this is especially

---

[29]Alex Tyson and Shiva Maniam. "Behind Trump's Victory: Divisions by Race, Gender, Education," Pew Research Center, November 9, 2016, www.pewresearch.org/fact-tank/2016/11/09/behind-trumps-victory-divisions-by-race-gender-education/.

[30]"Understanding the 2020 Electorate: AP VoteCast Survey," National Public Radio, November 3, 2020, www.npr.org/2020/11/03/929478378/understanding-the-2020-electorate-ap-votecast-survey.

[31]Jones and Cox, *America's Changing Religious Identity*, 27.

[32]Mark A. Noll, *The Scandal of the Evangelical Mind* (Grand Rapids, MI: Eerdmans, 1994).

[33]Ed Stetzer and Andrew MacDonald, "Why Evangelicals Voted Trump: Debunking the 81 Percent," *Christianity Today*, October 18, 2018, www.christianitytoday.com/ct/2018/october/why-evangelicals-trump-vote-81-percent-2016-election.html.

true of those without a college education; none of the leaders I spoke to expressed anything like this sentiment. They often expressed something closer to the opposite: that we should be especially vigilant to hold our leaders accountable. I interpret the difference this way: Evangelicals without a college degree are deferential to people in power—but they seem more attached to the person than to their purpose or qualifications. Trump seems to understand: he famously joked that he could "stand in the middle of 5th Avenue and shoot somebody and I wouldn't lose voters."[34] That is why some have warned that Trump's movement is tantamount to a cult of personality. Michael Horton, professor of systematic theology and apologetics at Westminster Seminary California, worried that some of Trump's supporters' attitudes were nearly "idolatrous."

In fact, there appears to be a demonstrable connection between some varieties of White evangelicalism and what one scholar has suggested are authoritarian tendencies—specifically, among evangelicals who do not have a high level of formal education. According to one scholar, "Although there is no inherent relationship between authoritarianism and religion itself, researchers have identified links between authoritarian values and the practice of 'conventional, unquestioned and unreflected religion,' commonly found among Evangelicals." Authoritarian leanings, such as aggression toward or intolerance of out groups, unquestioning submission to a leader, and inflexible policing of social norms are not necessary implications of evangelicalism, White or otherwise—in fact, Christianity should undermine, not reinforce, those tendencies—but they correlate with low levels of formal education, which is common within the evangelical world. The result is that these authoritarian tendencies broadly overlap with White evangelicalism insofar as evangelical religion is "conventional, unquestioned, and unreflected."

Decades ago a pair of scholars found that "mature faith development," as measured by, for example, a willingness to critically examine one's own faith, led to a *decrease* of authoritarian leanings, while the converse led to the opposite.[35] In today's context, I suggest that evangelicals who are taught habits

[34]Jeremy Diamond, "Trump: I Could 'Shoot Somebody and I Wouldn't Lose Any Votes,'" CNN, January 24, 2016, www.cnn.com/2016/01/23/politics/donald-trump-shoot-somebody-support/index.html.

[35]James McBride, "Authoritarianism and Religion: Trump and White American Evangelicals in Cultural Perspective," *The GCAS Review Journal* 1, no. 1 (2021), 5; Gary K, Leak and Brandy A. Randall, "Clarification of the Link Between Right Wing Authoritarianism and Religiousness:

of careful study, reflection, self-examination, and critical thinking—in line with the Bible's command to "take every thought captive" (2 Corinthians 10:5), "test everything" (1 Thessalonians 5:17), and "get wisdom, get insight" (Proverbs 4:5)—are less likely to have authoritarian sympathies compared to evangelical churches marked by lone celebrity pastors and a culture of anti-intellectualism.

The education divide is a complex problem because some skepticism of educated elites is justified. All humans are sinful, and the noetic effects of the fall afflict the highly educated as much as (and possibly more than) the rest. Highly educated people are just as prone to foolishness and arrogance, but the effects of their character faults are magnified through their privileged place in society—meaning that some scholarship is highly learned, well-read foolishness, and public policy made on the foundations of flawed scholarship is destructive and unjust.[36] Evangelical scholars working in secular universities are among the quickest to testify to the problems apparent in the contemporary university. Distrust of educated elites is also fueled by the perception that elites have been at the forefront of progressive social policy, such as abortion, gay marriage, and transgender rights—all antithetical to evangelicals' concerns.

But populist evangelicalism has turned a healthy skepticism of elites into a dogmatic ideology of anti-intellectualism and uncritical nationalism.[37] Some scholarship is foolish nonsense, but so is anti-intellectualism, nationalist ideology, and most of the content on TV, Facebook, TikTok, and Twitter: scholars and experts do not have a monopoly on foolishness (and scientific expertise, at least, is self-correcting). Ignoring experts is at least sometimes comprehensible, but treating the views of a reality TV star as equally valid is not—and turning the question of wearing masks during a global pandemic into a

---

The Role of Religious Maturity," *Journal for the Scientific Study of Religion* (1995): 245-52; Connor Friedersdorf, "What Ails the Right Isn't (Just) Racism," *The Atlantic*, August 9, 2019.

[36] For example, three scholars recently wrote and published a series of fake academic articles, successfully passing them off as serious scholarship through peer review to dramatize the vacuity of what they called "grievance studies." See Yascha Mounk, "What an Audacious Hoax Reveals About Academia." For a longer and deeper argument, see Harold Bloom, *The Closing of the American Mind* (New York: Simon & Schuster, 2008).

[37] For a defense of expert knowledge and the role experts play in society, see Tom Nichols, *The Death of Expertise*. See also Noll, *Jesus Christ and the Life of the Mind* (Grand Rapids, MI: Eerdmans, 2013); John Piper, *Think: The Life of the Mind and the Love of God* (Wheaton, IL: Crossway, 2010); and George Marsden, *The Outrageous Idea of Christian Scholarship* (New York: Oxford University Press, 1998).

cultural-war wedge issue is shockingly irresponsible. Citizens have a responsibility to weigh carefully what they hear and say rather than rely on crude
indicators, like someone's level of education or their job title, to serve as a
proxy for their trustworthiness.

Evangelicals do not need to go to college to protect themselves from the
deceptions of demagogues and nationalist con men. They need only remember
that the God whom we worship calls himself a God of the Word. He *spoke* the
universe into being; the Bible goes so far as to call Jesus Christ "the Word"
(John 1:1); and God inspired the authoritative record of his revelation of
himself in the form of a book. We ought to be extraordinarily careful with the
words he enables us to speak and extraordinarily careful whose words we
follow, like, retweet, and vote for. God commands us to "take every thought
captive to obey Christ" (2 Corinthians 10:5), to "let your speech always be
gracious" (Colossians 4:6) because "death and life are in the power of the
tongue" (Proverbs 18:21) and "out of the abundance of the heart" our mouths
speak (Luke 6:45). When spelling out the greatest commandment, God included the obligation to love him *with our minds* (Matthew 22:37). In light of
how highly God values our words and our thinking, excusing someone's
words because they are "just words" is careless and insensitive. Indulging in
cruel or deceitful language as a form of reprisal against perceived slights (to
"own the libs") or to provoke a reaction (trolling) is uncharitable and unbe-
coming of the Christian public witness and the American public square. And
centering one's political engagement on resentment of one's social location, as
much of the nationalist movement seems to do, is as spiritually dangerous as
it is politically counterproductive.

The *Christianity Today* editorial calling for Trump's removal in December
2019 was an accurate reflection of elite evangelical opinion—which is a very
small part of the broader movement. The same distrust of elites and institutions that has swept through American life in recent decades has, unsurpris-
ingly, affected evangelicals. The broader movement, like many social movements in the United States in a populist era, is adrift, unmoored from historic
sources of authority, guidance, or constraint. Many evangelicals have little
relationship with historic evangelical institutions—like *Christianity Today* or
the National Association of Evangelicals—and no inclination to defer to elite
evangelical opinion. The rift between evangelical laypersons and evangelical

elites has enabled the rise of a populist evangelical leadership class, including Robert Jeffries, Franklin Graham, Paula White, and others.

When Donald Trump accepted the label of nationalism in October 2018, he was drawing on a long and deep tradition in American history and American religion. He did not invent nationalism, but he did give it a major signal boost. Nationalism is an attitude as much as an ideology: a movement of emotion, resentment, wounded pride, and status anxiety. The words that politicians use to peddle nationalism are not words designed to persuade; they are words designed to anger, enflame, embitter, and frighten. Worse, they are words designed to deceive and distract, to pull attention away from one set of problems—such as racial justice, school reform, or the tax code—and focus on another (often exaggerated) set, including national pride, the right to say, "Merry Christmas," or the supposed threat from immigrants. Nationalism is a con game, a lie sold to empower one set of elites over against a different set of elites by manipulating the masses while rarely addressing any legitimate grievance.

Trump is expert at the game. Trump has given little indication that he believes in the tenets of Christian nationalism himself, but he made repeated and explicit appeals to Christian power and "traditional" notions of American identity and regularly used religious language. According to one scholar, "President Trump has used religious language at a higher rate than any president from the last 100 years." After analyzing hundreds of major presidential addresses since Franklin Roosevelt for the use of over a hundred specifically religious words, the scholar found that Trump averaged 7.3 religious terms per 1,000 words, nearly double the average of all presidents since Roosevelt. He found that Trump used more religious language in speeches given in more religious states; that Trump has increased his use of religious language over time; and that these patterns are consistent in both his speeches and his Twitter feed.[38] And, of course, Trump understood his base: he chose for his vice president a reliable and long-beloved member of the Christian Right.

---

[38]Ceri Hughes, "Appealing to Evangelicals, Trump Uses Religious Words and References to God at a Higher Rate Than Previous Presidents," *The Conversation*, October 13, 2020, https://thecon versation.com/appealing-to-evangelicals-trump-uses-religious-words-and-references-to-god -at-a-higher-rate-than-previous-presidents-146816; Ceri Hughes, "The God Card: Strategic Employment of Religious Language in US Presidential Discourse," *International Journal of Communication* 13 (2019): 22.

Everyone recognizes that Trump lies compulsively—that was one of the chief complaints from my interviewees—but the problem is not simply that Trump is a liar. He is a *demagogue*. The words of a demagogue are especially pernicious. A demagogue appeals directly to popular prejudices. In doing so he routinely lies, but the point of the lying is less to get away with falsehood than to construct an alternate social reality, one in which the leader is always right, his followers are always imperiled, and both ultimate victory and ultimate defeat are just around the corner (a good description of Trump's behavior especially in the aftermath the 2020 election). The con man may appeal to legitimate grievances—such as Trump's focus on economic anxiety or political correctness—but it is in his interest never to truly resolve them. Without the grievance, people do not need the strongman to protect them anymore. For his part, the con man uses crude techniques of psychological manipulation to seduce his followers, to get and keep power, whatever the cost. A good con man needs a good mark, and Trump found his ready and waiting.

CONCLUSION

The Christian Right emerged in the 1970s as a hybrid, seeming to articulate an ideology of Christian republicanism but also capitalizing on the long history and powerful sentiments of racially charged American nationalism with a Christianized gloss. I earlier suggested that Christians would eventually have to choose between the Christian republicanism that they professed and the Christian nationalism increasingly evident in evangelical circles. I suggested the test would come when Christians were faced with a choice between Christian power and Christian principle. The test came in the person of Donald Trump. Throughout his campaign and presidency, Trump openly championed nationalism and directly appealed to Christian power, promising to respect and restore Christian tradition, heritage, and influence while neglecting and violating principles of justice, equality, and democracy. He capitalized on the powerful desire among mostly White Christians to restore a vision of American nationhood in which White Christianity predominated. In exchange, Trump counted White Christians, especially non-college-educated White evangelicals, his strongest and most enthusiastic supporters for the duration of his presidency.

The danger in White evangelicals' embrace of nationalism and Donald Trump is not simply that they are thinking sloppily and making poor choices. Another danger is that, through uncritical support for Trump, Christian nationalists have become fellow travelers with overt White nationalists and racists—which is all too easy for opponents to play up given the history of White Christianity with American racism. Some of Trump's aides and advisers made openly racist appeals, including former White House Chief Strategist Steve Bannon, who told an audience to "let [critics] call you racist; wear it as a badge of honor," in May 2018. Former deputy assistant to the president for strategic communications Michael Anton during the 2016 election pseudonymously condemned "the ceaseless importation of Third World foreigners with no tradition of, taste for, or experience in liberty [which] means that the electorate grows more left, more Democratic, less Republican, less republican, and less traditionally American with every cycle. As does, of course, the US population,"[39] equating the Republican Party with republican principles and arguing that "Third World foreigners," would reject both.

And Trump himself occasionally seemed to go out of his way not to offend White nationalists, signal his desire for their approval, or hint that his agenda dovetailed with their view of the world. In a February 2016 interview with CNN, Trump initially claimed not to know who David Duke was (former Grand Wizard of the Ku Klux Klan) and, when asked, appeared to decline to condemn the Klan, the most notorious White supremacist organization in American history. (He later issued a disavowal of both.) Trump's infamous remarks after the protests and violence in Charlottesville, Virginia, in August 2017, that there was "blame on both sides" and that there were "very fine people on both sides," appeared to be a clear effort by Trump to exonerate and defend Confederate sympathizers. (Trump never retracted his Charlottesville statement; when asked, in April 2019, he reaffirmed it.) In July 2019, Trump tweeted that four non-White Congresswomen "who originally came from countries whose governments are a complete and total catastrophe," should "go back and help fix the totally broken and crime infested places from which they came," a clear suggestion that non-White Americans are not really "from"

---

[39]Michael Anton, "The Flight 93 Election," *Claremont Review of Books*, September 5, 2016, https://claremontreviewofbooks.com/digital/the-flight-93-election/ (published pseudonymously under the name "Publius Decius Mus").

America and do not belong here (only one of the four Congresswomen in question was actually born outside the United States). In 2020, during a debate with Vice President Biden, Trump was invited to condemn the Proud Boys, a right-wing agitation group with a history of violent protests and some links to White supremacists. Trump responded that the Boys should "stand back and stand by." (Some members of the Proud Boys were later charged with conspiracy in the January 6 Capitol attack.) And, of course, his years-long record of peddling a baseless conspiracy theory about President Barack Obama's birth certificate was a racially coded attack on the legitimacy of America's first non-White president.

In these and other incidents, Christian nationalists have tacitly accepted a wide range of nationalist fellow travelers, including White nationalists. In this, they are following a long tradition on the right of turning a blind eye to the sins of cobelligerents. Historian Dan Carter argued that "even though the streams of racial and economic conservatism have sometimes flowed in separate channels, they ultimately joined in the political coalition that reshaped American politics from the 1970s through the mid-1990s"[40] and beyond. Similarly, the Christian Right has, at least, not prioritized racial justice and, in its lack of urgency, conveyed insensitivity toward the issue—even tolerance for the perpetuation of racial inequalities, while making common cause with racist groups and individuals.

A critic may accuse me of smuggling race into this discussion. Between the 2016 and 2020 elections, Trump made small gains among non-Whites, especially Latino men (prompting some commentators to speculate about Latinos assimilating to Whiteness). But consider: while 76 to 81 percent of White evangelicals voted for Trump in 2016 and 2020, just 5 to 10 percent of Black Protestants did.[41] Nor was that unique to 2016: a majority of Whites voted for the Republican presidential candidate and three-quarters of non-Whites voted for the Democratic candidate in every election since at least 2004.[42] Set aside

---

[40]Dan T. Carter, *From George Wallace to Newt Gingrich: Race in the Conservative Counterrevolution, 1963-1994* (Baton Rouge, LA: LSU Press, 1996), xiv.

[41]Gregory A. Smith, "Among White Evangelicals, Regular Churchgoers Are the Most Supportive of Trump," Pew Research Center, April 26, 2017, www.pewresearch.org/fact-tank/2017/04/26/among-white-evangelicals-regular-churchgoers-are-the-most-supportive-of-trump/.

[42]"Election Night Surveys," Public Opinion Strategies, November 4, 2020, https://pos.org/wp-content/uploads/2020/11/2020-Post-Election-National-Survey-1.pdf.

Trump himself, it is clear that American nationalism is overwhelmingly a White Christian phenomenon. White Americans and non-White Americans see the world in starkly different terms, a difference that Christianity does not ameliorate and may actually worsen. White Christians and Black Christians show no greater consensus on politics than White and Black non-Christians. Race and ethnicity are stronger shapers of Americans' worldview than religion; or, put another way, Americans' religious views are themselves shaped by their racial identities—which should be felt as a stinging rebuke to every American Christian—and the ethnoreligious division strongly correlates with Americans' views toward nationalism.

The complicity of Trump-supporting Christians with nationalism, conspiracy theories, and political violence was dramatized at the end of Trump's presidency in two events. On December 12, 2020, thousands of protesters gathered in Washington, DC, in the "Jericho March." The event called on Christians to "pray, march, fast, and rally for election integrity," and protest what they claimed, baselessly, was a stolen election. Speakers at the march, including Metaxas, repeated the falsehood that the 2020 election had been rigged or stolen, that Trump had won a second term, and that Christians faced an urgent task of somehow ensuring Trump would stay in office. "It's like stealing the heart and soul of America," Metaxas said of the election during an interview the same week. "It's like holding a rusty knife to the throat of Lady Liberty. . . . We need to fight to the death, to the last drop of blood, because it's worth it."[43]

Less than a month later, some Trump supporters took Metaxas literally, egged on by Trump when he told them during a raucous address on Pennsylvania Avenue on January 6, 2021, to "fight" for the election and show "strength" to make their voices heard. Rioters walked from Trump's speech to the US Capitol, carried signs saying "Jesus saves," erected a cross—and a gallows—on the Capitol grounds, played Christian worship music, and chanted "Hang Mike Pence!" for his refusal to stop the certification of the election. Some forcibly broke into the Capitol building and, carrying the Christian flag and the Confederate flag, found their way to the floor of the US Senate. Some were armed with weapons and flex cuffs, evidently intending to kidnap or possibly

---

[43]Emma Green, "A Christian Insurrection," *The Atlantic*, January 8, 2021, www.theatlantic.com /politics/archive/2021/01/evangelicals-catholics-jericho-march-capitol/617591/; David French, "The Dangerous Idolatry of Christian Trumpism," *The Dispatch*, December 13, 2020, https:// frenchpress.thedispatch.com/p/the-dangerous-idolatry-of-christian.

assassinate members of Congress to prevent them from certifying the electoral college vote and formally recognizing Joe Biden's election to the presidency. In the Senate, they paused to pray: "Jesus Christ, we invoke your name!" The leader prayed, thanking God for the opportunity to send a message "that this is our nation . . . that we will not allow the America, the American way of the United States of America to go down. . . . Thank you for filling this chamber with patriots that love you, that love Christ. Thank you for allowing the United States of America to be reborn. . . . In Christ's holy name we pray, Amen!"[44]

Rioters invoked Jesus' name to bless an attempted terrorist attack on the US Congress, an attack intended to halt the constitutional transfer of power and overturn the result of a democratic election—because, as they prayed, "this is our nation." No clearer picture could emerge that Christian nationalism had triumphed over republicanism—nor could there be a clearer illustration of the movement's danger and authoritarianism. Nearly 150 DC and Capitol police were injured in the attack, and one protester was shot to death.

Critics will say, rightly, that it is unfair to place blame for the attack on all Trump supporters, all Christians, or all White evangelicals, most of whom condemned the violence, and I certainly do not intend to do so. The attack has so far been an aberration rather than the start of a wave of extremist violence (though some observers have warned that political violence and extralegal efforts to subvert elections may worsen in coming years).[45] That is true, but it is also true that Christian nationalism and Trump support led directly to the attack on the US Capitol on January 6, that they played a major role in inspiring the rioters, and that the attack was the logical culmination of Trumpist Christian nationalism. The widespread support for Trump and his vision of America and widespread belief in his conspiracy theories were the permission structures that enabled the attack to happen. In mid-November 2020, 52 percent of Republicans believed Trump had "rightfully won" the 2020 election and 68 percent said they were concerned the election was "rigged," according to a Reuters poll, despite that Trump's own head of the Department of Homeland Security's Cybersecurity and

---

[44]"A Reporter's Footage from Inside the Capitol Siege," *New Yorker*, January 17, 2021, available at www.youtube.com/watch?v=270F8s5TEKY&t=479s. The prayer begins at 7:55.

[45]Robert Kagan, "Our Constitutional Crisis Is Already Here," *Washington Post*, September 23, 2021.

Infrastructure Security Agency called it "the most secure election in American history."[46]

Those numbers are less surprising when we remember that nearly three-quarters of Republicans still doubted in 2016 that Barack Obama was born in the United States.[47] Such willful disregard for basic facts and human reason go hand-in-hand with the belief that Christian America faced an existential crisis in the 2016 and 2020 elections and that Donald Trump's reelection was somehow the last, best hope to preserve America's Christian heritage—beliefs that led some to reject all normal restrictions on political behavior and openly embrace violence and terrorism rather than accept legitimate defeat in a democratic election. Christian nationalism married to Donald Trump's political fortunes led its adherents, in the name of saving the American heritage, to trample the American creed.

[46]Chris Kahn, "Half of Republicans Say Biden Won Because of a 'Rigged' Election," Reuters, November 18, 2020, www.reuters.com/article/us-usa-election-poll/half-of-republicans-say-biden-won-because-of-a-rigged-election-reuters-ipsos-poll-idUSKBN27Y1AJ; Eric Tucker and Frank Bajak, "Repudiating Trump, Officials Say Election 'Most Secure,'" *Associated Press*, November 13, 2020, https://apnews.com/article/top-officials-elections-most-secure-66f9361084ccbc461e3bbf42861057a5.

[47]Josh Clinton and Carrie Roush, "Poll: Partisan Divide Over 'Birther' Question," NBCnews.com, August 10, 2016, www.nbcnews.com/politics/2016-election/poll-persistent-partisan-divide-over-birther-question-n627446?cid=sm_tw.

10

HOW TO THINK
OF NATION, GOSPEL,
AND CREED

IF WE REJECT NATIONALISM, we are confronted with several questions. What is the right way to think about American identity? How do we cultivate patriotism, loyalty, and affection for our country without succumbing to nationalism? Have we ever gotten it right? If nationalism is bad, how can we in good conscience be members of a nation, much less love our nations or cultivate loyalty and attachment to them?

In chapter six, we saw that the Bible presents humanity as ordered into social, cultural, and political groupings, including tribes, clans, peoples, families, nations, languages, kingdoms, and more. In Genesis 10, Deuteronomy 32:8, and Acts 17:26, we get a sense that our lived experience as members of these groups is, in some way, a natural part of creation, an experience that is sustained in some sense in the throne room of God in Revelation 5. (Only the division of humanity into distinct languages is presented as the result of sin—something never said of ethnic, national, or cultural divisions—but even the existence of plural languages cannot be intrinsically evil because Pentecost and Revelation suggest it will be redeemed and preserved in the new creation.) It is important to note that the Bible not only presents diverse groups, but diverse *kinds* of groups: at no point do we get the sense that God prefers one kind of group over others (e.g., clans as better than tribes, or tribes than nations), or that the boundary lines of our cultural groups must align with our political groups. That said, the Bible presents plural group identity as part of the normal, good, created order, and our group affinities are natural loves that can be affirmed but must be rightly ordered.

This has two implications: one upward, so to speak, about international politics, and one downward, about human nature. Oliver O'Donovan argues in the biblical vision of order, "at the international level there was to be no unitary mediator. . . . Yhwh's world order was plurally constituted."[1] The Bible has no aspiration for world government and accepts the plurality of nations. Second, and more importantly for my argument, this has implications for how we think of human personhood. The Bible presents human nature as defined at least partly by social, corporate, or group ties, not as the atomized individual of Enlightenment social-contract thinking. As God says, by way of creating the family, "it is not good that man should be alone" (Genesis 2:19). We are made for fellowship with other human beings and with God. Aristotle wrote, and virtually every theologian and philosopher in the Western tradition until the Enlightenment affirmed, that humans are social and political animals. Cicero argued that nature "prompts men to meet in companies, to form public assemblies and to take part in them themselves. . . . We are not born for ourselves alone, but our country claims a share of our being, and our friends a share."[2] Centuries later Thomas Aquinas would agree: "There is in man an inclination to good according to the nature of his reason, which nature is proper to him; thus man has a natural inclination to know the truth about God *and to live in society*."[3]

That we belong to social, cultural, and political groups is normal, healthy, and good. They are intrinsically good and need no other justification—but there are other benefits to them: they give us a sense of belonging; teach, protect, and educate us; and give us an orienting framework with which to encounter the world. That is why Nigel Biggar is right that "it is justifiable to feel affection, loyalty, and gratitude toward a nation whose customs and institutions have inducted us into created forms of human flourishing."[4] The

---

[1]Oliver O'Donovan, *The Desire of the Nations: Rediscovering the Roots of Political Theology* (Cambridge: Cambridge University Press, 1999), 72.

[2]Cicero, *On Duties [De Officiis]*, trans. Walter Miller, Loeb Classical Library (Cambridge, MA: Harvard University Press, 1913), 12, 55, 47.

[3]Thomas Aquinas, *Summa Theologica* I-II, Q94, article 2, in Aquinas, *On Law, Morality, and Politics*, ed. William P. Baumgarth and Richard J. Regan (Indianapolis: Hackett, 1988), 48, emphasis added.

[4]Nigel Biggar, *Between Kin and Cosmopolis: An Ethic of the Nation* (Eugene, OR: Wipf and Stock, 2014), 13.

libertarian view that humanity is best understood as a collection of individual free rational agents who form society by agreement to further their mutual advantage is philosophically shallow, as is cosmopolitanism that denies the legitimacy of cultural, national, or particular distinctiveness altogether.

That is also why I think R. R. Reno is partly right that the "strong gods" of public life are inescapable. I think his language is too strong, but he is more right than not that "the sacralizing impulse in public life is fundamental. Our social consensus always reaches for transcendent legitimacy," he wrote. (I would say "moral" legitimacy, not "transcendent.") "Public life requires the aroma of the sacred," in large part because of what kind of creatures we are. "To be human is to seek transcendent warrants and sacred sources for our social existence."[5] As I'll describe shortly, I prefer the language of "story" and "calling" to "sacredness" or "transcendence," but the effect is much the same. Because we are naturally social and political creatures, we are right to look to our communities as *a* source of meaning, purpose, and fulfillment (not *the* source, not the source of ultimate meaning or complete fulfillment).

Reno comes to the wrong conclusion and endorses modern nationalism as the best of our inevitable strong gods. Nonetheless, I think he is right that we cannot escape some kind of overarching story about who "we" are, a story that gives us meaning, purpose, and direction. Trying to avoid, deny, or defeat every strong god is, in fact, dangerously counterproductive: it triggers an immune system overreaction. When the body politic, or any part of it, feels its strong gods being attacked, it goes into a defensive, reactionary crouch and clings to the hardest, strongest, most extreme version of its gods. That is how political extremes of the right and left become parasitical symbionts of each other, each feeding on the other's extremism as justification for its own, their mutual warfare becoming an inescapable and self-reinforcing cycle, like fascism and communism in the 1930s and nationalism and progressivism today. The question is, how do we construct a political story about who we are that is safe and avoids the dangers of nationalism?

---

[5] R. R. Reno, *Return of the Strong Gods: Nationalism, Populism, and the Future of the West* (New York: Simon and Schuster, 2019), 136-39.

TOWARD A POSITIVE VISION OF NATIONALITY

To answer this, I want to draw on the work of Rogers Smith, a political scientist and political theorist at the University of Pennsylvania who previously served as the director of the university's Program on Democracy, Citizenship, and Constitutionalism. In his groundbreaking 2003 book, *Stories of Peoplehood*, Smith articulated the outlines of a theory of people making, which I think we can use as the groundwork for a positive vision of nationality. In Smith's view, governments only have a limited number of options to legitimize their rule. They can appeal to "economic or political power stories," that is, appeals to prosperity, administrative competence, or simple promises of power. But these appeals are almost never sufficient by themselves. Virtually all governments have to resort to what Smith calls "ethically constitutive stories," or stories that present "membership in a particular people as somehow intrinsic to who its members really are, because of traits that are imbued with ethical significance."[6] The stories that governments have, historically, invoked include quite a lot of dangerous, illiberal, and unjust stories, such as fascism, communism, and nationalism. The dangers of such stories are well known: "They include demands that all members gives total allegiance to a 'people's' sovereign authorities; disregard for the basic rights and interests of those dwelling within the bounds of a community, but not regarded as full members of that 'people'; and similar disdain, expressed either as aggression or neglect, toward the rights and interests of many of those outside its bounds."[7] This was my basic argument in chapter four about the inherent illiberality within nationalism. Most ideologies are dangerous and illiberal and lead to domestic oppression and international aggression.

Yet Smith rejects the idea that we can abolish ethically constitutive stories altogether. Like Reno's "strong gods," these stories are inevitable; they arise in essentially all polities; they seem to be an inescapable feature of human political community. "Ethically constitutive stories have not only always been part of the politics of people-making but always will be."[8] Part of their endurance is simply because they are powerful, popular, and successful, and the sheer logic of competition suggests that innovative political entrepreneurs will

---

[6] Rogers M. Smith, *Stories of Peoplehood: The Politics and Morals of Political Membership* (Cambridge: Cambridge University Press, 2003), 64.
[7] Smith, *Stories of Peoplehood*, 154.
[8] Smith, *Stories of Peoplehood*, 74.

have to resort to these stories to win support. "In the end nothing can really prevent aspiring leaders from summoning support by advancing compelling constitutive accounts of shared political identity. Such stories confer enough of a political advantage that at various times, their proponents are bound to gain the upper hand in the competitive politics of people-building that is part of any long-enduring society."[9]

These stories also thrive because they are not all bad; they meet enduring, deeply rooted human psychological needs. "Most people have profound philosophical and psychological needs to believe some sustaining ethically constitutive story. Most of us do need communities that endure and identities that feel secure if we are to be happy." Smith does not go into detail about the origins of these felt needs, but the biblical account of human communities suggests we need them because we are designed for them, and they for us. The stories that construct these communities, Smith continues, "provide sturdy anchors of morally compelling identity and worth amid the roiling seas of competitive community construction. They give us a sense of belonging, a sense of place in the world, a sense of partnership in a larger, meaningful collective existence and its shared endeavors. They help us make sense of our lives, intellectually and morally. And in so doing, they help to cement and sustain the communities that sustain us."[10]

Smith shows some similarities but a crucial difference with O'Donovan when the latter argues that a key component of political rule is the possession or inheritance of a tradition. O'Donovan's meaning is difficult, but I take him to mean that legitimate political authority is constituted in part by its role securing and perpetuating a nation's inheritance and traditions. Government exists in part to safeguard "something *possessed* and handed on from generation to generation," as Israel was to inherit and safeguard the Promised Land and the law of Moses.[11] I think Smith is correct that "stories" are inevitable and that governments ignore or repress them at their peril, and O'Donovan is right that acknowledging the influence of the past is one root of legitimate authority—but I am wary of O'Donovan's language of "inheritance" and "tradition," because of my earlier argument against enshrining one specific cultural template for the nation and in favor of "free culture"

---

[9]Smith, *Stories of Peoplehood*, 157.
[10]Smith, *Stories of Peoplehood*, 101.
[11]O'Donovan, *Desire of the Nations*, 41.

(see chap. 5). What is the difference? How do we sustain "stories" while also upholding the idea of "free culture"? I would locate the difference in our attitude toward the past. A story is open-ended and alive, available for retelling, reinterpretation, and remixing; a "tradition" is closed, fixed, essentialized, officious, and dead. Recall again Lowry's call to "preserve the cultural nation" by enshrining a quasi-official version of Anglo-Protestantism, or Orban's insistence that every nation "has the right to say that it does not want its country to change." That strikes me as misguided because it rigidifies the past in the name of preserving it. To celebrate our stories while respecting "free culture" does not mean we ignore the past or pretend it does not matter to who we are, but that we reexamine it afresh each generation for new insights and through new eyes.

Because ethically constitutive stories are inescapable, powerful, and sometimes good, we cannot and should not seek to banish them, even though they carry the danger of idolatry and oppression. Trying to banish them would be dangerous and counterproductive. "By seeking to remove from politics many of the things about which people care most, attempts to relegate constitutive stories to the margins only tend to weaken and falsify political life, making civic actions seem trivial and much public rhetoric disingenuous." For example, some thinkers have been in the habit of disdaining voters' concern for values and identity. Rational voters vote for their pocketbooks, these critics say, a clear material concern; appeals to "values" are a form of Marxian "false consciousness" that demagogues and capitalists use to keep the masses in line while exploiting them. This is the basic line of critique of books like *What's the Matter with Kansas?*[12] and this critique is notable both for its condescension toward most Americans and its ignorance about them.

Of course, the left has its own version of an ethically constitutive story and leans heavily on the language of values and identity, but its insistence that its story is beyond critique while others stories are beyond the pale almost certainly contributes to polarization and extremism: "Many contemporary proponents of extreme religious and racial views may experience strengthening senses of righteous indignation when they are told that their views are too unreasonable even to be debated on the merits in public arenas and that it is

---

[12]Thomas Frank, *What's the Matter with Kansas? How Conservatives Won the Heart of America* (New York: Picador, 2007).

'uncivil' for officials to discuss them seriously."[13] Trump's election was, in part, a rebellion against just this kind of shallow and insulting vision of political life stripped of meaningful debate about American national identity and national purpose. Smith wrote—a dozen years before Trump—a remarkable paragraph that reads like a prediction of the White working class responding to Trump's promise to "make America great again":

> Precisely because these stories can be foundational in the development of human identities, human psyches and sense of value and meaning, many people are likely to be made insecure *when the ideas, institutions, and practices expressive of established ethically constitutive stories are threatened*, from whatever source. Even persons whose statuses in prevailing arrangements are far from enviable may feel anxious when their world seems to be undergoing major upheavals and transformations. They are then likely to be responsive to elites who offer refurbished versions of the ideologies, institutions, and ways of life to which they feel allegiance.[14]

Trump's rise was a symptom of a deeper malady: the American political system had given up telling meaningful stories about who we are as a people, stories that are plausible, true, patriotic, inclusive, and that both resonate with our past yet make room for who we were becoming in the future. People need these stories. The left has no unifying story, in my view, stuck in the quagmire of identity politics. The right's story deteriorated into an endless call for more tax cuts and deregulation. Trump's distinctiveness was that he at least dared tell a story about restoring national greatness. It was not inclusive and only occasionally true, and a majority of Americans rightly rejected it in 2016 and 2020 and throughout his presidency, but it was almost the only effort by any major figure on the national stage to tell an ethically constitutive story, to make national identity mean something.

Trump's story resonated deeply with a plurality of Americans, and they embraced it with fervor—not the way a shopper rationally selects an item to purchase because they want it, but the way a stadium erupts when their underdog team scores an upset in the championship. We cannot do without national stories. We are wired for them. If we are not given a story, we will make one up. Absent alternatives, we will follow even the worst, most unjust and

---

[13]Smith, *Stories of Peoplehood*, 183.
[14]Smith, *Stories of Peoplehood*, 121.

illiberal ethically constitutive story if it is the only one in circulation. The solution, then, is to tame the stories; to vet them; to tell the right kind; not to stop telling them. To beat nationalism, we need to tell a better story.

Smith argues that we should tell a story rooted in history—he prefers a secular version of it—that draws on the truth of who we have been while aspiring to a better version of ourselves in the future. History is truthful, and "the inclusion of truthful elements is no guarantee of political success; but it is often advantageous, and it certainly contributes to the intellectual moral defensibility of the view."[15] The national story can and must include both triumphs and failures because that is the best way to include everyone—victor and victim alike—and to inspire people with a sense of responsibility. "I believe most people will be more strongly motivated, rather than alienated, if they see their political identities as partly constituted by histories displaying both good and bad elements. Such histories will indicate, quite authentically, that it is now largely up to them to determine in their shared political lives whether and how the best parts of their heritage will be continued and extended, and the worst parts overcome."[16] With specific reference to the United States, that means approaching our history of racism (and, I would add, sectarianism) in a certain way: "Rather than shrugging off America's criminal racial history as an aberration that still leaves us morally superior to all other peoples, the US as a political community and Americans as citizens should see themselves as possessing both distinctive responsibilities and distinctive opportunities to show that the poisonous legacies of racist institutions can be overcome."[17]

HISTORY AND AMERICAN IDENTITY

What does that look like in practice? The nationalist impulse rightly sees the need for a common identity—in contrast to the left, which often downplays that need in favor of various group identities—but it errs in how it defines the nation. Nationalism roots our common identity in enforced cultural unity and vests government with the responsibility to replicate and defend the national cultural identity—essentially, a large tribe. On the other hand, identity politics and multiculturalism amount to hypertribalism, sidelining the nation in favor

---

[15]Smith, *Stories of Peoplehood*, 189.
[16]Smith, *Stories of Peoplehood*, 160.
[17]Smith, *Stories of Peoplehood*, 200.

of racial, sexual, or class-based subgroupings. I affirmed in chapter two that tribalism is natural and can be put to good use if it is harnessed to something higher than itself. But tribalism alone, by itself, is dangerous. It is consistent with neither an open society nor with human flourishing. Reducing human social life to the reenactment of the premodern tribe is denigrating to human dignity, ignorant of the realities of modern polities, and willfully blind to the history of tribalism's dangers. We must *embrace and transcend* our tribal identities, living in the tension between our primordial, tribal origins and our universal, transcendent purpose.

This is hardly a novel insight. Thirty years ago Benjamin Barber argued we were living in an age of "Jihad vs. McWorld," a contest between the forces of tribalism (Jihad) and globalism (McWorld), between the centripetal and centrifugal forces in political life, and argued that we needed to find a way to tame both.[18] Nor was Barber wholly original. Political theorists argue about the relative merits of regimes ruled by the one, the few, and the many, and generally argued in favor of mixed regimes that blended aspects of all types. Medieval scholastics took the debate in more abstract directions into the realm of epistemology, arguing over nominalism (in favor of particulars) against realism (in favor of the reality of universals). Before them, Plato and Aristotle argued over whether the universal or the particular was the ground of all reality, knowledge, and truth. This is a perennial debate in human life. Shall our politics be grounded most fundamentally in the universal (globalism) or particular (tribalism and nationalism)?

Some readers will be drawn to argue for one or the other side. But mere partisanship in this debate is a sign of intellectual blindness in philosophy as much as in politics. If you cannot see the merit in your opponent's point of view, the eyes of your heart and mind are not truly open yet. Jesus counseled us to look to the plank in our own eyes before worrying about the speck in our neighbor's eye. I think Jesus' wisdom applies just as well to the life of the mind as to matters of the spirit (because I do not think there is as much of a distinction between them as we often assume). Jesus' counsel to practice self-examination holds true in argumentation. Look for the weaknesses in what you believe before worrying about the weaknesses of the other side.

---

[18]Benjamin Barber, *Jihad vs. McWorld: Terrorism's Challenge to Democracy* (New York: Ballantine, 2010).

One of my great frustrations in public debate is how often people assume that to point out the errors of one side is to affirm the virtue of the other. Americans have been drilled into a stupefying habit of binary thinking because of our two-party system: if one is bad, the other must be good. That is obviously not true for the simple reason that both sides could both be wrong at the same time, and usually are—and both sides might also contain germs of truth, and usually do. Nationalists rightly recognize the failings and errors of progressivism, which says precisely nothing about the merits of nationalism. Globalists and tribalists are wrong about most things they affirm, but their critique of each other is spot on. Plato, though he was a partisan for the universal, nonetheless rightly counseled the practice of dialectic reasoning, a kind of habit of seeing both sides, rooted in the character traits of curiosity, broadmindedness, and intellectual hospitality. To put it in more Christian terms, we see but dimly, which suggests we should cultivate intellectual humility and a continuous openness to learn, to revise our convictions, and to treat those with whom we disagree not as enemies but as potential teachers. The quest for justice is not a two-party system.

What does this mean for our efforts to rethink our identity as Americans? One side affirms our tribal identity as Anglo-Protestants; the other side damns Anglo-Protestantism and wants to turn its back on that history altogether. Of course both are wrong: we should *embrace and transcend* our Anglo-Protestant cultural heritage, embrace it as our history, and transcend it in our future. This means recognizing and celebrating the best of our Anglo-Protestant past, recognizing its continuing salience to who we are—even when "we" include non-Whites and non-Protestants—while rejecting the simplistic tribalism of treating our heritage as the beginning and end of our national identity. In Frederick Douglass's famous 1852 Independence Day address, he told his White audience that "I will unite with you to honor [the founders'] memory," and called the founders "our fathers," claiming their history as his own story, as I share below. We, all of us, share in the Anglo-Protestant past; it is our history, a history that includes some good things that *all people* can celebrate. Even non-Anglos and non-Protestants live in a polity founded, shaped, and defined by Anglo-Protestants for most of American history. We collectively benefit from the sacrifice and heroism of the best of them even as we heal from the abuse and oppression of the worst of them.

A vital part of embracing Anglo-Protestantism as our originating tribe is to know our history—including the history of our achievements and our sins. This is how we stay grounded in the particular and accept the inevitable tribalism that constitutes part (but only part) of all public life. It is hard to have a shared sense of who "we" are unless we have a shared story. Our understanding of that story will differ greatly depending on our social location, especially our racial or ethnic backgrounds. That's fine: I do not think we need a common place in our national story, but at least a common knowledge about it, a common sense of what went right, a common desire to cultivate the best of it, and a common desire to continue the story. We have to accept that the American past, for better and worse, as the inescapable antecedent narrative to which we are heirs, and our heirdom comes with the responsibility to act as responsible stewards and caretakers of the national story.

Some on the left seem to want to reject national history, teach the history of subgroups and marginalized peoples, or study national history only insofar as it is necessary to catalog what we did wrong, a kind of history best exemplified by Howard Zinn's widely popular *A People's History of the United States*. Such works have helpfully uncovered the history of many people who were not in power or whose contributions were overlooked. They have also helped correct the older tradition of writing history as hagiography. But the allergy to celebrating national achievement or national identity leaves their history books incomplete at best; more often, like Zinn's book, they are exercises in cherry-picking the historical evidence to present the worst possible version of history that is corrosive of a healthy patriotism and national sentiment because it undermines any sense of a shared historical achievement, experience, or identity.

This is dangerous. People must have something in which to take pride; if we deny them the ability to take pride in their nation, they will simply shift the locus of their loyalty to a subgroup, such as their ethnic or racial group. Relentlessly deconstructing American patriotism is likely to fuel White nationalism on the one side and identity politics for minority groups on the other. National identity grounded in common history is far safer than identity grounded in race, ethnicity, religion, tradition, or "heritage." Max Weber highlighted the importance of "memories of a common political destiny,"[19] in his rumination

---

[19]Max Weber, "The Nation," in *Readings and Commentary on Modernity*, ed. Stephen Kalberg (Oxford: Blackwell, 2005).

on national identity. Ernest Renan wrote in one of the earliest (1882) and still best discussions of the definition of nations that a nation requires two things:

> One is the possession in common of a rich legacy of memories; the other is present consent, the desire to live together, the desire to continue to invest in the heritage that we have jointly received. . . . The nation, like the individual, is the outcome of a long past of efforts, sacrifices, and devotions. . . . A heroic past with great men and glory (I mean true glory) is the social capital upon which the national idea rests. These are the essential conditions of being a people: having common glories in the past and a will to continue them in the present; having made great things together and wishing to make them again.[20]

C. S. Lewis exhorted his readers to cultivate "a particular attitude to our country's past," an attitude of honor toward "the great deeds of our ancestors," whose example we strive to uphold, emulate, and improve upon—even as he wanted to question and study the past with open eyes for the nation's sins.[21] Or as Amanda Gorman's poem "The Hill We Climb" says, "Being America is more than a pride we inherit. / It's the past we step into and how we repair it." To cite another great work of literature, as Alfred the Great, the ninth-century Anglo-Saxon king, says in the Netflix show *The Last Kingdom*, "A country is its history, the sum of all its stories. We are what our fathers made us."[22] America has done great things in the past and has many more to do in the future.

Being an American means, in part, knowing and celebrating the history of our great deeds, appropriating them as one's own, and pledging to participate in future ones—and it means knowing and lamenting the history of our misdeeds and committing to work for justice in the future. White Americans can celebrate Frederick Douglass's vision of American nationhood, including his damnation of hypocritical White American Christianity, and African Americans can celebrate the words of a Declaration written by a White Anglo-Protestant slaveowner. The African American writer James Baldwin discovered his common Americanness with White Americans as an expatriate in France in 1959; he saw White Europeans differed from White Americans, and thus how he was similar to the latter. Recognizing their mutual alienation from

---

[20]Ernest Renan, "What Is a Nation?," in *Becoming National: A Reader*, ed. Geoff Eley and Ronald Grigor Suny (New York: Oxford University Press, 1996), 52.

[21]C. S. Lewis, *The Four Loves* (New York: Harcourt and Brace, 1960), 42.

[22]*The Last Kingdom*, season 2, episode 8, 4:23, Netflix, www.netflix.com/watch/80164474.

Europe meant "we would no longer need to cling to the shame and bitterness which had divided us so long." This realization helped Baldwin feel "released from the illusion that I hated America." Baldwin rejected that hate and chose instead to recognize that he, like everyone, will always carry the mark of his origins, and he chose to "find it a matter for rejoicing."[23]

Embracing and rejoicing in our shared history and shared identity means, I think, publicly honoring the American founders and other Americans who made irreplaceable and positive contributions to our nation. It probably also means establishing something like a truth and reconciliation commission to help educate Americans—especially White Americans—about the uglier realities of our past. Knowing history truthfully means a full and well-rounded education that does not turn a blind eye to our failings and hypocrisies. As Smith argues, such stories help increase citizens' sense of civic responsibility because they

> present membership in the American political community as participation in a larger entity with an existence and meaning that simultaneously transcend and inform the individual lives of its citizens. Historical stories also have a natural propensity to strengthen senses of civic responsibility and to affirm the propriety of democratic self-governance. For in presenting the political community as something to which citizens have given shape and meaning in the past, these stories make it clear that the decisions of American political leaders and their active constituents today can play a large role in determining their nation's current and future significance—especially if they take their powers and opportunities to do so seriously.[24]

This approach to national identity may also mean recognizing English as the language of our public life. Weber thought so: "Of those cultural elements that represent the most important positive basis for the formation of national sentiment everywhere, a common language takes first place." Weber believed this was becoming even more important under the political and economic conditions of modernity because a common language helped bind together the masses who did not participate in elite culture and facilitated a national economic life.[25] I am personally torn about this. America is functionally a bilingual country. One of America's strengths is the presence of immigrants

---

[23]James Baldwin, *Nobody Knows My Name* (New York: Dell, 1961), 18-19, 22.
[24]Smith, *Stories of Peoplehood*, 189
[25]Weber, "The Nation."

who speak scores upon scores of languages: that helps us understand the world better and train better businessmen, diplomats, statesmen, and spies. Many who argue for English as the national language use English as a proxy for European culture: for them, recognizing the national language is a way of signaling a national commitment to a Western or British heritage.

I prefer to think of a "public" language rather than a "national" language to indicate that all languages are welcome, but we use English for our common life, including our public schools and government. I suggest a public language not as Trojan horse to smuggle European culture into the definition of American identity, but in recognition that the ability to speak to one another and communicate in the public square is an important prerequisite to a shared political endeavor, and it is an important part of our history. The history of America was enacted in English and its great words were written in English. It is hard to imagine connecting with that history, deriving some sense of continuity with it, and founding our national identity (partly) in it without shared fluency in English. The US naturalization process currently requires immigrants to "be able to read, write, and speak basic English," "have a basic understanding of US history and government," and "demonstrate an attachment to the principles and ideals of the US Constitution." These seem to me reasonable membership criteria for American nationality, neither too restrictive nor too lax (though I am not sure how well these criteria are actually enforced). They emphatically do not include Christianity, European ancestry, or Anglo-Protestant culture.

Our history is part of our identity, whether we want it or not. We cannot uncritically celebrate everything in the past, of course, but neither can we pretend that we have the ability to reject history altogether and start the world anew. I've argued in favor of taking down Confederate statues and monuments, but taking down the statues of George Washington, Thomas Jefferson, and Ulysses S. Grant, as mobs inexplicably did in the summer of 2020, or Benjamin Franklin, as a Washington, DC, commission recommended, is historically illiterate and comes off as a trivial performative revolution in service of a fantasized puritanical utopia so detached from reality it is functionally nihilistic. Unlike Confederate leaders, Washington and Jefferson did great deeds worthy of celebration and honor, deeds from which we continue to benefit; their sins tarnished, but did not destroy, their achievements. We cannot denude our public square of any historical figure who did anything wrong or who ever disagreed with today's prevailing moral standards, much less anyone who ever disagreed with the ever-shifting moral standards of the left. Such an effort would amount to a declaration that there are no heroes, no figures in the past worth veneration—which is tantamount to saying that there is no story of great deeds that binds us together, no shared history, and thus no nation.

THE AMERICAN CREED

But if we are to both honor and critique the founders, the founders are not the final authority of justice and not the sole source of our national identity. We can only recognize our misdeeds if we have a standard outside and above our tribe to judge it. Our American identity cannot end with Anglo-Protestant tribalism. We must embrace our Anglo-Protestant past, but we can and should allow ourselves to grow beyond Anglo-Protestantism. We must aspire to incorporate universal ideals which grow us beyond the provincialism of our tribe, challenge us to see beyond the horizon within which we were raised, and hold us accountable even for crimes our tribe may condone. That is why American identity should be founded first and foremost on the ideals of the American experiment as reflected in the US Constitution, the Declaration of Independence, the writings of Abraham Lincoln and Frederick Douglass, the sermons and speeches of Martin Luther King Jr., and others of the great papers of American history. If you do not know or do not agree with the American creed, in an important sense you are not truly or fully American, even if you hold American citizenship.

Rich Lowry, whose book on nationalism I reviewed in chapter three, argued that "the criterion for citizenship in the United States is not attachment to a set of ideas but birth within our borders."[26] Simply as a matter of law, he is wrong: legal immigrants are not born within our borders but gain citizenship through naturalization which *does* require express agreement to the Constitution. As a matter of political theory and American history, he is even more wrong. The leaders of the Confederacy were born in America and inherited the same Anglo-Protestant cultural heritage as the leaders of the Union, yet they explicitly rejected the American creed, committed treason against the US Constitution, and repudiated the Declaration of Independence and its

---

[26]Rich Lowry, *The Case for Nationalism: How It Made Us Rich, Powerful, and Free* (New York: Broadside, 2019), loc. 395, Kindle.

assertion that "all men are created equal." During the war the Confederate leaders *were not Americans*: they did not share the same sense of national identity as the Unionists, were not part of the national "we," and forsook their rights of citizenship—until they surrendered their arms, gave up their rebellion, received amnesty for their treason, and swore an oath to "faithfully support and defend the Constitution of the United States." Throughout the era, before the war as they argued over slavery, during the secession crisis and the war itself as hundreds of thousands of Americans died, the White citizens of the North and South shared the same birth, culture, language, heritage, and even religion. The only thing that divided them was whether or not they accepted the principles of the Constitution and the Declaration. Those principles—*not* differences of religion, culture, or language—are what distinguished North from South, Unionists from Confederates, Americans from traitors. It is to these ideals immigrants can be asked to assimilate, not to European culture or Protestant Christianity. The ideas of the Constitution and Declaration, as practiced in this particular land, are the bedrock, the fundament of any possible working definition of what it means to be an American.

Throughout American history, nativists and nationalists have worried that some kinds of people might not be capable of upholding the American creed: Catholics, they said, because of their loyalty to the pope; or Jews, because of a supposed global plot to undermine Christendom; the Germans, because of their general barbarism; the Irish, because of their drunkenness; Eastern Europeans, because of their illiteracy or lack of experience with Enlightenment thought; Chinese, because they are not Christians; Native Americans and Hispanics, because they were supposedly not suited to an Anglo work ethic; and above all Africans, because of any and every possible excuse that could be imagined. What is remarkable is that American history is the history of disproving every one of these bigotries. That story of overcoming—coming ever closer to our ideals and forming a more perfect Union—is what it means to be American. It is the ethically constitutive story of who we are.

But nationalists are correct in one respect: some people do not support or agree with the ideals of the American experiment, and in an important sense they do threaten national identity. Who are these people? Not any one ethnic or religious group, but nationalists themselves. Nationalism in its ideal form is precisely the set of ideas that rejects the American creed as the foundational principle of American identity. Nationalists do not reject the creed; they reject its *primacy in defining American identity*. But the creed must be *the dispositive fact* of American identity, or it is functionally toothless. Nationalism defines American identity *first* by shared race, religion, or (today) culture; to them, the creed is good secondarily, derivatively, only because and insofar as it came from our Anglo-Protestant culture. If that is how you view the creed, you do not actually understand the creed at all. The creed describes itself in universal, not parochial, terms. "All men" are created equal, not White men, Christian men, or European men. "Government" exists to defend our rights—not Western governments, White governments, or Christian governments. To treat the creed as a mere cultural artifact is to reject what the creed says about itself. To be true to the creed, we define America by the basic requirements of citizenship, the most basic of which is loyalty to the principles of our shared life together, the principles of our Constitution, coupled with an awareness of our history and a commitment to a shared future. The creed cannot be the sole source of American national identity, but it must be the preeminent source. American nationhood is best understood neither as our history alone, nor our creed alone, but as the *story of our creed* in this land by a diverse collection of people attempting to live out its principles together.

The creed is a principle of exclusion; but some form of exclusion is inevitable and necessary. The question is *on what basis* will we exclude. Nationalists are fond of saying that without a border, we don't have a country. They are correct. Borders are essential for defining who "we" are and who isn't part of "us." All groups need an exclusion principle for the group to exist and cohere. Churches do not admit Muslims as members, and mosques rightly reciprocate by excluding Christians. On what principle will we exclude people from full membership in the American nation? Will we exclude people because they do not assimilate to Anglo-Protestantism? That would exclude quite a lot of Americans. The Constitution and Declaration are the proper borders of American identity. Excluding people based on disloyalty to the Constitution is far better than excluding them based on their cultural identity or accepting them on the basis of their mere physical presence on American soil.

"ANGLO-SAXON DESTINY AND RESPONSIBILITY"

Invoking the creed, and thus America's best virtue, raises one final danger: hubris, complacency, and moral deafness because of the superiority of a national identity based on timeless values. After the encounter with the rich young ruler, Jesus told his disciples that "only with difficulty will a rich person enter the kingdom of heaven" (Matthew 19:23). Wealth tempts us to believe we can be independent; it faintly echoes Satan's temptation in the garden that "you will be like God" (Genesis 3:5). When we have much of what the world esteems, we feel like gods, and are far less apt to heed the living God. America has so much of what the world esteems, including wealth, power, dynamism, natural beauty, and more. But in the creed, America has its greatest source of worldly wealth: it has an actual claim to authentic political morality. After thousands of years of philosophers debating the true nature of justice and the shape of the ideal regime, the United States (and United Kingdom) can, with a straight face, claim to have come closer to the answer than any other people or nation in history—which is precisely why Americans can be so pig-headed, prideful, and obtuse.

I wonder if there is almost a natural law at work here: the power of a false idol is in direct proportion to its goodness if rightly ordered. All things are originally good, and all loves good if rightly ordered, but all things can become idols, and all loves idolatry, if disordered. Precisely to the degree that something is actually good, to that same extent it becomes dangerous and powerful when loved too strongly. Satan was the highest of angels; thus, in his fall, he becomes the prince of demons. The American experiment is—and I mean this without exaggeration—simply one of the greatest things ever to happen in human history, which is exactly why it is so hard not to idolize America, and why American nationalism—the religion of American greatness—is so dangerous. This is obviously true in cases of American wickedness. Here I want to emphasize that when America *is at its best*, pursuing just causes like the War for Independence, the Civil War, the World Wars, and the Cold War, our virtue and success feed a sense of national self-righteousness and blunts Christians' public witness. American Christians can become deaf to rebuke and flippant about past historical sins because of our justifiable pride in American identity and American achievements. The problem is acute for Americans because, for us, there is much of which to be justly proud.

In other words, "The pride of a virtuous nation cannot be humbled by moral and political criticisms because in comparative terms it may actually be virtuous."[27] So wrote Reinhold Niebuhr in his profound essay on "Anglo-Saxon Destiny and Responsibility." Written in October 1943, as the Allies were turning the tide of war against the Axis powers, Niebuhr recognized that the United States and Great Britain would emerge from World War II as the most powerful states in the world, and that they professed to be dedicated to principles of freedom and human dignity. As such, they had a special responsibility to safeguard those principles at home and abroad. This is the "destiny and responsibility" of his title. But Niebuhr recognized the tension: the two great powers really were the best hope for world order, even as the United States imposed a Jim Crow system of racial apartheid against African Americans and the United Kingdom sustained a global empire over vast swaths of the world. In 1943 they were quite literally the last, best hope for mankind, waging total war against the genocidal Nazi and Imperial Japanese campaigns for world conquest, but their just cause did not mean they were terribly exemplary in the sight of God.

That is why Niebuhr cautioned the great democratic powers from believing that their position of greatness was because of superior merit. "The fact is that no nation or individual is ever good enough to deserve the position of leadership that some nations and individuals achieve," he wrote, warning against the spirit of pharisaism that takes hold when one believes staunchly in one's own righteous power.[28] He argued that if we take a fair look at our history, we would recognize that accident and fortune—or God's providence—played as much a role as our own virtue in creating our power. We should welcome such providence as a gift of grace, not an occasion for prideful boasting. If states ignore the evidence of grace in their history, then "Those who achieve a special position in history claim a right to it either by virtue of their power"—like the Nazis or Soviets—"or by virtue of their goodness," which is the besetting pride of the Anglo-Americans.[29]

Niebuhr offers us some essential perspective on a difficult debate today. Oftentimes the left takes America's historical sins as proof against American exceptionalism. America is nothing special, they say; we are just as capable of cruelty, oppression, and injustice as anyone else. The nationalist right responds

---

[27]Reinhold Niebuhr, *Love and Justice: Selections from the Shorter Writings of Reinhold Niebuhr* (Louisville, KY: Westminster John Knox, 1992), 186.

[28]Niebuhr, *Love and Justice*, 185.

[29]Niebuhr, *Love and Justice*, 186.

with a wearisome and belligerent insistence on America's unique righteousness. Niebuhr enters this debate on neither side. Yes, he says, America really is something special. Britain and America actually are, in historical terms, the greatest nations in the world and probably the greatest in world history. But we should not pretend that our greatness is simply because of our goodness. We have been given—we have not earned—our position of greatness. With that gift comes unprecedented responsibility. A student of mine once called this the Spider-Man doctrine of international affairs: with great power comes great responsibility. But Uncle Ben borrowed the idea from Jesus: "Everyone to whom much was given, of him much will be required, and from him to whom they entrusted much, they will demand the more" (Luke 12:48).

It is precisely because we actually are the greatest nation in the history of the world that we are in a position of unique spiritual danger. "We ought not derive either special security or special advantages from our high historical mission. The real fact is that we are placed in a precarious moral and historical position by our special mission," Niebuhr warns.[30] The difficulty is that Americans are, by historical standards and compared to the other great powers of ages past, relatively good. That very goodness means that we can always turn away any rebuke or criticism by pointing at others' greater sins, playing a game of geopolitical "whataboutism." And, thus, "The pride of a virtuous nation cannot be humbled by moral and political criticisms because in comparative terms it may actually be virtuous." The best nations are the most prideful and least responsive to rebuke and correction because they can always point to someone else who is worse than they are. Great virtue yields a great dilemma: we should not give in to false humility and pretend we are worse than we are, but the reality of our own virtue can blind us to the sins that remain.

We can tell a true story about how the United States is superior to the empires of Rome, the Ottomans, China, Germany, Japan and Russia, the empires of the caliphs and Moghuls, the sultans, czars, Caesars, and Sun Kings, because of our greater devotion to accountable governance, to universal principles of human equality and freedom. But, frankly, that is a low bar: no empire in history has a terribly good track record of honoring human dignity. All too often we use the story of our comparative morality to justify moral apathy and ignore persistent oppression and injustice. Powerful and virtuous states are

---

[30]Niebuhr, *Love and Justice*, 187.

prone to view righteousness in comparative, relative terms, the "competitive prestige" that Orwell condemned: so long as we can plausibly claim to be better than the other guy, we give ourselves permission to be as bad as necessary or to avert our eyes from our own failings.

This story is the tension between different kinds of American exceptionalism: "open" exceptionalism, in which America holds itself up as a moral exemplar of liberty and justice and challenges itself to high moral aspirations, versus "closed" exceptionalism of self-righteousness, moral preening, and national belligerence.[31] Understood rightly, the story of American exceptionalism is a challenge, a standard against which we always fall short, and an aspiration to do better. Open American exceptionalism is best understood as Plato's "noble lie," a myth we tell ourselves to inspire loyalty and patriotism, educate our youth, and construct a sense of national identity and national mission. But the myth must remain grounded in fact: only a version of the myth that includes our national sins and failings can resonate with all Americans and avoid the self-righteousness all too common in American history.

Americans have rarely practiced Niebuhrian humility. To take one example: during the Civil War, the Union, though it was on the right side of that conflict, fully embodied the tradition of American nationalism. In fact, being in the right fueled the North's sense of messianic mission and righteous calling. On the eve of the Civil War, the North "had long adopted the rhetoric of the 'New Israel' as its own. By 1861, it was deeply ingrained and as instinctual to elite opinion shapers as to ordinary men and women," according to historian Harry Stout. The "new Israel" theology was a way of thinking about America that "spelled out America's sacred identity as a 'redeemer nation' engaged in a special 'covenant' with God to save the world."[32] For many northerners, the Civil War was plainly a righteous war against the evil slave power—which it indeed was—but their righteous self-confidence had the side-effect of confirming their sense that God had destined America to be his instrument for bringing the gospel of liberty to all the world. Julia Ward Howe's "Battle Hymn of the Republic," written in the midst of the Civil War, draws a direct parallel between Jesus and the American soldier: "As he died to make men holy, let us

---

[31]John D. Wilsey, *American Exceptionalism and Civil Religion: Reassessing the History of an Idea* (Downers Grove, IL: InterVarsity Press, 2015).

[32]Harry S. Stout, *Upon the Altar of the Nation: A Moral History of the Civil War* (New York: Penguin, 2007), 38.

die to make men free." As Stout argued, "Howe's anthem helped transform the war's meaning into a moral crusade for freedom . . . it turned the war into something holy, hence beyond moral critique. . . . The hymn is an urgent call to arms and promises victory over the enemies of Israel."[33]

The Civil War was so destructive that Americans felt the need to ascribe some apocalyptic, even eschatological, meaning to the nation for whose existence they sacrificed so much. Preachers and mourning citizens regularly spoke of the "baptism in blood" the nation was undergoing. During and after the war, "patriotism itself became sacralized to the point that it enjoyed co-equal or even superior status to conventional denominational faiths," feeding into a particular brand of American messianism.[34] "The adoption of emancipation occurred alongside the transformation of the conflict from limited war to total war, even holy war," because northern clergy "sanctified, in the most explicitly religious terms both the Northern cause and the United States itself," according to Andrew Preston.[35] The starkness of death called out for transcendent interpretation to make it bearable. "The Civil War was indeed the crimson baptism of our nationalism," in Stout's conclusion, "Americans in the North and the South came to believe that their bloodletting contained a profound religious meaning for their collective life as a nation."[36] After the war, Horace Bushnell gave voice to this sentiment. The American experiment "will be no more thought of as a mere human contact, or composition . . . but it will be that bond of common life which God has touched with blood; a sacredly heroic, Providentially tragic unity . . . and the sense of nationality becomes even a kind of religion."[37]

American nationalism became a kind of religion through the Civil War. The war to defeat slavery was plainly just, but—not for the last time—the nation's rightful pursuit of justice gave it a wrongful belief that it had a unique commission and destiny from God. Worse, the nation wove a myth about national righteousness out of the war that has hardened the nation against moral critique ever since. The case of the Civil War shows how it can be especially

---

[33]Stout, *Upon the Altar of the Nation*, 116.

[34]Stout, *Upon the Altar of the Nation*, xviii-xx.

[35]Andrew Preston, *Sword of the Spirit, Shield of Faith: Religion in American War and Diplomacy* (New York: Knopf, 2012), 163, 167, 171.

[36]Stout, *Upon the Altar of the Nation*, 459.

[37]Quoted in Mark A. Noll, *America's God: From Jonathan Edwards to Abraham Lincoln* (New York: Oxford University Press, 2002), 423.

difficult for Christians to keep their sacred and secular loyalties separate when America is at its best: precisely *because* the Union triumphed and *because* we can take collective pride in having defeated the Confederacy and vanquished slavery, it is that much harder to subject the righteous Union to theological critique, to hold fast to the belief that we are just one nation among nations in the sight of God.

FREDERICK DOUGLASS

Hard, but not impossible. Frederick Douglass, the preeminent African American writer, orator, and abolitionist of the nineteenth century, is an excellent example of how to hold onto a critical patriotism that does not give in to a crusading, belligerent nationalism nor to a cynical, antinational despair, a voice we need to hear today. Douglass was born enslaved on a Maryland plantation in 1817 or 1818. He escaped to freedom when he was twenty or twenty-one years old. Ordained in the African Methodist Episcopal Church, Douglass spent his adult, free life as an activist, writer, publisher, journalist, commentator, lobbyist, and ambassador. He initially aligned himself with William Lloyd Garrison, who discovered him on the abolitionist lecture circuit in the early 1840s. Following the Garrisonian line, Douglass condemned the US Constitution and the Union with slaveholding states throughout the 1840s. But Douglass gradually came to change his views, publicly announcing them in his newspaper in May 1851, leading to an open break with Garrison. Throughout his life, Douglass wrestled with the meaning of the American experiment, especially whether and to what extent his Christianity and his dedication to political liberty allowed him to identify with the United States and to what extent they obligated him to condemn it.[38]

Douglass's faith in the United States was not easy, and he did not avow it earlier in his life. In an 1847 speech, when he still counted himself a Garrisonian, he essentially disavowed the United States. "I have no love for America, as such; I have no patriotism. I have no country," he exclaimed. The existence of slavery made the country and its constitution abhorrent to him. "The Institutions of this Country do not know me—do not recognize me as a man. I am not thought of, spoken of, in any direction, out of the Anti-Slavery ranks, as a man," because of which he felt no loyalty to the United States. "I am not

---

[38]David W. Blight, *Frederick Douglass: Prophet of Freedom* (New York: Simon & Schuster, 2020).

thought of or spoken of, except as a piece of property belonging to some Christian Slaveholder, and all the Religious and Political Institutions of this Country alike pronounce me a Slave and a chattel. Now, in such a country as this I cannot have patriotism." Douglass reviewed the record of slavery and its cruelties to conclude,

> How can I, I say, love a country thus cursed, thus bedewed with the blood of my brethren? A Country, the Church of which, and the Government of which, and the Constitution of which are in favor of supporting and perpetuating this monstrous system of injustice and blood? I have not, I cannot have, any love for this country, as such, or for its Constitution. I desire to see it overthrown as speedily as possible and its Constitution shivered in a thousand fragments.[39]

Yet even in 1847 he spoke favorably of "American principles," while condemning the "bastard Democracy" of American practice.

Douglass came to change his views in part because he disliked agreeing to the slavers' interpretation of the Constitution as a proslavery document. After his break with Garrison, Douglass embraced American patriotism, a move we see in his famous Fourth of July address in 1852 (actually delivered on the fifth). The speech is often quoted for its famous condemnation of America—but the full speech contains a deeper celebration of America's promise. Douglass, addressing a White audience, began by noting that the Fourth is "the birthday of your National Independence" the beginning of "your political freedom," accomplished by "your fathers," noting that "the freedom gained is yours; and you, therefore, may properly celebrate this anniversary," stressing his audience's ownership to subtly distance himself from it. He celebrated America's youth in hopes that the long years ahead of it might be the occasion to learn greater wisdom.

Importantly, Douglass affirmed the rightness of the Revolutionary generation's cause against Britain. He avowed respect for the founding generation: for their bravery, great deeds, patriotism, self-sacrifice, public spiritedness, and "admiration for liberty," and he pledged that "I will unite with you to honor their memory," striking a patriotic note and an allegiance to the nation whose sins he is about to denounce. Douglass concluded his opening by affirming the Declaration of Independence and pleading with America to stand by it: "The

---

[39]Frederick Douglass, "Country, Conscience, and the Anti-Slavery Cause," May 11, 1847, https://glc.yale.edu/country-conscience-and-anti-slavery-cause.

principles contained in [the Declaration of Independence] are saving principles. Stand by those principles, be true to them on all occasions, in all places, against all foes, and at whatever cost."

Then Douglass brings the hammer: "What have I, or those I represent, to do with your national independence?" he asked. "Are the great principles of political freedom and of natural justice, embodied in that Declaration of Independence, extended to us?" A Black man standing in front of a White audience speaking of American independence, Douglass asked questions that should have been obvious, but that had been repressed, driven out of polite company. "I am not included within the pale of this glorious anniversary! Your high independence only reveals the immeasurable distance between us." Because of that distance, "This Fourth of July is *yours,* not *mine.* You may rejoice, I must mourn." Douglass's call to mourn inescapably affected his view of American identity: he could not but mourn when he dwelt on American hypocrisy and oppression. "Whether we turn to the declarations of the past, or to the professions of the present, the conduct of the nation seems equally hideous and revolting. America is false to the past, false to the present, and solemnly binds herself to be false to the future," he said, just moments after promising to join with his audience to celebrate the Declaration. Douglass, celebrating and damning America is the same breath, drove his point home: "What, to the American slave, is your 4th of July?"

Douglass went further. The continued existence of slavery in a nation overwhelmingly populated by Christians made Christianity itself and its churches complicit in the peculiar institution. "The [slave] power is co-extensive with the star-spangled banner, and American Christianity," he said. If churches took a stand against slavery, it would vanish immediately because of the overwhelming power of religion in American life. That slavery endured was proof of the church's cowardice, complicity, or collaboration with slave holders. Even worse, for Douglass, was the fugitive slave law which obligated northerners to cooperate in hunting down and returning escaped slaves, even against the objections of northerners' consciences. Northerners' failure to revolt against the law meant their conscience did not compel them to act for justice, showing their religion to be hollow. "The fact that the church of our country, (with fractional exceptions) does not esteem 'the Fugitive Slave Law' as a declaration of war against religious liberty, implies that that church regards religion simply as a form of worship, an empty ceremony, and *not* a vital principle, requiring active benevolence, justice, love and good will towards man," Douglass thundered, a direct rebuke of the slaveholders' insistence that Christianity imposed no obligation on its adherents to work for justice.

Douglass damned White American Christians' spiritual excuse-making and deflection. American Christianity, even when it avowed abolitionism, was tacitly complicit because of its failure to make justice and antislavery central to its gospel message and to demand its adherents to *act* in accordance with this message. American Christianity preached a false gospel of inner, individualistic spirituality matched with disregard for external works, solidarity, or justice. For Douglass, the American church "has made itself the bulwark of American slavery, and the shield of American slave-hunters. Many of its most eloquent Divines, who stand as the very lights of the church, have shamelessly given the sanction of religion, and the bible, to the whole slave system."

But note that Douglass indicted White Americans with their own religion and their own political ideals—which required him to validate their fundamental integrity and justice. Americans professed Christianity and failed to practice it, interpreting it in such a way as to excuse them from taking any significant action to work for justice on behalf of enslaved Africans. Similarly, Americans professed political liberty yet denied it to enslaved Africans. Douglass did not evade the conclusion: "The existence of slavery in this country brands your republicanism as a sham, your humanity as a base pretense, and your Christianity as a lie." But Douglass was himself a Christian: he did not let White Christians' sin drive him from faith in Jesus, a non-White man. Douglass himself affirmed the Declaration; he did not let White Americans' hypocrisy destroy his faith in the potential of the United States.

Crucially, Douglass argued not that American ideals or the Christian religion were wrong, but that Americans failed to understand and practice them. The Constitution, properly understood, "is a glorious liberty document," he said. In 1860, he debated the proposition of whether the Constitution was a pro- or antislavery document. He took the position that it was, fundamentally, an antislavery document because it gave to the free states every advantage over the slaveholding South and provided the best means for the abolition of slavery through its republican frame and democratic processes.[40] He admired the Declaration and challenged Americans to "stand by those principles, be true to them on all occasions, in all places, against all foes, and at whatever cost." He believed the founders were right to stand up for their ideals against the British and right to proclaim their principles throughout the world.

That is why he admitted, in his conclusion, that "I do not despair of this country." There was always hope that the United States might turn away from its received practice and choose to become a better nation—a hope he expressed, remarkably, before the Civil War and more than a decade before abolition was finally accomplished. In this respect, Douglass is the perfect example of using the American creed to critique American practice, to reject America as it actually was in favor of what America rightly aspired to be, and of subjecting America to withering criticism in service of a deeper, hopeful patriotism. Douglass was able to do so because he understood America to be defined by its creed, not by its heritage; by the ideals it proclaimed, not the culture that surrounded it; by Christian principle, not "Christian" power. And he understood that the culture predominant within White American Christianity was, in his time, the enemy of true Christianity.[41]

A decade later, amid the Civil War, Douglass gave another July 4 address in which he embraced the American past even more strongly and openly. With the Civil War, "we are only continuing the tremendous struggle, which your fathers and my fathers began eighty-six years ago." Throughout the address Douglass speaks of "our fathers," a notable difference from 1852 when he pointedly told his White audience that the day celebrated "your political freedom" accomplished by "your fathers." David Blight, a biographer of Douglass, argues that in 1862, in contrast to the more famous 1852 address, Douglass "took ownership in the special day and gave it new meaning. . . . It was now his age, his duty, and especially *his* country." Blight notes that "Douglass had never before called the American founders his 'fathers,'" a shift that indicated how far Douglass was willing to embrace the American story as his own.[42] The Civil War was a continuation of the fight for the ideals of the

---

[40]Frederick Douglass, "The Constitution of the United States: Is It Pro-Slavery or Anti-Slavery?," March 26, 1860, https://teachingamericanhistory.org/library/document/the-constitution-of-the-united-states-is-it-pro-slavery-or-anti-slavery/.
[41]Frederick Douglass, "Oration Delivered in Corinthian Hall, Rochester," July 5, 1852, https://rbscp.lib.rochester.edu/2945.
[42]Blight, *Prophet of Freedom*, 368.

Declaration. Douglass grew even more fulsome in his praise: "No people ever entered upon the pathway of nations, with higher and [greater] ideas of justice, liberty and humanity than ourselves," he said. "There are principles in the Declaration of Independence which would release every slave in the world and prepare the earth for a millennium of righteousness and peace."[43] Having borne the full brunt of America's worst sins, he also witnessed the United States making untold sacrifice to live up to his highest hopes. Here is Douglass embracing the American story as his story, finding himself to be an American. To readers who only know of Douglass's jeremiad of 1852 and its famous line— "What, to the American slave, is your 4th of July?"—the Douglass of 1862 is a striking evolution. Douglass repeated these themes again in yet another July 4 speech, in 1875, affirming the rightful place of African Americans in the American story and their co-ownership of its ideals.

Douglass explicitly drew a contrast between American principles and White culture. Reflecting in April 1862 on "The War and How to End It," Douglass asks why the South hates the North so intensely. "You are of the same race, the same language, the same sacred historic memories," he said. But if the two sides share the same tradition, heritage, and history, "Why do they hate you?" Douglass concludes it is because the two sides have fundamentally different views of what America means, and that the South was captive to its false and self-limiting understanding of America as the White Republic. Douglass, astonishingly, put himself in the shoes of the slave masters in an act of imaginative empathy, considering that he would believe as they did if in their position. "If I were a slaveholder, and was determined to remain such, I would equal the worst, both in cruelty to the slave and in hatred to the north," he argues, to show how slavery is opposed to the basic ideas of the United States, "I should hate the Declaration of Independence, hate the Constitution, hate the Golden rule, hate free schools, free speech, free press, and every other form of freedom. Because in them all, I should see an enemy to my claim of property in man." The difference between the North and South was not a difference of Christian tradition, British heritage, or European culture: it was the political ideals of liberty and equality, and the Constitution and Declaration on which they rested. Douglass might have said that the difference was

---

[43] Frederick Douglass, "The Slaveholders' Rebellion," July 4, 1826, https://teachingamericanhistory .org/library/document/the-slaveholders-rebellion/.

indeed Christianity—but not in the way that the defenders of the culturally Christian South believed.

The Civil War was a conflict of two rival visions of American identity. Both cloaked themselves in Christian language. But in one, to use Roger Williams' phrase, the Christian culture swallowed up the reality of the Christian faith. The South's version was not simply mistaken, it was self-defeating, un-American, and unchristian. Consequently, the war was not an effort by the North to conquer the South, but to save it. Slavery "makes slaves of the negroes, vassals of the poor Whites and tyrants of the masters," Douglass said, and tyranny, of course, is inimical to republican freedom. "Pride, injustice, ingratitude, lust of dominion, cruelty, scorn, and contempt are the qualities of this rebellion, and slavery breeds them all." The war would set free the slaves, but as importantly it would liberate their masters from the curse of being tyrants. White southerners were never free to enjoy true republican freedom until slavery was abolished. Douglass's concern to recognize the humanity of the slavers and work for their true freedom is a remarkable contrapuntal note to the slavers' refusal to do the same for him.

CONCLUSION

OUR LONGING FOR COMMUNITY will never be fulfilled by a large, impersonal, pluralistic national polity. Unfortunately, the United States is now trapped between two movements, the progressive left and the nationalist right, who both want to make our nation serve that purpose. American politics since the 1970s has been a wearying clash between those who want to enshrine and rigidify the Eisenhower-era American national identity—Reagan, the Moral Majority, the Christian Coalition, the Tea Party, the MAGA voters—and those who reject it out of hand as a mask for the racism, sexism, neo-Confederate nostalgia, and homophobia of the alt-right. One side wants to "make America great again" and the other is suspicious about what "again" refers to.

The debate has deteriorated into raw tribalism because the iterated contest, rehashed every four years, has nearly destroyed all sense of trust and common citizenship between the two sides. There is virtually no sense of shared history or a shared meaning of justice among Americans. Within living memory we could at least agree to disagree so long as everyone followed the rules of democratic contestation. Now we accuse each other (not without reason) of hijacking the rules to rig the game, in which case agreeing to disagree is tantamount to surrender. Each new round feels like the final one. We tell ourselves that the stakes are existential, and we claim that casting a vote in a ballot box is akin to charging the cockpit of a hijacked airliner. In that metaphor, our political opponents are terrorists.

Though I have not focused on it in this book, the progressive left bears a burden of responsibility for our current impasse. Progressivism is best understood as a philosophy of history, a belief that history unfolds in the direction of progressive policy preferences. Today's progressive elites act like a self-appointed vanguard commissioned by history to open up the next chapter in our story. Such a self-congratulatory, self-aggrandizing narrative has no moral horizon or framework and no way to justify what its policy preferences are, other than vague appeals to "the children," "the future," and "the right side of history," which mean whatever they want those empty phrases to mean. Shorn of any fixed moral commitments, progressivism deteriorates into the lowest common denominator available within the rhetoric of freedom: individual autonomy, personal discovery, self-expression, fulfillment, and empowerment. But what is there to discover within the empty progressive self? What is there to express? The lonely progressive self gravitates to the only commitments and attachments available in a world stripped of God, nature, reason, community, and tradition: commonalities of race, class, and gender, which are experienced both as inescapable, essential defining attributes *and* as constricting burdens that must be transcended, transgressed, redefined, and thrown off in a never-ending replay of personal liberation. In this light, the progressive commitments to abortion, the sexual revolution, and identity politics are a feature, not a bug, of the movement. They express the fundamental core of what progressivism is: a rebellion against any and all constraints and limitations on personal independence, including the limits of nature itself. Similarly, the hectoring, authoritarian temperament that gives rise to speech codes and cancel culture flows naturally from progressivism. Progressivism is a religion, but one without grace. It is a return to Puritan roots in the worst sense of the word, an endless crusade of moral reform with no forgiveness, no atonement, and no savior.

But as much as the progressive left is at fault, the nationalist right is too, as I hope I have shown throughout this book. White American Christians bear substantial responsibility for the damage done to trust and common citizenship in the United States. By politicizing our religion and insisting that it is central to American identity while turning a blind eye to the continuing realities of racial injustice, or in past centuries actually defending slavery and segregation, we gave non-Christians and non-Whites little reason to trust us or believe they could peacefully share a country with us. Our resistance to the loss of White Protestant influence at every stage in American history has not endeared us to others. Our willingness to wage culture war to preserve our tribe's historical perks and privileges justifiably makes others wonder if the liberal ideals we helped invent are nothing more than a fantasy we told the world to make them feel comfortable with White Protestant hegemony.

Conservative White Christians believe that the left is the aggressor in the culture war and that conservative efforts since then have been a justified, defensive attempt to preserve something good and decent from the civilization we inherited. There is some truth to that belief, but only some. White Christians can only convince ourselves that we were not the aggressors if we view our previous dominance in American life as something natural, providential, and good. But the pre-1960s Anglo-Protestant dominance in American history was itself a standing aggression: most obviously against Catholics, Native Americans, and especially African Americans, but also an aggression against American ideals and thus in principle *against every single American*. The effort by non-Whites and non-Christians—joined by some faithful White Christians who prioritized Christian principle over Christian power—to fight for equal justice was not wrong, and it was only an aggression in the sense that a counteroffensive is a tactical aggression in the service of strategic defense. And it is important to recognize that greater equality and justice will be equal justice for White Christians as well, in the same way that Douglass wanted his oppressors to experience the blessing of true democratic citizenship.

None of this is to excuse the left, which has hijacked the legitimate agenda of the oppressed and disenfranchised, unjustifiably claimed to be their representative, spun a fable about how the Democratic Party platform is the necessary fulfillment of their aspirations, and arrogated to itself the mantle of moral leadership that it never earned. It is vital to recognize the distinction between righteous reform movements, like the civil rights movement, and the ideology of the left. The Democratic Party claims they are the same and argues that without their party we have no reform and no liberation for the oppressed. Such distortions are the germ of truth to the right's narrative, and these and other elements in its ideology—above all, its uncompromising crusade to entrench every facet of the sexual revolution and its increasingly troubling stance on religious liberty—are real cultural aggressions worth fighting against.

The only possible way out of this impasse is nothing new. I do not have a new ideology, a new "-ism" to sell, in part because there is nothing new under the sun, but also because I think we do not need to invent new ideas when old ones would serve just as well. Classical liberalism, civic republicanism, Christian republicanism, and federalism are old ideas, but they are good ones, and Americans might want to try using them sometime. Federalism, in particular, holds out promise as a way for diverse people who do not agree on justice to nonetheless share a country together. What if the people in San Francisco wanted to defund the police and turn their city-state into a green, eco-communist, pot-smoking, drag-queen-dancing hippie utopia? What if Texans wanted to abolish most bureaucracies, regulations, and taxes, and turn their state into the world's most well-armed anarcho-libertarian paradise? Why should I care, and why should I stop them? More to the point, why should Washington, DC, stop them? Diversity and pluralism mean more than a diversity of skin colors—they also mean a diversity of *ways of living*, a diversity of communities, subcultures, and ideas for how to govern.[1]

Ordered liberty and human dignity are the best and only viable anchors for political order. There is no viable alternative to some form of classical liberalism or civic republicanism that can keep the peace among citizens who disagree about the nature of justice. The left has yet to offer a meaningful explanation about what they would like to see in place of American institutions, which they believe to be irredeemably broken by systemic injustice and racism. The nationalist right has been equally vague about what its endgame is, or how their vision of a revitalized Western civilization or Christian nationhood can be made consistent with the fact of American pluralism. Nor is it clear to me that any of the critique of democracy from the right or left should be taken seriously. The ideals of limited government and representative institutions are still the best means for ordered liberty, domestic tranquility, and human flourishing at home and abroad—and Christians can and should be a distinctive voice making this case to our fellow Americans.

The Christian Right was a failed attempt to answer the left and turn back its flawed vision of American identity—failed, because its own vision of America was also flawed. Certainly, some Christian activists are sincerely motivated by

---

[1]David French develops this idea in *Divided We Fall: America's Secession Threat and How to Restore Our Nation* (New York: St. Martin's Press, 2020).

Christian principle to work for justice, ordered liberty and republican freedom. Those parts of the movement limp along, fragmented into a number of single-issue crusades, including the generational crusade against abortion, the perennial fight for religious liberty, and smaller efforts to fight sex trafficking or poverty and push for criminal justice reform or immigrants' rights. These movements may gain tactical victories here and there amid the larger movement's collapse.

And the larger movement is collapsing. It was never solely about Christian principle, equal justice, or republicanism. Such language was used in past generations as the rhetorical window-dressing of White supremacy and Protestant sectarianism. Whether from historical habit, cultural inertia, group insecurity, or demographic destiny, the Christian Right has continued its predecessors' habits of using the rhetoric of republicanism to advance an agenda of Christian power under the mistaken belief that Christianity was the sole source of civic virtue and political liberty. The Christian Right was, above all, an effort to assert ownership over American identity, to define America as a Christian nation, and to see that national self-understanding recognized, affirmed, and codified in public symbolism, in the teaching of American history, and in the rhetoric of American statesmen. That turned the Christian Right from a movement of social conservatism to a movement of American nationalism; from political liberty to political victory; from Christian principle to Christian power. The movement deteriorated from a community of principle ostensibly devoted to the common good to a provincially-minded, ethnoreligious sect devoted to its own power, prestige, and defense. When I say that the movement is collapsing, I do not necessarily mean in numbers or success but in moral aspiration, intellectual depth, and political vision.

In this light, the Christian Right's relationship with Donald Trump is straightforward and not at all mysterious. He promised a restoration of Christian power, a promise that resonated deeply with White Christians. (Black Christians, who never had power in the first place, understood the promise of restoration was not aimed at them.) At the same time, during the Trump presidency the movement gave almost no voice at all to their originating project of civic republicanism, political freedom, the rule of law, constitutionalism, limited government, or equal justice for all, the ideals which are among the greatest legacies of American Christianity. The Christian Right was instead mostly silent in the face of the Trump presidency's demagoguery, criminality, and illiberal nationalism.

By 2016, if not before, the Christian Right had lost whatever intellectual tradition it once had to recognize and warn against the dangers of American nationalism. Instead, it embraced the contrary tradition, the one that saw in nationalism, not danger, but opportunity; the tradition in which White American Christianity served as the chaplaincy of American nationalism, not the prophetic voice holding it accountable. Only in defeat will there be opportunity to recover an older, wiser Christian prophetic voice, one that loves America but does not worship her, one that articulates the old idea of Christian republicanism in good and sincere faith as an ethic of equal justice for all. Such a recovery would use the residual cultural power of American Christianity to pursue the common good—but would not confuse or conflate the two and, if ever they conflict, would prioritize the latter over the former. The common good—ordered liberty and human flourishing, not the pursuit of our own tribe's power and privilege—must be the animating vision of Christian participation in American democracy.

A PASTORAL NOTE

The difference between unhealthy Christian nationalism and healthy Christian political witness is clear in the big picture. If you believe that the government should do things to ensure America continues to be a Christian nation, you are a Christian nationalist. If you want to use immigration policy or school curriculum to create or reinforce the idea of a Christian nation, you are a Christian nationalist. But there is a real dilemma: Christians who reject Christian nationalism nonetheless want to see the US government govern justly, wisely, even righteously, because "righteousness exalts a nation." So long as we live in a democracy, it is good to love our neighbors politically by pursuing justice together in the public square. That means it is right for Christians to pursue and use political power and to influence public policy—so long as we are doing it for justice and peace for all people. The difference between this stance and Christian nationalism can be subtle, sometimes a matter of our inner motivation and the orientation of our hearts. We might pursue the same policies—school reform, say, or religious liberty—for republican motives or for nationalist motives. How do we know when we have fallen into Christian nationalism? And how do we guard against it?

The best answer I can give is a series of question we should ask ourselves. What is driving our political activism? Is it fear of losing power, or is it gratitude for the freedom we have and a desire to steward it for the next generation? Is it about protecting what we believe to be ours, or giving to others what is rightfully theirs? It is discomfort with change, or proactive effort to steer change in the right direction? Is it about restoring the past, or building something better in the future? Is it self-centered, or other-directed? What do your non-White and non-Christian friends think about your political convictions? (Do you have non-White and non-Christian friends?) Most importantly, When our self-interest conflicts with the common good, which do we choose? Perhaps we do not face stark tradeoffs between competing values the way these questions imply, and we can pursue both self-interest and the common good roughly in tandem. In that case the question is, Where do our priorities lie? What is the ultimate value we choose above others? Which one is the cause, and which the effect? Which is shaping, and which shaped? Which is the cart, and which the horse? I expect for most of us, if we are honest, our motives are mixed, and it can be difficult to parse our own deceitful hearts.

That is why our political witness should be shaped in community, with accountability, and with the shepherding guidance of elders, teachers, and pastors (along with input from experts and professionals). That means our churches and our pastors, elders, and teachers should be actively involved in helping us shape our political witness—even, for some churches, actively involved in organizing local political activism. Only with the unavoidable accountability of working with fellow Christians—hopefully including from different walks of life—can we become aware of our blind spots and our motives. Some pastors may be uncomfortable with the role I suggest they and their churches take on here as shapers of Christians' political witness. Some White pastors argue they should avoid politics and "just preach the gospel," because it could cause division (a claim they rarely make when it comes time to preach about abortion or religious liberty, and a claim Black pastors rarely make because the Black church has always been essential to the Black Christian political witness). Others may think pastors are already too political—and that politicized religion is exactly the problem we are trying to avoid, not double-down on. It may seem that my prescription is simply more of the disease I've warned about throughout this book.

I do not think the problem is that pastors talk about politics too much or too little, and the solution is not to adjust a knob regulating how much they talk about politics. The problem is that evangelical pastors and teachers tend to talk about politics piecemeal, focusing on favored causes; act as partisans; or they talk about politics generically, with an occasional sermon on Romans 13 or Matthew 22, exhorting the congregation to respect the authorities when our party is in power, or Acts 5, exhorting the congregation to steel itself for persecution when our party is out of power. What our churches seem to lack is a biblical political theology, a holistic approach to secular order and corporate identities as presented across the whole narrative of the Bible, from which we can preach specific exhortations throughout the year and throughout the election cycle—in, through, and during every other sermon. The gospel of individual, spiritual salvation is true and important, but we must apply and live out its saving message to the world as a measure of love for our neighbors and obedience to a God who loves justice. Living out the gospel has implications beyond the individual, which means it has implications for relationships, for living together in groups and in society, implications for the broader culture, and thus implications for politics.

We are political animals, and few issues that pastors address lack corporate, social, or political dimensions. Pastors need to bring out that dimension and teach on it because Americans are palpably malformed in this area, particularly given the individualism and relationalism of the White evangelical toolkit. Alan Jacobs, a professor of the humanities at Baylor University, told me that he wants churches to talk about politics, "not in the sense of policies or who to vote for, but politics in the much broader sense: What does it mean to be a political animal? What does it mean to be someone who is in the midst of a vast and complex society full of people who disagree with you in all sorts of ways? And what does it mean to be faithful and Christian in that world?" People need to be taught how to live as part of a body, how to understand and live out our roles as a member of a church, citizen of a nation, and resident of a community. In our self-centered, narcissistic, individualistic, expressionist age, we are incompetent in the arts of living together. We may be naturally social and political animals, but we still have to acquire the cultivated virtues of citizens.[2] Churches must help form us into better political animals. We cannot leave that job only to families and schools unless we believe that Jesus has nothing to say about our political lives—which is false.

To do this well, our pastors, elders, and teachers need to know something of the world we live in, especially the specific social, cultural, historical context that makes up our vast and complex society. That is part of what shepherding means: to know the field where your sheep are grazing and understand if they need to be led to a healthier pasture. To teach us how to be better political animals, pastors have to understand what kind of political animals we have been trained to be by the world around us and what kind of social, cultural, and political fields we have been grazing in. Put more abstractly: Pastors must be aware of the antecedent narrative to which we are all heirs, the story we are living, so that they can speak specifically and directly to the sins and tragedies of that story and guide and shepherd us to write a better chapter.

That may seem like an unrealistic expectation to put on pastors and teachers in the church. On the one hand, all I am suggesting is that pastors and teachers have a working knowledge of the basic realities of American history and culture so that they can help their congregations understand what it means to be a faithful Christian in America. But on the other hand, perhaps it is a large demand because many White pastors—reflecting their congregations—avoid or deny some of the biggest facts of American history and culture. A large part of the history of Christians in America is the story of White Christians confusing their sacred and secular loyalties, seeking to build the kingdom of God on earth, viewing America as a new Israel and chosen nation, of misapplying 2 Chronicles 7:14 and Psalm 33:12 to the United States—and, in doing so, using a myth of American righteousness to turn a blind eye to, or actually justify, White supremacy, slavery, and segregation. That is the field in which White evangelicalism has been grazing, the context in which the White evangelical

---

[2]We do not lack for good academic political theology, but that theology is not getting to the pews because pastors are not transmitting it. For just a few examples, see Jonathan Leeman, *Political Church: The Local Assembly as Embassy of Christ's Rule* (Downers Grove, IL: InterVarsity Press, 2016); Oliver O'Donovan, *The Desire of the Nations: Rediscovering the Roots of Political Theology* (Cambridge: Cambridge University Press, 1999); David Van Drunen, *Politics after Christendom: Political Theology in a Fractured World* (Grand Rapids, MI: Zondervan Academic, 2020); Michael Gerson and Peter Wehner, *City of Man: Religion and Politics in a New Era* (Chicago: Moody Publishers, 2010); James Davison Hunter, *To Change the World: The Irony, Tragedy, and Possibility of Christianity in the Late Modern World* (New York: Oxford University Press, 2010).

political animal was shaped. When pastors ignore, deny, or even support these myths, they deform their congregation's political identities and allow preexisting deformations to go unchallenged.

Churches must play a role in challenging Christian nationalism. Practically, there is no more credible voice to confront an unhealthy Christian political witness than the healthy kind. Theologically, Jesus gave authority to his church to proclaim his message and represent his name. When his name and his message are misrepresented, the church must be at the forefront of saying so and correcting the record—which means preaching about how to be a better political animal is a legitimate function for the church. Pastors cannot effectively shepherd their congregations if they absent themselves from the social, cultural, and political lives of their people—aspects that take up a large part of human life. It is not enough that we simply stop preaching these falsehoods and try to turn the page. The story has still been told and it does not become untold by ignoring the past. Pastors must actively preach against these falsehoods to help our congregations see where we have implicitly continued them, to recognize the lasting damage they have done, and to recognize whatever responsibility we may have for beginning the work of repair.

RECOMMENDED RESOURCES

Ahmari, Sohrab. "Against David French-ism." *First Things*, May 29, 2019. www.firstthings
.com/web-exclusives/2019/05/against-david-french-ism.

Alter, Peter. *Nationalism*. 2nd ed. New York: Hodder Education, 1994.

Anderson, Benedict. *Imagined Communities: Reflections on the Origin and Spread of Nationalism*. New York: Verso, 2006.

Anton, Michael. "The Flight 93 Election." *Claremont Review of Books*, September 5, 2016. https://claremontreviewofbooks.com/digital/the-flight-93-election/ (published pseudonymously under the name "Publius Decius Mus").

Aquinas, Thomas. *Political Writings*. Edited by R. W. Dyson. Cambridge: Cambridge University Press, 2002.

Augustine. *The City of God Against the Pagans*. Edited by Robert W. Dyson. Cambridge: Cambridge University Press, 1998.

Balmer, Randall. "The Real Origins of the Religious Right." *Politico*, May 27, 2014. www.politico.com/magazine/story/2014/05/religious-right-real-origins-107133.

Barber, Benjamin. *Jihad vs. McWorld: Terrorism's Challenge to Democracy*. New York: Ballantine, 2010.

Barr, David. "Evangelical Support for Donald Trump as a Moral Project: Description and Critique." *Religion & Culture Forum*, January 16, 2018. https://voices.uchicago.edu /religionculture/2018/01/16/evangelical-support-for-trump-as-a-moral-project -description-and-critique/.

Bellah, Robert N. *The Broken Covenant: American Civil Religion in Time of Trial*. Chicago: University of Chicago Press, 1992.

———. "Civil Religion in America." *Daedalus* (1967): 1-21.

Biggar, Nigel. *Between Kin and Cosmopolis: An Ethic of the Nation*. Eugene, OR: Wipf and Stock, 2014.

Billig, Michael. *Banal Nationalism*. London: Sage, 1995.

Blight, David W. *Frederick Douglass: Prophet of Freedom*. New York: Simon & Schuster, 2020.

Bloom, Harold. *The Closing of the American Mind*. New York: Simon & Schuster, 2008.

Blum, Edward J. *Reforging the White Republic: Race, Religion, and American Nationalism, 1865–1898*. Baton Rouge, LA: LSU Press, 2015.

Bonikowski, Bart, and Paul DiMaggio. "Varieties of American Popular Nationalism." *American Sociological Review* 81, no. 5 (2016): 949-80.

Boot, Max. *The Corrosion of Conservatism: Why I Left the Right*. New York: Liveright, 2018.

Bosworth, R. J. B. *Nationalism*. New York: Routledge, 2007.

Carter, Dan T. *From George Wallace to Newt Gingrich: Race in the Conservative Counter-revolution, 1963-1994*. Baton Rouge, LA: LSU Press, 1996.

Cherry, Conrad, ed. *God's New Israel: Religious Interpretations of American Destiny*. Chapel Hill: UNC Press, 1998.

Citrin, Jack, Ernst B. Haas, Christopher Muste, and Beth Reingold. "Is American Nationalism Changing? Implications for Foreign Policy." *International Studies Quarterly* 38, no. 1 (1994): 1-31.

Clinton, Josh and Carrie Roush. "Poll: Partisan Divide Over 'Birther' Question." NBCnews.com, August 10, 2016. www.nbcnews.com/politics/2016-election/poll-persistent-partisan-divide-over-birther-question-n627446?cid=sm_tw.

Deneen, Patrick J. *Why Liberalism Failed*. New Haven, CT: Yale University Press, 2019.

Dochuk, Darren. *From Bible Belt to Sunbelt: Plain-Folk Religion, Grassroots Politics, and the Rise of Evangelical Conservatism*. New York: Norton, 2010.

Douglass, Frederick. "The Constitution of the United States: Is It Pro-Slavery or Anti-Slavery?" March 26, 1860. https://teachingamericanhistory.org/library/document/the-constitution-of-the-united-states-is-it-pro-slavery-or-anti-slavery/.

———. "Country, Conscience, and the Anti-Slavery Cause." May 11, 1847. https://glc.yale.edu/country-conscience-and-anti-slavery-cause.

———. "The Dred Scott Decision." May 14, 1857. https://rbscp.lib.rochester.edu/4399.

———. "Oration Delivered in Corinthian Hall, Rochester." July 5, 1852. https://rbscp.lib.rochester.edu/2945.

———. "The Slaveholders' Rebellion." July 4, 1826. https://teachingamericanhistory.org/library/document/the-slaveholders-rebellion/.

———. "The War and How to End It." March 25, 1862. https://rbscp.lib.rochester.edu/4394.

Dowland, Seth. *Family Values and the Rise of the Christian Right*. Philadelphia: University of Pennsylvania Press, 2015.

Drakeman, Donald L. *Church, State, and Original Intent*. Cambridge: Cambridge University Press, 2009.

Dreher, Rod. *The Benedict Option: A Strategy for Christians in a Post-Christian Nation.* New York: Penguin, 2017.

Du Mez, Kristin Kobes. *Jesus and John Wayne: How White Evangelicals Corrupted a Faith and Fractured a Nation.* New York: Liveright, 2020.

Eley, Geoff, and Ronald Grigor Suny, eds. *Becoming National: A Reader.* New York: Oxford University Press, 1996.

Emerson, Michael O., and Christian Smith. *Divided by Faith: Evangelical Religion and the Problem of Race in America.* New York: Oxford University Press, 2001.

Evans, Curtis J. "White Evangelical Protestant Responses to the Civil Rights Movement." *The Harvard Theological Review* 102, no. 2 (2009): 245-73.

Falwell, Jerry. *Listen, America!* New York: Doubleday, 1980.

Fea, John. *Believe Me: The Evangelical Road to Donald Trump.* Grand Rapids, MI: Eerdmans, 2018.

———. *Was America Founded as a Christian Nation? A Historical Introduction.* Revised edition. Louisville, KY: Westminster John Knox Press, 2016.

Fichte, Johann Gottlieb. "Addresses to the German Nation," in *From Absolutism to Napoleon, 1648—1815.* Vol 2. of German History in Documents and Images. Washington, DC: German Historical Institute. http://germanhistorydocs.ghi-dc.org/pdf/eng/12_EnlightPhilos_Doc.8_English.pdf.

Fitzgerald, Frances. *The Evangelicals: The Struggle to Shape America.* New York: Simon and Schuster, 2017.

Frank, Thomas. *What's the Matter with Kansas? How Conservatives Won the Heart of America.* New York: Picador, 2007.

Freedom House, "Freedom in the World." Washington, DC, 2017. https://freedomhouse.org/sites/default/files/FH_FIW_2017_Report_Final.pdf

French, David. *Divided We Fall: America's Secession Threat and How to Restore Our Nation.* New York: St. Martin's Press, 2020.

Fukuyama, Francis. *Identity: The Demand for Dignity and the Politics of Resentment.* New York: Farrar, Straus and Giroux, 2018.

Gaston, K. Healan. *Imagining Judeo-Christian America: Religion, Secularism, and the Redefinition of Democracy.* Chicago: University of Chicago Press, 2019.

Gellner, Ernest. *Nations and Nationalism.* Ithaca, NY: Cornell University Press, 2008.

Glenn, Gary D. "Forgotten Purposes of the First Amendment Religion Clauses." *The Review of Politics* (1987): 340-67.

Gloege, Timothy. *Guaranteed Pure: The Moody Bible Institute, Business, and the Making of Modern Evangelicalism.* Chapel Hill: UNC Press, 2015.

Goldberg, Jonah. *Suicide of the West: How the Rebirth of Tribalism, Nationalism, and Socialism Is Destroying American Democracy.* New York: Crown Forum, 2020.

Goldberg, Michelle. *Kingdom Coming: The Rise of Christian Nationalism.* New York: Norton, 2006.

Gorski, Philip. "Why Evangelicals Voted for Trump: A Critical Cultural Sociology." In *Politics of Meaning/Meaning of Politics*, edited by Jason Mast and Jeffrey C. Alexander, 165-83. New York: Palgrave Macmillan, 2019.

Green, Steven K. *The Third Disestablishment: Church, State, and American Culture, 1940–1975*. New York: Oxford University Press, 2018.

Greenfeld, Liah. *Nationalism and the Mind: Essays on Modern Culture*. London: Oneworld, 2006.

Hall, Mark David. *Did America Have a Christian Founding?* Nashville: Nelson, 2019.

———. *Roger Sherman and the Creation of the American Republic*. New York: Oxford University Press, 2013.

Hanby, Michael. "The Civic Project of American Christianity." *First Things*, February 2015.

Hays, J. Daniel. *From Every People and Nation: A Biblical Theology of Race*. Downers Grove, IL: InterVarsity Press, 2003.

Hazony, Yoram. *The Virtue of Nationalism*. London: Hachette, 2018.

Hedges, Chris. *American Fascists: The Christian Right and the War on America*. New York: Simon and Schuster, 2008.

Hobsbawm, Eric J. *Nations and Nationalism Since 1780: Programme, Myth, Reality*. Cambridge: Cambridge University Press, 2012.

Hochschild, Arlie Russell. *Strangers in Their Own Land: Anger and Mourning on the American Right*. New York: The New Press, 2018.

Hughes, Ceri. "Appealing to Evangelicals, Trump Uses Religious Words and References to God at a Higher Rate Than Previous Presidents." *The Conversation*, October 13, 2020. https://theconversation.com/appealing-to-evangelicals-trump-uses-religious -words-and-references-to-god-at-a-higher-rate-than-previous-presidents-146816.

———. "The God Card: Strategic Employment of Religious Language in US Presidential Discourse." *International Journal of Communication* 13 (2019): 22.

Hunter, James Davison. *To Change the World: The Irony, Tragedy, and Possibility of Christianity in the Late Modern World*. New York: Oxford University Press, 2010.

Huntington, Samuel P. *Who Are We?: The Challenges to America's National Identity*. New York: Simon and Schuster, 2004.

Jones, Robert P. *White Too Long: The Legacy of White Supremacy in American Christianity*. New York: Simon & Schuster, 2020.

Jones, Robert P., and Daniel Cox. *America's Changing Religious Identity*. Public Religion Research Institute, September 6, 2017. www.prri.org/research/american -religious-landscape-christian-religiously-unaffiliated/.

Kaufmann, Eric. "Ethnic or Civic Nation? Theorizing the American Case." *Canadian Review of Studies in Nationalism* 27, no. 1/2 (2000): 133-55.

Keller, Timothy. *Generous Justice: How God's Grace Makes Us Just*. New York: Penguin, 2012.

Kohn, Hans. *The Idea of Nationalism: A Study of the Origins and Background*. New York: Macmillan, 1944.

Kruse, Kevin M. *One Nation Under God: How Corporate America Invented Christian America*. New York: Basic Books, 2015.

Lilla, Mark. *The Once and Future Liberal: After Identity Politics*. New York: Oxford University Press, 2018.

Lind, Michael. *Next American Nation: The New Nationalism and the Fourth American Revolution*. New York: Simon and Schuster, 2010.

Loury, Glenn C. *The Anatomy of Racial Inequality*. Cambridge, MA: Harvard University Press, 2009.

———. "Why Does Racial Inequality Persist? Culture, Causation, and Responsibility." *The Manhattan Institute*, May 2019. https://media4.manhattan-institute.org/sites/default /files/R-0519-GL.pdf.

Lowndes, Joseph E. *From the New Deal to the New Right: Race and the Southern Origins of Modern Conservatism*. New Haven, CT: Yale University Press, 2008.

Lowry, Rich. *The Case for Nationalism: How It Made Us Rich, Powerful, and Free*. New York: Broadside, 2019.

Lynerd, Benjamin. "On Political Theology and Religious Nationalism." *Religion and Culture Forum*, January 26, 2018. https://voices.uchicago.edu/religion-culture/2018/01/26/on-political-theology-and-religious-nationalism-a-response/.

MacIntyre, Alasdair. *After Virtue: A Study in Moral Theology*. Notre Dame, IN: University of Notre Dame Press, 1984.

Marsden, George M. *Fundamentalism and American Culture*. New York: Oxford University Press, 2006.

———. *Religion and American Culture: A Brief History*. Grand Rapids, MI: Eerdmans 2018.

McGirr, Lisa. *Suburban Warriors: The Origins of the New American Right-Updated Edition*. Princeton, NJ: Princeton University Press, 2015.

Mead, Walter Russell. *God and Gold: Britain, America, and the Making of the Modern World*. New York: Vintage, 2008.

———. *Special Providence: American Foreign Policy and How It Changed the World*. New York: Routledge, 2013.

Mearsheimer, John J. *The Great Delusion: Liberal Dreams and International Realities*. New Haven, CT: Yale University Press, 2018.

Miller, Paul D. "Non-'Western' Liberalism and the Resilience of the Liberal International Order." *The Washington Quarterly* 41, no. 2 (2018): 137-53.

———. "Politics is More than Abortion vs. Character." *Mere Orthodoxy*, November 2, 2020.

———. "The Twenty-First Century Federalist." *Perspectives on Politics* 46, no. 1 (2017): 51-57.

Niebuhr, Reinhold. *The Children of Light and the Children of Darkness: A Vindication of Democracy and a Critique of Its Traditional Defense*. Chicago: University of Chicago Press, 2011.

———. *Love and Justice: Selections from the Shorter Writings of Reinhold Niebuhr*. Louisville, KY: Westminster John Knox Press, 1992.

Noll, Mark A. *America's God: From Jonathan Edwards to Abraham Lincoln*. New York: Oxford University Press, 2002.

———. *God and Race in American Politics: A Short History*. Princeton, NJ: Princeton University Press, 2010.

O'Donovan, Oliver. *The Desire of the Nations: Rediscovering the Roots of Political Theology*. Cambridge: Cambridge University Press, 1999.

Orwell, George. "Notes on Nationalism." Orwell Foundation. www.orwellfoundation .com/the-orwell-foundation/orwell/essays-and-other-works/notes-on-nationalism/.

Philpott, Daniel. "In Defense of Self-Determination." *Ethics* 105, no. 2 (1995): 352-85.

Preston, Andrew. *Sword of the Spirit, Shield of faith: Religion in American War and Diplomacy*. New York: Knopf, 2012.

Reno, R. R. *Return of the Strong Gods: Nationalism, Populism, and the Future of the West*. New York: Simon and Schuster, 2019.

Smith, Anthony. *Chosen Peoples: Sacred Sources of National Identity*. New York: Oxford University Press, 2003.

———. *National Identity*. Reno: University of Nevada Press, 1991.

———. *Nationalism: Theory, Ideology, History*. 2nd edition. New York: Polity, 2010.

Smith, Rogers M. *Civic Ideals: Conflicting Visions of Citizenship in US History*. New Haven, CT: Yale University Press, 1997.

———. *Stories of Peoplehood: The Politics and Morals of Political Membership*. Cambridge: Cambridge University Press, 2003.

Speiser, Ephraim A. "'People' and 'Nation' of Israel." *Journal of Biblical Literature* (1960): 157-63.

Stackhouse, John. "American Evangelical Support for Donald Trump: Mostly American, and Only Sort-of 'Evangelical.'" *Religion and Culture Forum*, February 2, 2018. https:// voices.uchicago.edu/religionculture/2018/02/02/american-evangelical-support -for-donald-trump-mostly-american-and-only-sort-of-evangelical-a-response/.

Stewart, Katherine. *The Power Worshippers: Inside the Dangerous Rise of Religious Nationalism*. New York: Bloomsbury, 2020.

Stout, Harry S. *Upon the Altar of the Nation: A Moral History of the Civil War*. New York: Penguin, 2007.

Sutton, Matthew Avery. *American Apocalypse*. Cambridge, MA: Harvard University Press, 2014.

Thompson, Derek. "The Deep Story of Trumpism." *The Atlantic*, December 29, 2020. www.theatlantic.com/ideas/archive/2020/12/deep-story-trumpism/617498/.

Tuveson, Ernest Lee. *Redeemer Nation: The Idea of America's Millennial Role*. Chicago: University of Chicago Press, 1980.

Van Engen, Abram C. *City on a Hill: A History of American Exceptionalism*. New Haven, CT: Yale University Press, 2020.

Vermeule, Adrian. "Beyond Originalism." *The Atlantic*, March 31, 2020.

Weber, Max. *Readings and Commentary on Modernity*. Edited by Stephen Kalberg. Oxford: Blackwell, 2005.

Whitehead, Andrew L., and Samuel L. Perry. *Taking America Back for God: Christian Nationalism in the United States*. New York: Oxford University Press, 2020.

Wilcox, Clyde and Carin Robinson. *Onward Christian Soldiers? The Religious Right in American Politics*. New York: Routledge, 2018.

Williams, Daniel K. *God's Own Party: The Making of the Christian Right*. New York: Oxford University Press, 2012.

Williams, Roger. *The Bloudy Tenent of Persecution for Cause of Conscience Discussed and Mr. Cotton's Letter Examined and Answered*. Edited by Edward Bean Underhill. London: Haddon, 1848.

Wilsey, John D. *American Exceptionalism and Civil Religion: Reassessing the History of an Idea*. Downers Grove, IL: InterVarsity Press, 2015.

———. *One Nation Under God? An Evangelical Critique of Christian America*. Eugene, OR: Wipf and Stock, 2011.

Winship, Michael Paul. *Godly Republicanism*. Cambridge, MA: Harvard University Press, 2012.

Witte, John, and Joel A. Nichols. *Religion and the American Constitutional Experiment*. New York: Oxford University Press, 2016.

Wright, Matthew, Jack Citrin, and Jonathan Wand. "Alternative Measures of American National Identity: Implications for the Civic-Ethnic distinction." *Political Psychology* 33, no. 4 (2012): 469-82.

GENERAL INDEX

SCRIPTURE INDEX